Ancient Faith and American-Born Churches

Ancient Faith and American-Born Churches

DIALOGUES BETWEEN CHRISTIAN TRADITIONS

EDITED BY

Ted A. Campbell

Ann K. Riggs

Gilbert W. Stafford

WITH ASSISTANCE FROM *Charles Hikaru Simpson*

NATIONAL COUNCIL OF THE CHURCHES OF CHRIST
IN THE USA
FAITH AND ORDER COMMISSION THEOLOGICAL SERIES

Ann K. Riggs, General Editor

Paulist Press
New York/Mahwah, N.J.

Cover design by Mike Velthaus
Book design by Lynn Else

Library of Congress Cataloging-in-Publication Data

Ancient faith and American-born churches : dialogues between Christian traditions / edited by Ted A. Campbell, Ann K. Riggs, Gilbert W. Stafford ; with assistance from Charles Hikaru Simpson.
    p. cm.—(Faith and order commission theological series)
    ISBN 0-8091-4321-6 (alk. paper)
    1. Church—Congresses. 2. Christian union—United States—Congresses. I. Campbell, Ted. II. Riggs, Ann, 1950- III. Stafford, Gilbert W. (Gilbert Wayne), 1938- IV. Simpson, Charles Hikaru. V. Series
BV600.3.A48 2005
280'.042–dc22

                                        2005017181

Published by Paulist Press
997 Macarthur Boulevard
Mahwah, New Jersey 07430

www.paulistpress.com

Printed and bound in the
United States of America

CONTENTS

DIALOGUE 2
The Hermeneutics of Reconciliation in Worship:
A Dialogue between Holiness and Eastern Orthodox Traditions

DIALOGUE 3
Apostolicity: A Dialogue between the Roman Catholic Tradition and
the Stone-Campbell Restoration Tradition

DIALOGUE 4
The Role of Creeds and Confessions: A Dialogue among Reformed,
Methodist, and Quaker Traditions

CONTENTS

DIALOGUE 7
The Authority and Function of Scripture: A Dialogue among
Roman Catholic, Lutheran, and Reformed Traditions

DIALOGUE 8
Eschatology and Mission: A Dialogue between
Anglican and Adventist Traditions

FOREWORD

Thomas F. Best

This book, the first in the NCCCUSA Faith and Order Commission Theological Series, invites Christians and churches into a *dialogue of discovery*.

It is an antidote to the limited understandings of the Christian faith, and of the churches, that are only too prevalent today: to an understanding of the churches as one-dimensional and monolithic, all basically the same in thought and practice; or of the churches as formed into competing, if not opposing, camps identified as conservative and liberal, or "culture-bound" and countercultural; or of the churches as so different, and indeed divided, that they can offer no coherent witness to the faith. In the first view the churches have no need to dialogue among themselves; in the second they have no desire to do so; in the third they could not do so, for want of a common language.

But from these pages emerges a different picture: one of churches in dialogue, sharing their own distinctive faith convictions and practices, learning about the cherished beliefs of others and, in the process, learning more about their own cherished beliefs. We see churches as they accept a new vulnerability without compromising their own convictions, opening themselves to others, to new perspectives and possibilities for the life of faith. We are privileged observers, present at the moment when ignorance and fear is replaced by knowledge; when the stranger becomes a partner in a mutual journey in faith; when the familiar ecclesial landscape, dotted with churches grown comfortable and self-sufficient in their division, is challenged by Christ's call that they be visibly one (John 17:21).

It is no accident that we speak of the ecumenical *movement:* it is not mainly a matter of persons, or congregations, or committees, or texts, or official positions, but rather of the interaction, over time, of those and other factors in a process of individual and institutional growth. A creative and sensitive process enables growth. This book is the result of such a process; and two of its most creative aspects deserve, I believe, special mention.

The first is the method used to pair the partners in dialogue, or sometimes to bring them into groupings of three. Thus, churches that associate themselves with councils of churches found themselves in dialogue with churches that traditionally distance themselves from such ecumenical bodies. Churches originating in pre-American (here used to mean United States) experience were brought into dialogue with churches originating in the American experience. And churches with explicit, more complex written doctrinal systems were brought together with those functioning more through commonly agreed understandings, mainly orally expressed. In these conditions routine or merely polite behavior was not an option, and dialogue anything but obvious. It took courage to pursue such a process; but it has worked.

The second creative aspect of the process is that it required the partners to deal with the full range of their reactions to one another's belief and practice. The partners were to note not only areas of agreement or disagreement, but also areas of disconnection, points at which the language of the other simply made no sense or at which the position of the other seemed, frankly, to be nonsense. This approach opened up for dialogue a whole range of issues that, in most dialogues, would have been politely avoided. Surprise, puzzlement, the sense of "do they actually mean *that?*"—in this process, all these reactions could be brought to the table and shared within the context of commitment to the dialogue process. Again, a fresh approach proved valid in the doing.

This book and the process behind it is, then, an admirable example of the dialogue of discovery. In its method, in the breadth and commitment of its participants, and in the quality of its results it exemplifies much of what is best in the modern ecumenical movement. May the churches take its lessons to heart, even as they journey in dialogue together toward visible unity.

PREFACE

Ann K. Riggs

In *Parcours de la Reconnaissance,* Paul Ricoeur recounts his intellectual wanderings as he considers the notion of *reconnaissance,* "recognition."[1] He observes that there are both active and passive dimensions to recognition: we both recognize and are recognized. Recognition can be a process of observation and assessment of the other when, for example, we recognize a person whom we have not seen for a long while as still being the same person. Recognition can be a process through which we come to distinguish between that which is consistent with an identity we are considering and that which is not consistent with it. Ricoeur's account focuses particularly on the recognition of oneself/ourselves as oneself/ourselves through capacity and act, memory and promise, collective practices and agency. Finally, recognition is mutual. In its fullest expression, mutual recognition is evident in, through, and after formal acts of mutuality.

Ricoeur's reflections and examples have vivid applicability to the processes of dialogue among Christians and Christian communities. In coming to know and understand one another, we seek to recognize the full Christian ecclesiality of others and be recognized by others as fully church. In some cases, this means processes through which we come to see others as once again familiar. In some cases, this means processes of self-recognition that exclude what is extraneous, restore what has been diminished, and locate self-identity in the capacities, acts, memories, promises, collective practices, and agency that accurately define ourselves as church. In some cases, this means processes of formal mutual recognition. In the texts that are the results of international ecumenical dialogue, examples of each of these types of recognition can be found.

In "The Common Declaration of John Paul II and Catholicos Karekin I" of 1996, the two primates together affirm having recognized one another again after the passage of time:

> Pope John Paul II and Catholicos Karekin I recognize the deep spiritual communion which already unites them and the Bishops, clergy and lay faithful of their Churches. It is a communion which finds its roots in the common faith in the Holy and Life-giving Trinity proclaimed by the Apostles and transmitted down the centuries by the many Fathers and Doctors of the Church and the Bishops, priests, and martyrs who have followed them. They rejoice in the fact that recent developments of ecumenical relations and theological discussions carried out in the spirit of Christian love and fellowship have dispelled many misunderstandings inherited from the controversies and dissensions of the past. Such dialogues and encounters have prepared a healthy situation of mutual understanding and recovery of the deeper spiritual communion based on the common faith in the Holy Trinity that they have been given through the Gospel of Christ and in the Holy Tradition of the Church.[2]

In *Baptism, Eucharist and Ministry*, a text of the World Council of Churches' Faith and Order Commission, the churches of the world are asked to assess "the extent to which your church can recognize in this text the faith of the Church through the ages."[3] Assuming that those to whom the question is addressed will recognize their own churches as holding "the faith of the Church through the ages," they are asked to what extent they recognize themselves in this new text.

The final paragraph of *Baptism, Eucharist and Ministry* speaks of the goal of mutual ecclesial recognition among the churches:

> The mutual recognition of churches and their ministries implies decision by the appropriate authorities and a liturgical act from which point unity would be publicly manifest. Several forms of such public act have been proposed: mutual laying on of hands, eucharistic concelebration, solemn worship without a particular rite of recognition, the reading of a text of union during the course of a celebration. No one

liturgical form would be absolutely required, but in any case it would be necessary to proclaim the accomplishments of mutual recognition publicly. The common celebration of the eucharist would certainly be the place for such an act.[4]

The process of reaching formal, mutual, ecclesial recognition is a long one, involving many preliminary moments of recognition of self and recognition of the other. In the United States, the number of churches in relationships of diverse forms of mutual recognition is growing. But there are, as well, many communities that are at much more preliminary stages of mutuality with one another. In many cases, churches that are in relationships of extensive formal mutuality with some communities are at the very earliest stages of conversation with other communities.

The early stages of dialogue present particular difficulties. How do those who know little of one another's thought patterns and self-understandings speak productively together? How do we speak with one another rather than past one another? In addition to the openness and commitment that are required in any dialogue situation, dialogues between highly disparate or thoroughly unfamiliar partners also require special methodological care.

The work of the 1996–99 quadrennium of the Ecclesiology Study Group of the Faith and Order Commission of the National Council of the Churches of Christ in the USA was particularly aimed at increasing the communicative successes of the most preliminary steps toward mutuality among churches in the United States, so that more developed stages of recognition will become possible in years to come. The work presented here is offered as a gift of hope to the future of our ecclesial relationships of mutuality and recognition and with gratitude to those who have come before us in this work.

Participants in one or more aspects of the work of the Ecclesiology Study Group of the Faith and Order Commission of the National Council of the Churches of Christ in the USA, 1996–99, included:

Charles W. Brockwell Jr., United Methodist Church
Ted A. Campbell, United Methodist Church

O. C. Edwards, Episcopal Church
John H. Erickson, Orthodox Church in America
John T. Ford, CSC, Roman Catholic Church
Denis Fortin, Seventh-day Adventist Church
Douglas A. Foster, Churches of Christ
Dean Freiday, Friends General Conference
Jeffrey Gros, FSC, Roman Catholic Church
Norman A. Hjelm, Evangelical Lutheran Church in America
Paul Janssen, Reformed Church in America
Rosemary Jermann, Roman Catholic Church
Michael Kinnamon, Christian Church (Disciples of Christ)
Theresa F. Koernke, IHM, Roman Catholic Church
Philip Krey, Evangelical Lutheran Church in America
David J. Lull, United Methodist Church
Melanie A. May, Church of the Brethren
Kevin McMorrow, SA, Roman Catholic Church
Paul Meyendorff, Orthodox Church in America
Samuel H. Nafzger, Lutheran Church–Missouri Synod
Ann K. Riggs, Friends General Conference
Cecil M. Robeck Jr., Society for Pentecostal Studies
Paul E. Robertson, Southern Baptist Convention
William G. Rusch, Evangelical Lutheran Church in America
Joseph D. Small, Presbyterian Church (USA)
Gilbert W. Stafford, Church of God, Anderson, IN
Clyde J. Steckel, United Church of Christ
Eugene G. Turner, Presbyterian Church (USA)
George Vandervelde, Christian Reformed Church

Our special thanks go to William G. Rusch, the director of the Faith and Order Commission during the period of this study; Joanne Barbieri, the commission's program assistant at that time; and R. Keelan Downton, Faith and Order Post-doctoral Fellow, 2005–06.

Unless otherwise indicated, biblical quotations are from the New Revised Standard Version.

NOTES

1. Paul Ricoeur, *Parcours de la Reconnaissance: Trois études* (Paris: Stock, 2004).

2. "Common Declaration of John Paul II and Catholicos Karekin I," Rome, December 13, 1996, available at http://www.vatican.va/roman_curia/pontifical_councils/chrstuni/anc-orient-ch-docs/rc_pc_christuni_doc_19961213_jp-ii-karekin-i_en.html.

3. Faith and Order Commission, World Council of Churches, *Baptism, Eucharist and Ministry,* Faith and Order Paper 111 (Geneva: World Council of Churches, 1982), x.

4. Ibid., par. 55, p. 32.

INTRODUCTION

Gilbert W. Stafford

CHURCHES IN "ANYWHERE," USA

Welcome to "Anywhere," USA! One finds in "Anywhere" many traditions of the Christian faith. These traditions are, in many ways, widely divergent in their doctrinal emphases, in the ways they live out their faith, and in their corporate worship. At the Church of Christ, for example, one finds a cappella singing of four-part harmony songs, in a plain meeting house, and with a Bible-study sermon. At the Orthodox Church the atmosphere is very different with its brightly colored icons of Christ and the saints, with incense filling the air, and with two processions—the Little Entrance with the Bible, and the Great Entrance with the holy gifts for the Eucharist.

If we were to attend the services of the Pentecostal and the Presbyterian churches in Anywhere, we would find significant differences between them as well. In the first, one would very likely find exuberant singing accompanied by hand clapping, maybe some tongues speaking, and spontaneous expressions both of joy and of concerns. In the Presbyterian Church, one would likely find a carefully ordered service with congregational responses already scripted for unison reading, a pastoral prayer with no spontaneous expressions from the congregation, and a sermon crafted as the centerpiece of the service.

Let us go to four additional churches in Anywhere. At the Roman Catholic Church the culmination of the service is the Eucharist with the whole congregation going forward to receive the holy sacrifice. However, at the Southern Baptist Church the culmination of the service is the altar call, during which time

1

persons are called to make a decision for Christ. At the nonpro-grammed Friends Meeting, the congregants sit in silence until someone, moved by the Spirit, speaks. In fact, it might be that the greater part of the meeting time is spent in silence. Not so at the Episcopal Church: there the whole service is full of words and actions. And if one wants to worship with the Seventh-day Adventist Church one must do it on Saturday.

The examples of other churches in Anywhere, of course, could be greatly expanded. In terms of external expressions, it is as though one is in a different world in each of these churches. In too many instances, the churches in Anywhere do, in fact, func-tion as though they are in completely different worlds. And yet when one looks beyond the obvious differences one finds in all of them the one faith in Jesus the Christ as Savior and Lord. But how can the churches of this one Lord deal with their divisive issues? What kind of conversation will lead to mutual enrichment and the end of functioning as though the churches in Anywhere were in different religious worlds? The Faith and Order Movement is a worldwide endeavor to answer these questions.

THE FAITH AND ORDER MOVEMENT

In the 1910 World Missionary Conference in Edinburgh, Scotland, widely divergent churches and other missionary-sending agencies came together to consider how they could unite their witness around the world. The participants in the Edinburgh Conference were there as official representatives of their respective churches or agencies, and not merely because, as individuals, they had the desire to attend a missionary conference.

Near the end of the conference, Bishop Charles H. Brent of the Protestant Episcopal Church in the United States—at that time, he was bishop of the Philippine Islands—issued a challenge. He pled for the churches to convene in the future for the purpose of addressing not only missionary concerns but doctrinal concerns as well. That was the seed that eventually grew into what we now know as the Faith and Order Movement. Faith and Order has, from the beginning, been a forum where churches with very different histories, emphases, and traditions come together for the purpose of dealing with church-dividing doctrinal issues. Participants trust that as they study divergent histories and confessional understandings, and as they write about and discuss them, the Lord of the church will bring about a new tangible expression of the unity of the faith. The first World Conference on Faith and Order was held in Lausanne, Switzerland, in 1927, with subsequent conferences in Edinburgh (1937), Lund, Sweden (1952), Montreal, Canada (1963), and Santiago de Compostela, Spain (1993). Faith and Order work, particularly for churches in the United States and Canada, began in 1957 with a meeting on September 3–19 of that year, in Oberlin, Ohio.

Since 1957 churches associated with the World Council of Churches and with the National Council of Churches of Christ in the USA, as well as churches associated with neither, have come to the Faith and Order table for discussion. The Church of God (Anderson, Indiana), which I represent, has participated in Faith and Order from Oberlin onward, even though it is a member of neither council of churches.

Over the years, this North American contingent of the Faith and Order Movement has included conversation partners from a wide variety of Christian traditions. The traditions represented include both the ancient ones such as the Roman Catholic and Orthodox, and younger ones such as Pentecostal and Adventist. At the table are churches of both the magisterial Reformation as well as of the radical Reformation. It includes a spectrum of churches with historical connections to England: Episcopal, Methodist, and Quakers. While most of the traditions were born in the European context, others were born in the American context, for example, Disciples, Churches of Christ, Assembly of God, and Seventh-day Adventist. Over the course of years, one finds traditions as divergent as the Lutheran Church–Missouri Synod, the Southern Baptist, and the United Church of Christ. Here one finds both the historic Black churches and the historic Peace churches. Or, to look at the diversity another way, participants represent generic groupings of Christians: Catholic, Orthodox, Anglican, Lutheran, Reformed, Anabaptist, Wesleyan, Holiness, Evangelical, Pentecostal, Restorationist, and Adventist.

One of the many learning opportunities in Faith and Order is how to talk with each other about differing traditions of "like precious faith." It is the opportunity for the national entities related to the local churches in Anywhere to enter into each other's world. The environment is provided for seeing others not as enemies of the faith but as friends in the faith "once for all delivered to the saints" (see Jude 3). As friends they learn to help each other explore those treasures of the faith, which, heretofore, had been despised, ignored, or overlooked.

A SPECIAL PROJECT

A few years ago the Ecclesiology Study Group of Faith and Order, of which I am a part, began asking itself a cluster of important questions. Were we being intentional enough about focusing our conversational skills on the issues and perspectives brought to the table by churches that relate differently to the two councils of churches? As indicated above, some churches are either members of the councils or, if not members, at least involved at the highest levels of official conversations. Other churches are not members of the council due to official church policy and religious priorities. In light of these two different kinds of relationships the churches at the table have to the councils, we decided to devise a way whereby representatives of both kinds of churches could participate on an equal footing in the conversation. We did not want to have meetings at which some mainly listened while others talked. We did not want a church's official relationship to the councils to determine whether it was an insider or an outsider to the conversation at the table.

Were we being intentional enough in fully engaging those churches that were specific to the U.S. context with other churches? Were there particular conversations that would occur in our commission which would occur nowhere else in the world?

Finally, were we being intentional enough in engaging churches with very different styles of articulating their self-understanding? Churches with clear doctrinal texts have ways to engage one another based upon those texts. For example: What does the *Book of Concord* say about topic X? What do the documents of the Council of Trent say on that topic? Communities that arise from the same theological and churchly movement discuss issues among themselves in terms of the characteristic concerns of that movement. For example: The Churches of Christ and the Christian Church (Disciples of Christ) talk with one another within the shared heritage of the Stone-Campbell movement. But how do the Churches of Christ and the Roman Catholic Church most productively pick up the discussion with one another?

In order to accomplish our goal of being more intentional in these dimensions of ecumenical discussion, we chose the dialogue partners, the methodology, and the topics. This book is a product of those conversations.

THE DIALOGUE PARTNERS

First, let us consider the dialogue partners. The differences we attempted to engage are multivalent. Seen from one set of coordinates we have here dialogue partnerships that consist of a study group member who comes from a church tradition that, on the whole, distances itself from the World and National Councils of Churches (indicated below with a minus mark), and one or more members who comes from a church tradition that is closely associated with them, either by membership or by ecclesiastical association (indicated by a plus). With that general guideline, the pairings included Church of God (Anderson) (–) and Roman Catholic (+); Church of God (Anderson) (–) and Orthodox Church in America (+); Churches of Christ (–) and Roman Catholic (+); Southern Baptist (–) and Roman Catholic (+); Lutheran Church–Missouri Synod (–), United Church of Christ (+), and Roman Catholic (+); and Seventh-day Adventist (–) and Episcopal (+). Over the course of the four years during which these conversations took place they were enriched also by persons representing the Assemblies of God and the Christian Reformed Church, neither of which holds membership in the councils, and by persons representing the United Methodist Church, the

Presbyterian Church (USA), Friends General Conference, the Evangelical Lutheran Church in America, the Reformed Church in America, and the Christian Church (Disciples of Christ), each of which holds membership in the World Council of Churches and is either a member or a longtime associate of the National Council of Churches.

Another dimension of the pairings was discussion between a church rooted in pre-American experience—the Evangelical Lutheran Church in America—and a church originated as well as rooted in the American experience—the Christian Church (Disciples of Christ). The same dynamic of differences applies in the pairings and triads listed above. Roman Catholic (pre-American origin) and Church of God (Anderson) (American origin); Orthodox Church in America (pre-American origin) and Church of God (Anderson) (American origin); Roman Catholic (pre-American origin) and Churches of Christ (American origin); Roman Catholic (pre-American origin) and Southern Baptist (American origin); Episcopal (pre-American origin) and Seventh-day Adventist (American origin).

Of course, all the churches in the U.S. religious landscape have been distinctively shaped by historical development within the United States. Two triads demonstrate something of the ways that churches with pre-American roots are at the same time distinctively shaped by their historical experiences and development in the United States: Lutheran Church–Missouri Synod, United Church of Christ, and Roman Catholic; and United Methodist Church, the Presbyterian Church (USA), and Friends General Conference.

A last dynamic of difference we engaged in our pairings and triads was difference in theological style and intellectual accessibility among the churches in dialogue. Some of the churches in our study have highly articulated and carefully monitored written doctrinal systems. Other communities function much more as oral traditions, with shared understandings and insights, well known to those within the community, but hard to document and explain to outsiders. We hope that the record presented here of our interactions can serve as a resource for others seeking mutual understanding across these differences in community style.

METHODOLOGY

Now let us say a word about the methodology. John T. Ford, CSC, proposed, and we accepted, the following plan. Each member of the pairings would set forth the position of his or her tradition on the assigned subject. This was not to be the author's own personal position but the historic position of the tradition being represented.

Each member of the pairings/triologues, then, would submit his or her paper to the other member(s) of the pairing (or triad). A response was to be written under three headings. The first is *resonance*. What did each find in the other's paper with which one, out of his or her own tradition, could readily affirm? To what in the other tradition(s) does one's own tradition say Amen? The object is to identify areas of commonality, similarities, and points of convergence, if not in terms of the language used, at least in terms of the general emphasis or broad concepts.

The second heading is *dissonance*. What does each find that is contrary to his or her tradition's understanding of the faith? Under this heading the respondent was to deal with issues with which he or she, though understanding the position taken, disagrees. This is where one tradition says to another: "We think that you are off track with this perspective." The assumption here is that in order for ecumenical dialogue to be beneficial it always must be honest. The commitment is to bring differences out into the open so that they can be discussed, not swept under the rug of bland congeniality.

The third heading is *non-sonance, non-sense*. This is the part of the other's presentation that one finds nonsensical. This part of the other's presentation is like listening to a language that one does not know; it is like hearing a discourse from a discipline whose vocabulary one has never studied. Non-sonance, non-sense may be due to not knowing the vocabulary itself. Or, it may be because one is not acquainted with the basic assumptions for what is being said, or one is not familiar with the theological environment in which the language is used. Consequently, it is an "unknown tongue" that needs to be interpreted.

Having read each other's original and response papers, the members of each pairing or triad came to the meeting of the whole study group prepared to talk face-to-face about issues raised in the written work. After the authors of the papers clarified issues, raised new questions, and received interpretations for that which was not clear, the whole study group, then, entered into the discussion. One of the values of this approach was that the whole group had the benefit of a focused discussion that was already in process, into which they, then, could enter.

TOPICS

Third are the topics—we chose the following: the nature of the church's holiness, the reconciling nature of worship, apostolicity, and the role of creeds and confessions in the life of the church, Christian initiation, ecclesiastical authority, the authority and function of scripture, mission, and eschatology. We chose the pairings and the topics progressively through our four years of biennial meetings. We did it this way so that we could take into account issues that emerged in the course of our work together. "Where to from here?" was the question at every meeting. "What needs to be addressed next? And who among us represents significantly different approaches to the subject?"

VALUES

What, then, are the values of conversations of this sort?

First, they are mutually enriching not only for the persons directly involved but also indirectly for the traditions they represent. Each tradition has the opportunity:

- to affirm common emphases with others of "like precious faith,"

- to ask probing questions about matters of disagreement, and

- to receive the interpretation of "unknown tongues."

Those professors of the history of Christianity and of theology who are involved in Faith and Order discussions, then, are apt to be in a better position to interpret more accurately other Christian traditions to their students, to the congregations where they preach, and to the readers of their books and articles. Eventually, in the normal cycle of church life, these informed discussions could have a positive impact on the churches in Anywhere.

Churches in every venue too often live in theological isolation. Isolation leads to misunderstanding, and misunderstanding breeds contempt. The mutual enrichment at the Faith and Order table not only is for the benefit of the persons directly involved but is a metaphor of the kind of mutual enrichment that can take place among the churches in Anywhere. It is the hope of those involved in this project that, in fact, that will be the case. This book is not, therefore, simply a report about what several of us have done; it is the issuance of an invitation for the churches in every venue of their existence together to enter into focused conversations something like these. We issue this invitation because we are firmly convinced that enrichment awaits those churches in whatever venue—congregational or denominational—that will invest themselves in such conversations.

Second, these focused discussions provide the opportunity for questions to be raised by outsiders about issues that insiders are too close to see. When given the liberty to do so, outsiders can ask questions that insiders find uncomfortable. Each tradition needs to be stretched by such inquiries, instead of spending all of its energy dealing only with the comfortable questions from inside the ranks. Having to deal with the uncomfortable questions posed by outsiders sharpens our understanding of our own tradition in God's economy. It is the environment in which we become aware of those dimensions of our particular faith community that need further reflection. In some instances we may find that we are called to a deepening of our understandings by thinking more carefully about those dimensions of our tradition that, while precious, are held with theological naiveté. In other instances, we may be called to the broadening of our understandings to include dimensions to which traditionally we have given little or no attention. In still others, we may be called to the revision of our understandings in light of perspectives from the wider church that make our traditionally held positions untenable.

Third, these focused discussions provide an opportunity for the surprising work of the Holy Spirit. We may find the Holy Spirit giving us new paradigms: paradigms for the way we think about certain issues of the faith, new paradigms for how we go about being church, and new paradigms for how each of our traditions can relate to the one, holy, catholic, and apostolic church. I think that it is correct that for most, if not all, of the participants in Faith and Order new appreciation is gained for the multiple ways there are for being church. Perhaps one of the first steps toward reconciliation between the churches is the realization that in the economy of God there is much variegation in the texture of our church life. And, furthermore, it is important to realize that to the extent that this rich texture manifests the one, holy, catholic, and apostolic church, it is the work of the Holy Spirit.

Fourth, this exercise introduces participants to new vocabulary in the lexicon of the wider church. Words, phrases, and concepts that each tradition uses without definition or explanation when conversing in-house often need both definition and explanation when used in the broader church. The point is not that all traditions should use all the language of others. The point is that the unique vocabulary of each tradition opens windows on the richness of the Christian faith. Words, phrases, and concepts symbolize the reflective life of other traditions in their respective understandings of the "faith once for all delivered to the saints."

Fifth, sitting at the table of discourse brings with it a mystical experience of the oneness of the body of Christ. At the table for this particular discourse were representatives from Catholic, Orthodox, liberal Protestant, and conservative Protestant churches. Both the more liberal Lutherans and the more conservative Lutherans were represented. Both Holiness and Pentecostal churches were present. Representatives from both ends of the spectrum of the Restorationist Movement—the a cappella Churches of Christ and the Disciples—were sitting side by side affirming a common heritage. The range of sacramental theologies was there, from the Catholic, Orthodox, and Anglican understandings to the Quaker understanding, and in between were Protestants whose theology on the subject, while not Catholic, Orthodox, or Anglican, nevertheless uses sacramental language, as well as those who avoid sacramental language, preferring ordinance language. Also a range of spiritual pieties characterized the group. In addition, the positions on church governance and polity ranged from the hierarchical to the strictly egalitarian. However, as we sat at the table of discourse, even with all of these differences and many more, we functioned on the assumption that this was the discourse of brothers and sisters who have the same Lord. We prayed with each other and for each other. When one shared a hurt it was in the atmosphere of sharing it with the fellowship of Christ gathered at that table. Though we live and work in different ecclesial communities we experienced the mystical body of Christ that is more comprehensive than the ecclesial demarcations of any one of our several traditions.

Sixth, it is the hope that this Faith and Order exercise will encourage the churches in Anywhere to do the same kind of thing; will give confidence to church traditions that as yet are not involved at the national level in such dialogues to become involved; will prompt state, regional, and local groupings of churches to devise plans whereby they can have focused discussions about theological and doctrinal issues; and will serve as an example of at least one way it can be done.

Seventh, this kind of dialogue dispels the misconception circulated in some quarters that the ecumenical movement is about finding the lowest common denominator for Christian understandings of the faith. Faith and Order is not about watered down doctrine and theology. It is about robust doctrine and theology. It is not about easy solutions to thorny issues. It is not about sweeping differences under the rug. It is about living with those differences, respecting them, and seeking to find what "the Spirit says to the churches" (e.g., the traditions) so that we may hear more fully what the Spirit is saying both to each tradition and to the whole church.

Eighth, we are reminded that when we are in settings like this, our role is not that of espousing our own personal theologies. Our role is to enunciate our best understanding of our respective traditions. Such dialogues are not about personal positions but about the dogmatic, doctrinal, confessional, and theological understandings of various church traditions. It is about their respective histories and operational modes. It is as though in one room, whole traditions themselves come together to converse about the faith. Whole traditions with thousands of years of history sit with whole traditions that are in the hundreds range. Whole traditions rooted in the European context converse with whole traditions rooted in the American context. The person across the table from me, for example, is not simply a person with a personal name. Yes, that to be sure! But that person is the embodiment of a whole tradition. I expect him or her to represent that tradition to me. In this context it is not what he or she thinks that is of greatest interest to me, but what his or her tradition holds.

Ninth, this exercise reminds us of a crucial guideline for all discourse of this type. We are to seek understanding of another tradition in light of its most recent reflective work and on the basis of its best and most official thinking. Each of our traditions has poor exponents who espouse distorted self-understandings. It is unfortunate whenever we look at another tradition in its poorest light instead of its best.

This raises the issue of the credibility of the spokespersons for a tradition. Is he or she well informed about the tradition? Does the tradition itself place its stamp of approval on him or her as one who is capable of speaking intelligently, accurately, and appreciatively of the tradition? Such credentials are given in a wide variety of ways in the respective traditions. In some traditions it is by *denominational appointment;* the initiative is taken by the denomination itself. In others it is by *denominational consent.* A professor, for example, desires to be part of Faith and Order and receives denominational consent to serve. In this case the person takes the initiative. In others it is by *approval from or at the request of a representative entity* (e.g., a college, a learned society, a religious community) of the tradition. An individual may see the importance of such dialogue but no denominational structure exists to facilitate it and so the person appeals to a seminary, for example, to approve participation.

Faith and Order itself, in the last analysis, however, must monitor who participates in order to make sure that, in its view, the participants do meet the criteria set forth above. In other venues for such discussions, the same kind of monitoring has to be maintained if, indeed, the dialogue is to function at its optimal level.

And finally, such conversations as this book reports is one sign that our Lord's prayer, "that they may all be one," is being answered to the end "that the world may believe that you have sent me" (John 17:21). They are a response to the Pauline injunction to bear with one another in love, "making every effort to maintain the unity of the Spirit in the bond of peace" (Eph 4:2–3). In a world that so obviously stands in need of the reconciling love of God, the church is called to new endeavors that show this kind of love in the way our many traditions relate to each other. What we do at our tables of discussion influence what we do at our tables of communion. And what we do at our tables of communion influences the world either for the good of the kingdom, or as a detriment.

THEOLOGICAL LANGUAGE AND ECUMENICAL METHODOLOGY

John T. Ford, CSC

Participating in ecumenical dialogue is often similar to learning a new language. Sometimes ecumenical conversation goes smoothly, just as the process of learning grammar and acquiring vocabulary can be an enjoyable activity: learning a new language can be as entertaining as learning a new game.

At other times, however, language learning is tedious. We can become discouraged by the drudgery of learning vocabulary, just as we can be clumsy in trying to learn a new sport. Similarly, ecumenical conversations are sometimes frustrated by awkward misunderstandings. At still other times, language learning can be quite puzzling, especially when we sense that a word is being used in a way that we don't quite understand; it's like playing a game whose rules are unfamiliar. Similarly, some ecumenical conversations get stalled when one group of participants is using terms that their counterparts do not really understand.

When learning a foreign language, most people anticipate or at least adjust to such difficulties. However, when an ecumenical conversation is in our own language, we often fail to notice that similar language dynamics can be operative—until at some point, the dialogue comes to a standstill. Then we are puzzled about why a conversation that previously was going well has suddenly and unexpectedly become problematic. However, there are three dynamics of language learning that are often operative, and occasionally obstructive, in ecumenical dialogue: (1) resonance; (2) dissonance; (3) non-sonance.

RESONANCE

Perhaps the most obvious challenge in learning another language is the acquisition of vocabulary. However, much vocabulary learning seems mainly a matter of diligence, *if* the vocabulary refers to concrete realities. For example, with minimal effort, a student can learn the word for *father* in German *(Vater)*, French *(père)*, or Spanish (padre); the words are different, but the reality designated by the words is the same.

One can have similar experiences in ecumenical conversations. For example, during the "get-acquainted" reception at the very first ecumenical dialogue that I ever attended, a Lutheran professor of New Testament and I, a historical-systematic theologian, began to talk about "Justification"—in retrospect, such a topic seems almost predestined as a conversation piece for Lutherans and Roman Catholics. In any case, what surprised me—and encouraged future ecumenical conversations—was our mutual discovery that behind his description of justification based on the New Testament and my understanding of justification grounded in the Council of Trent was a great deal of commonality.

Like the beginning language student who learns the word for father in another language, we had discovered that while our words were different, the reality behind the words was much the same. In spite of the differences in vocabulary, we were able to detect an echoing or *resonance* in regard to the reality.

However, a word of caution is necessary here: experiences are never completely identical. There are always nuances—sometimes historical, sometimes cultural, sometimes personal—that can catch us off guard. For example, while I can learn the word for father in another language, I still tend to base my understanding of *father* on my personal relationship with my own father. Thus, I tend to speak of my father in another language in the same way that I speak of him in English. However, in some other cultures this may not be appropriate; for example, in some cultures, one is expected to address one's father in formal terms; in other languages, such formality would be considered inappropriate, since one should speak to one's father in the most familiar of terms. Such usage can be perplexing to English speakers, since the distinction between formal and familiar address has practically disappeared from English.[1]

A comparable difference in usage may perplex ecumenical conversations. For example, in speaking of *sacrament,* those coming from Catholic traditions will usually mean "an outward sign of interior grace." In contrast, some (but not all) Protestants find the term *sacrament* uncongenial, even unclear, and prefer to use a term like *ordinance* to describe baptism as a rite in which a person publicly professes belief in the Trinity and is received into membership in the Church.

While such language usage is also current in Catholic traditions, it can become problematic when one begins to discuss the age for the reception of baptism. For those with a sacramental understanding, baptism not only marks the baptized's entry into the Church, but is also a conferral of interior grace, and thus should be, indeed must be, conferred on infants; *not* to baptize infants would be a type of ecclesial child neglect: depriving a child of baptism is comparable to depriving a child of food.

In contrast, for those who emphasize the need for personal conversion and commitment as necessary predispositions, baptism witnesses an individual's decision for Christ, and thus should be administered only to adults; to baptize infants would be a form of ecclesial child manipulation: baptism should not be forced on anyone.

The anomaly in ecumenical discussions about baptism arises from the fact that baptism is a *concrete* rite at the heart of the Church's life: although the ceremonies vary from one church to the next, baptism is readily recognized, since it is generally administered with water and the invocation of the Trinity. Nonetheless, this very "concreteness" in the case of the age of baptism presents an irresolvable dilemma: at what age should a person be baptized?[2] Thus, while the term baptism is a common word in Christian vocabulary, the apparent resonance is deceptive, insofar as there is considerable difference among Christians in explaining its theological meaning.

DISSONANCE

Another frequent experience in learning a language is what a friend calls "fractured French"—for example, seeing the word *coin* in French and presuming that it refers to money, rather than "corner." However as much as such words "look alike," they are basically different in meaning. There are multiple examples of such linguistic dissonance: it is tempting to equate *compromiso* in Spanish with "compromise" instead of its real meaning of "commitment"; this type of misunderstanding can become dangerous if, for example, one supposes that the German *Gift* means "present," when it actually means "poison."

Similar confusion can easily emerge in ecumenical conversation. On one occasion, a participant in a multilateral dialogue kept speaking of "Jesus as *verily* God." At first, I presumed that this was his personal way of expressing the ancient Christological confession that Jesus Christ is "true God of true God." Then another participant raised a question about the relationship of the humanity and divinity of Christ and it became apparent from the speaker's reply that he considered Jesus a human person who had an unusually insightful knowledge of God, in other words, Jesus was a person with extraordinary perceptions about the divine, but not personally divine. My initial presumption of agreement was shattered. From the similarity of words, I had assumed agreement when it did not actually exist.

This type of experience is frequently encountered in discussing "agreed statements." On the one hand, the writers of such documents usually seek to draft statements to which all participants can subscribe. Thus, an agreed statement represents a *convergence* of various philosophical and theological viewpoints. In other words, an agreed statement is sort of a condensation or reduction of a variety of views that in their fuller systematic development might well be incompatible.

Accordingly, agreed statements can usually be interpreted in a variety of ways. At their ecumenical best, such statements can resolve long-standing divisions. Yet, such statements simultaneously have the potential of unraveling, if a reader attempts—as readers almost inevitably do—to analyze the statement from a

18

specific theological perspective. Thus, for example, it is not surprising that the report of the World Council of Churches on *Baptism, Eucharist and Ministry* not only has received wide-ranging acceptance, but also has been critiqued from specifically different denominational viewpoints.[3]

This is not to say that such agreed statements should not be drafted. Much less is it to accuse such statements of dishonesty. However, it is necessary to recognize that words that are used in ecumenical documents often have cognates in denominational traditions, where the meanings are not necessarily the same, indeed where they are sometimes decidedly different. Apparent ecumenical convergence can conceal theological dissonance.

NON-SONANCE

Even after a person has mastered the basics of another language, it is not uncommon to come across words that are not easily translated into English; one needs more than the standard dictionary in order to understand them. For example, it is hard to find good translations for *raison d'être* (literally, "reason of being"), or *das Gegenüber* (literally "the over-againstness"), or *mestizaje* (literally, "mixture"). As an illustration of the last example, Virgil Elizondo has entitled his autobiographical reflections on crossing cultural and theological frontiers *The Future Is Mestizo*—an enigmatic title that arouses a reader's curiosity, which would not quite be the case were the title "The Future Is Mixed."[4]

Such terms have a certain *non-sonance,* even *non-sense*—it is comparatively easy to learn the word, but more difficult to identify the concept or reality behind the name: such words lack resonance with my personal experience. Thus, such terms are usually not simply idiomatic ways of speaking, they are embedded in the culture of a people. For example, while a student in Europe, I looked forward to the weekly edition of a French newspaper that featured a "British Joke of the Week"—first of all, the British sense of humor was sometimes perplexing, but it was even more humorous to read several lengthy columns in French explaining why the joke was funny. In short, to appreciate the humor of other languages, one must try to understand the culture in which it is used.

The same may be said for ecumenical dialogue, where the words of one's ecumenical partners must be understood from their theological perspective. For example, when Protestants speak of *sola scriptura*, it is not always clear to a Roman Catholic whether they are advocating a fundamentally personal interpretation of scripture given to each individual under the guidance of the Holy Spirit, or whether they are maintaining that any and every doctrine taught by the Church must have some type of warranty in scripture, or some combination of these positions.

A similar difficulty arises when Roman Catholics speak of *magisterium,* which can refer to church teaching, to the level of authority connected with a particular teaching, or to church teachers or their teaching function—in a variety of combinations depending on context.[5] Thus, it is hardly surprising that ecumenical conversations sometimes get entangled in lengthy, intricate, and usually frustrating discussion about the meaning of such expressions as *sola scriptura* and *magisterium*—precisely because such terms are so deeply embedded in their respective theological traditions that their true meaning may not be immediately evident to an outsider.

As in the example of the British jokes, it is often difficult for an outsider to understand, much less to appreciate, the meaning and the importance that such expressions have within another denominational tradition. Thus, ecumenical dialogue needs to follow the standard advice of language teachers: "when in doubt, ask a native speaker for clarification." And even then, since languages operate differently, one may simply not understand the explanation: in ecumenical dialogue, it is not always possible to overcome *non-sonance*—cases where an idea is so embedded in a particular denominational tradition that outsiders do not find it easy to comprehend.

ECUMENICAL METHODOLOGY

Most people learn to speak another language by trial and error: What does this sentence really mean? Do I really understand what is being said? Or have I missed the main point? Admittedly, such a process exposes the novice linguist to a variety of potential embarrassments. Who hasn't managed to say the opposite of what one was trying to say? Who hasn't misunderstood what the other person was trying to say? Who hasn't been dumbfounded about the meaning of a sentence? Yet under the guidance of a fluent teacher, and with at least a modicum of humility, the process is usually constructive, if not always congenial.

A similar process can be productive in ecumenical dialogue; for example, the Ecclesiology Study Group of the Faith and Order Commission of the National Council of Churches has found it helpful to ask participants to raise three questions in their discussions: (1) resonance: where do we agree? (2) dissonance: where do we disagree? (3) non-sonance: where don't we understand each other?

Such simple questions have multiple benefits:

1. The effort to identify areas of consensus sometimes uncovers previously unsuspected resonance behind quite different theological language; for example, Evangelicals and Catholics have discovered more commonalties than either would have suspected prior to engaging in dialogue.

2. Nonetheless, in searching for consensus, one occasionally finds unexpected disagreement; for example, although Orthodox and Catholic theologians find much in common about sacramental ministry, agreement about the papacy remains a difficult, even neuralgic topic.

3. In ecumenical dialogue, as in other conversations, sometimes the participants use words "full of sound" but "signifying nothing" as far as their dialogue partners are concerned; for example, Roman Catholic discussions of complex theological topics like transubstantiation are sometimes soporific.

A major benefit from language study is that it requires students to reexamine the vocabulary and grammar of their own language. A similar benefit accrues in ecumenical dialogue, where the questions of one's dialogue partners often prompt a person to rethink personal philosophical presuppositions, to reconsider denominational terminology, and even to restructure a systematic theology that has been inherited without critique.

Finally, the study of a foreign language provides an entrée into a new and different world, a new Weltanschauung or theological worldview, but especially an *encuentro* between people of different cultures. Similarly in ecumenical conversation, one experiences a broadening of theological horizons, new ways of appreciating the Christian message, and most of all, friendship with other committed Christians.

The real joy in learning another language is that it opens a door to encountering people of another culture; in effect, language learning provides opportunities for personal enrichment unavailable in one's own language. Ecumenical dialogue promises a similar gift: to learn about the beliefs of fellow Christians—not merely through written texts, whose meaning may not always be clear—but through persons who live and witness the Christian tradition represented by those texts. After all, the real test of language proficiency is one's ability to converse with native speakers in their own language.

The real benefit of ecumenical dialogue is its "exchange of gifts"—through ecumenical dialogue, each participant is enriched by new insights into the Gospel, experiences new ways of living the Christian life, and becomes deeply committed to the ecumenical quest that "all may be one" (John 17:21).[6]

NOTES

An earlier version of this essay appeared as "Learning the Language of Ecumenism," *Ecumenical Trends* 26, no. 9 (October 1997): 139–43.

1. The contrast between formality and familiarity is readily available in German *(Sie, du)*, French *(vous, tu)*, and Spanish *(Usted, tú)* but has largely been lost in English with the virtual disappearance of "Thou."

2. A useful work for comparing the teachings of different confessional traditions on Baptism, as well as many other doc-

trines, is Ted A. Campbell, *Christian Confessions: A Historical Introduction* (Louisville, KY: Westminster John Knox Press, 1996).

3. See *Baptism, Eucharist and Ministry 1982–1990: Report on the Process and Responses,* Faith and Order Paper 149 (Geneva: World Council of Churches, 1990).

4. Virgil Elizondo, *The Future Is Mestizo: Life Where Cultures Meet* (Bloomington, IN: Meyer-Stone Books, 1988), uses *mestizaje* as a basic concept for constructing a cross-cultural theology.

5. Helpful explanations of the complex meanings of *magisterium* are given in two works by Francis A. Sullivan, *Magisterium: Teaching Authority in the Catholic Church* (New York/Ramsey, NJ: Paulist Press, 1983) and *Creative Fidelity: Weighing and Interpreting Documents of the Magisterium* (New York/Mahwah, NJ: Paulist Press, 1996).

6. See the thought-provoking description of Margaret O'Gara, *The Ecumenical Gift Exchange* (Collegeville, MN: Liturgical Press, 1998), vii–xi.

DIALOGUE 1

THE UNITIVE POWER OF HOLINESS:
A DIALOGUE BETWEEN HOLINESS AND
ROMAN CATHOLIC TRADITIONS

HOLINESS AS UNDERSTOOD BY THE WESLEYAN/HOLINESS TRADITION

Gilbert W. Stafford

In the Wesleyan/Holiness tradition to which I belong, holiness is understood to be the divine quality of life to which all believers are called. Basic to our understanding is that we are holy by virtue of our faith in Christ. This is a holiness of relationship; it is a holiness of status before God. By virtue of our faith identification with God in Christ, we are set apart for participation in the divine mission through Christ. This new identity is God's gift through Christ.

But not only is holiness a gift; it is a pursuit. "Pursue peace with everyone, and the holiness without which no one will see the Lord" (Heb 12:14). Believers are called to commit themselves to being shaped in the image of Christ. The holiness of the Church's corporate life is directly related to individual believers making holiness of life their own personal pursuit. Such holiness of life is characterized by the following: the settledness of believers' hearts and minds on God, the integration of one's whole self around Christ and his mission in the world, loving relationships with those both inside and outside the community of faith, and readiness for the Lord's return. Our part in this spiritual pursuit is the offering of ourselves as living sacrifices to God (see Rom 12:1–2). God's part is to empower us with the Spirit for this pursuit and to so work within us that we will become in the wholeness of our being committed to and involved with divine service in the world. "The one who calls you is faithful, and he will do this," Paul says (1 Thess 5:24).

From the beginning, the relational dimensions of holiness have been stressed in the Wesleyan/Holiness tradition. The unity of the people of God is understood to be the natural consequence of true holiness; furthermore, it is assumed that true unity is impossible apart from hearts that are purified in love by the Spirit's work. This understanding is expressed in a late-nineteenth-century Holiness song, "The Bond of Perfectness," the refrain of which is "O brethren, how this perfect love Unites us all in Jesus! One heart, and soul, and mind; we prove The union heaven gave us" (D. S. Warner).

WHAT THIS MEANS IN TERMS OF THOSE OUTSIDE THE FAITH

Personal holiness is understood to be not for the individual's self-satisfaction but for the purpose of the divine mission in the world. The missionary impulse is seen as a natural outgrowth of heart holiness. Pentecost is viewed as the empowerment and cleansing of the church for the gospel mission "in Jerusalem, in all Judea and Samaria, and to the ends of the earth" (Acts 1:8).

The church empowered by the Holy Spirit is herald, priest, and representative. It is the herald of the message of saving grace. It is the priest introducing the blessings of God to the world and representing the world to God in its intercessory prayers. It is the representative of the reigning presence of God in human history.

The church's connection to the world is seen in Jesus' prayer in John 17. Verse 17 is a petition that his disciples would be sanctified in the truth. The resulting oneness is, Jesus says, "so that the world may know that you have sent me and have loved them even as you have loved me" (verse 23).

The Wesleyan/Holiness tradition understands this relationship to the world to be a matter not only of gospel telling but also of gospel living. John Wesley was deeply committed to ministry to the poor in eighteenth-century England. He was a major influence on William Wilberforce in the struggle to outlaw human slavery. From the very beginning of the Wesleyan movement, personal holiness has been understood to imply both sensitivity and commitment to the needs of the marginalized. The Salvation Army is the most visible expression of this connection between personal holiness and social responsibility.

In the United States, the Wesleyan Church's earliest history is connected with the protest against slavery. The Church of the Nazarene came into existence under the influence of P. F. Bresee's passionate desire to minister to the marginalized. The United Methodist Church has a strong emphasis on sensitivity to societal issues and on social action. All of this is directly related to the Wesleyan/Holiness understanding about what it means to live the holy life.

W. T. Purkiser, a Nazarene writer, puts it well: "We cannot choose between doctrine and ethics, between creed and life, between inner experience and outer conduct, between individual salvation and social action. Both are in the New Testament and are not divided. 'What God has joined together, let...[no one] put asunder.'"[1]

WHAT THIS MEANS ECUMENICALLY

One of John Wesley's well-known sermons is on the "Catholic Spirit." His text is 2 Kings 10:15: "Is thine heart right, as my heart is with thy heart? And Jehonadab answered, It is. If it be, give me thine hand" (KJV). In the sermon, Wesley spells out what he has in mind by one's heart being right: it is right with God; it believes in the Lord Jesus Christ; it is "filled with the energy of love"; it is doing the will of God; it serves the Lord with reverence; it is right toward one's neighbor; and it shows love by what it does.

This catholic spirit is to be expressed toward those both outside the faith and within. Regarding those outside the faith, Wesley says that the person with a catholic spirit "embraces with strong and cordial affection neighbors and strangers, friends and enemies. This is catholic, or universal, love. And he that has this is of a catholic spirit. For love alone gives the title to this character: catholic love is a catholic spirit" (III.4).

Following this consideration, Wesley then deals with the catholic spirit in relation to fellow believers. He refers to love for all "whatever opinion or worship or congregation, who believe in the Lord Jesus Christ, who love God and man, who, rejoicing to please and fearing to offend God, are careful to abstain from evil and zealous of good works." Continuing, Wesley says that the one who is of a truly catholic spirit,

> having an unspeakable tenderness for their persons and longing for their welfare, does not cease to commend them to God in prayer as well as to plead their cause before men; who speaks comfortably to them and labours by all his words to strengthen their hands in God. He assists them to the uttermost of his power in all things, spiritual and temporal. He is ready 'to spend and be spent for them' [see 2 Cor 12:15 KJV], yea, 'to lay down his life for' their sake [John 15:13 KJV]. (III.5)[2]

The Wesleyan understanding of the dynamic of Christian unity is that first and foremost it is inspired by the Holy Spirit in the human heart. The sanctifying presence of the Spirit cleanses believers of contrary spirits and moves them to reach out in Christian fellowship to those whose hearts are right with God through faith in Jesus Christ. Christian unity, then, is first and foremost an attitude of the holy heart.

This Wesleyan understanding of catholicity was expressed by an early-twentieth-century American Holiness songwriter, Charles W. Naylor, in "The Church's Jubilee," one stanza of which goes: "The day of sects and creeds for us forevermore is past, Our brotherhood are all the saints upon the world so vast; We reach our hands in fellowship to every blood-washed one, While love entwines about each heart in which God's will is done."

Perhaps three of the most significant contributions that the Wesleyan/Holiness tradition can make to the Church at large are these: the idealism of a church that is both committed to the historic Christian faith and accepting of those within the faith whose traditions are different; holiness of heart as the necessary personal dynamic of Christian unity; and the cruciality of unity being a personal attitude before it can be a social reality.

NOTES

1. W. T. Purkiser, *Interpreting Christian Holiness* (Kansas City: Beacon Hill, 1971), 61–62.

2. *John Wesley,* ed. Albert C. Outler (New York: Oxford University Press, 1964), 91–104.

HOLINESS AS UNDERSTOOD IN THE ROMAN CATHOLIC TRADITION

Kevin McMorrow, SA

According to Roman Catholic teaching, holiness is the gift of Godself. It consists in love of God and neighbor. Our love of God is itself God's gift and has as its principal effect our being made into "participants of the divine nature" (2 Pet 1:4). Relative to neighbor this one love finds expression in the upbuilding of others especially through prayer and service. This service is meant to be exercised especially on behalf of the poor and downtrodden. In Catholic teaching holiness is one and therefore there is not one kind of holiness for ordained ministers and then a second for members of the Jesuit community and a third kind for laity. This one holiness precisely as God's gift (and not due therefore to our own works or merits) is always subject to growth and ongoing perfection until the moment of death. Love of God and neighbor is that in which holiness consists but it always remains unfinished, and involves a daily process: "As God's chosen ones, holy and beloved, clothe yourselves with compassion, kindness, humility, meekness, and patience" (Col 3:12).

The source of holiness is the Trinity. The Father's will that all people enter into communion of life with him is effected through the redemptive ministry of Jesus inclusive especially of his death, resurrection, and sending of the Holy Spirit. To the Holy Spirit is attributed the daily growth in holiness residing as the Spirit does in the hearts of the faithful and in the church as in a temple. In Catholic teaching the prompting of the Spirit leading to more intense love of God and neighbor requires the cooperation or assent of the faithful. Contemporary Catholic teaching is insistent that this very cooperation is made possible through the divine initiative or grace. However the latter may be explained by theologians (uncreated/created grace), the aim or thrust is unitive, that is, greater or more intense communion of life between God and his people and between people themselves. In addition to stressing the need of cooperation, Catholic teaching also stresses the need of sacraments both in the initial reception of holiness and in the ongoing pursuit of holiness of life. The two principal sacraments are baptism and Eucharist (Lord's Supper). The principal minister of all sacraments is Jesus Christ and having been adopted as sons in the Son through baptism, the other sacraments are understood as configuring or shaping us to be more perfect sons/daughters in the Son.

WHAT THIS MEANS IN TERMS OF THOSE OUTSIDE THE FAITH

As my esteemed colleague has written: "Personal holiness is understood to be not for the individual's self-satisfaction but for the purpose of the divine mission in the world." Catholic teaching resonates with this as is evidenced from the following:

> The faithful, therefore, must learn the deepest meaning and the value of all creation, as well as its role in the harmonious praise of God. They must assist each other to live holier lives even in their daily occupations. In this way the world may be permeated by the spirit of Christ and it may more effectively fulfill its purpose in justice, charity and peace" (Vatican Council II, Dogmatic Constitution on the Church, *Lumen Gentium [LG]*, chap. IV, par. 36).[1]

The holiness of individuals and the holiness of the Church is intended to be extended to all "without distinction of race, creed, or social condition: it looks for neither gain nor gratitude" (Vatican Council II, Decree on the Church's Missionary Activity, *Ad Gentes [AG]*, chap. II, par. 12).

This inclusive aspect of holiness (its universality) is a topic treated by John Paul II in his encyclical letter *Redemptoris Missio.* I ask the reader to substitute the word *holiness* where the Pope uses the word *salvation.* "The universality of salvation means that it is granted not only to those who explicitly believe in Christ and have entered the Church....For such people salvation in Christ is accessible by virtue of a grace, while having a mysterious relationship to the Church, does not make them formally part of the Church....This grace comes from Christ; it is the result of his Sacrifice and is communicated by the Holy Spirit. It enables each person to attain salvation through his or her free cooperation" (John Paul II, *Redemptoris Missio,* par. 8).[2]

WHAT THIS MEANS ECUMENICALLY

From the Catholic perspective the holiness of those baptized into Christ as well as the holiness of their churches or communities definitely unites them with the Catholic faithful. Such Christians are to be considered as brothers and sisters by the children of the Catholic Church precisely because of the holiness of their baptism and because "in some real way they are joined with us in the Holy Spirit, for to them too He gives His gifts and graces whereby He is operative among them with His sanctifying power. Some indeed He has strengthened to the extent of the shedding of their blood" (*LG,* par. 15). John Paul II views this shedding of blood as already constituting a perfect communion between all Christians:

> God preserves communion among the baptized in the supreme demand of faith, manifested in the sacrifice of life itself....I now add that this communion is already perfect in what we all consider the highest point of the life of grace, *martyria* unto death, the truest communion possible with Christ who shed his Blood, and by that sacrifice brings near those who once were far off." (see Eph 2:13)[3]

Finally, Catholic thinking stresses that if holiness is to be a unitive power it definitely involves both personal and communal conversion with all that such implies, for "there can be no

ecumenism worthy of the name without a change of heart"
(Vatican Council II, Decree on Ecumenism, *Unitatis redintegratio [UR]*, par. 7).

In summary, the Catholic understanding of holiness suggests
the following: (1) the holiness that unites people with God and
with each other is by its very nature unitive; (2) it is God's gift to
all people and when gratefully received can contribute to the solidarity and betterment of all people and of the whole of creation;
(3) it is especially incumbent upon all of the baptized to bring this
holiness (the riches of Jesus Christ) to greater perfection within
themselves so "that the world may believe" (John 17:21).

NOTES

1. Quotations from the documents of the Second Vatican
Council in the present chapter are from the Vatican website,
http://www.vatican.va/archive/hist_councils/ii_vatican_council/

2. John Paul II, Encyclical Letter *Redemptoris Missio,*
December 7, 1990, available at http://www.vatican.va/
holy_father/john_paul_ii/encyclicals/documents/hf_jp-
ii_enc_07121990_redemptoris-missio_en.html.

3. John Paul II, *Ut unum sint: On Commitment to Ecumenism*
(UUS), available in *Origins* 25 (June 8, 1995): 49–72, par. 84.

RESPONSE

Gilbert W. Stafford

I appreciate the fine work of my esteemed colleague in dialogue. In keeping with our agreed procedure, I shall respond at three levels.

RESONANCE

Much of the paper falls in the category of points of resonance between what he says and what I believe to be the case from the perspective of my tradition. Two examples are the following.

In paragraph one he states that "holiness is *one* and therefore there is not one kind of holiness for ordained ministers and then a second for members of the Jesuit community and a third kind for laity." This perspective is at the heart of the Wesleyan/ Holiness tradition, namely, that the holiness to which God calls us is for every believer, none excepted. Multiple levels of holiness do not exist, one for each kind of Christian.

I also agree with the emphasis that living a holy life requires our cooperation. While it is made possible by God and is of grace, it does not become integral to us apart from our volitional responsiveness. Both the divine initiative spoken of in 1 Thessalonians 5:24 ("The one who calls you is faithful, and he will do this") and the human action spoken of in Romans 12:1 ("Present your bodies as a living sacrifice") make up the divine economy of holiness.

DIFFERENCES

Differences between our two traditions are seen in the following. The strong emphasis on the sacraments as the means of the "initial reception of holiness" and in "the ongoing pursuit of it" is not an emphasis in my tradition. Instead, the emphasis is on the immediacy of the converting and sanctifying grace of God, neither work of which is confined to the reception of sacraments. The emphasis is on the "strangely warmed" heart and on the cleansing and empowering work of the Holy Spirit. Of primary importance is the personal experience of grace that is not dependent on the sacraments. To be sure, baptism, the Lord's Supper, and, for some in the Holiness tradition, foot washing are understood to be part and parcel of the economy of holiness, but not the definitive mode by which it is experienced. The emphasis is on the Holy Spirit who has immediate access to us and who is the one and only agent bringing the holiness of the Triune God into our lives. The difference between our two traditions has to do with the priority of emphasis. This difference is *not* between the Holy Spirit without sacraments (as though that were the Wesleyan/Holiness view) and sacraments without the Holy Spirit (as though that were the Roman Catholic view). Rather, it is a difference between an emphasis on the immediacy of the Holy Spirit and an emphasis on the cruciality of the sacraments. (However, see point 5 below.)

Another difference has to do with the last sentence in my colleague's paper: "It is especially incumbent upon all of the baptized to bring this holiness (the riches of Jesus Christ) to greater perfection within themselves so 'that the world may believe.'" My tradition would be more likely to say something like this: "It is the will of God for all believers to yield themselves to the work of the Holy Spirit who then will perfect our love for God so that we may be God's servant people in the world." Both of us agree that we are to cooperate with God. But at least at this point we appear to have differing emphases regarding who the agent of the perfecting endeavor is.

LACK OF UNDERSTANDING

The points at which I do not understand the language of a different Christian tradition are:

1. In the first paragraph, the sentence "Love of God and neighbor is that in which holiness consists but it always remains unfinished." If this means that we are to continually grow in love of God and neighbor, thereby growing in holiness, I understand it. But is that what is meant by "it always remains unfinished"? I need clarification in understanding the concept of unfinished love, unfinished holiness.

2. At another point, reference is made to "uncreated/created grace." I need further information about this terminology.

3. I am unclear about the idea concerning the extension of "the holiness of individuals and the holiness of the church" to all. Does this refer to the spread of the call to holiness, or does it refer to the spread of people's personal influence and the Church's influence? If the latter, what kind of influence is to be extended? Some possibilities that come to mind are the influence of a particular form of church life, the influence of love, the influence of social action, the influence of a particular doctrinal stance. I need additional discussion at this point.

4. Reference is made to "communal conversion with all that such implies." What is communal conversion? And what does it imply?

5. I do not know how to put together the strong emphasis on sacraments alongside the position taken to the effect that holiness is granted to those beyond the church, and, consequently, without the benefit of the sacraments. I need help in the reconciliation of these two perspectives.

RESPONSE

Kevin McMorrow, SA

In my response to Gilbert Stafford's paper I have been asked to identify three things: (1) points of resonance concerning what holiness means in the Wesleyan/Holiness tradition and the Catholic tradition; (2) differences that might exist in the meaning of holiness between the two traditions; (3) areas in which we simply do not understand each other relative to the meaning of holiness.

The same three things—resonance, difference, lack of understanding—are to be applied also to the following areas: What holiness means in terms of those outside the faith; and what holiness means ecumenically. The three areas: (1) holiness as understood in the Wesleyan/Holiness tradition and in the Catholic tradition; (2) what holiness means in terms of those outside the faith from the Wesleyan/Holiness and Catholic tradition; (3) what holiness means ecumenically from the Wesleyan/Holiness and Catholic traditions, fall under the general heading: "The Unitive Power of Holiness."

My reading of Stafford's paper leads me to say that I do not see any area or point in his presentation that I simply do not understand. I do see resonances or agreements and while there may be differences, I am not sure if such are real differences or simply differences of emphasis and differences that emerge from word formulations that often leave unsaid things that are taken for granted. Needless to say, a presentation on the meaning of holiness and other topics that is limited to about three pages necessarily means that much is left unsaid.

POINTS OF RESONANCE AND DIFFERENCE: THE MEANING OF HOLINESS

1. The Wesleyan/Holiness tradition describes holiness as the divine quality of life. It seems to me that this is in harmony with the Catholic perspective, namely, that holiness is the gift of God.

2. The Wesleyan/Holiness tradition stresses that holiness is present in individuals by virtue of their faith in Christ. Catholic teaching says that all holiness is merited by Christ and so faith in Christ informed by charity indeed renders a person holy.

3. The Wesleyan/Holiness tradition describes holiness, a result of faith in Christ, as establishing a status before God, a holiness of relationship that in turn sets believers apart "for participation in the divine mission through Christ." I believe that Catholic teaching would concur with this but would add that the relationship with God involves the indwelling of the Trinity. Participation in the divine mission flows from the dwelling of Father, Son, and Holy Spirit in the hearts of the faithful.

4. I think there is more emphasis in the Wesleyan/Holiness tradition on holiness consisting in faith in Christ than there is in the Catholic tradition. While the latter emphasizes the centrality of faith in Christ, it sees holiness as consisting in love of God and neighbor. Such love, of course, exists outside of the community of Christian believers. Within the community of believers this love of God and neighbor would be shaped both by the teaching of Jesus on love and by his filial sentiments of praise, thanksgiving, obedience, and so on.

5. Catholic teaching would agree with what Stafford has written: "But not only is holiness a gift; it is a pursuit." And both traditions would agree that the pursuit of holiness is due to the empowerment of the Holy Spirit. The Catholic tradition would bring sacramental grace into this

pursuit more than does the Wesleyan/Holiness tradition as I understand the latter. The free cooperation or assent underlined in the Catholic tradition resonates perfectly with what Stafford has written: "Our part in this spiritual pursuit is the offering of ourselves as living sacrifices to God" (Rom. 12:1–2).

POINTS OF RESONANCE AND DIFFERENCE: WHAT THIS MEANS IN TERMS OF THOSE OUTSIDE THE FAITH

1. The Wesleyan/Holiness tradition and the Catholic tradition are at one in their insistence that holiness is "for the purpose of divine mission in the world."

2. Both traditions, employing perhaps different language, would see the church as herald (sacrament) of that holiness which invites all peoples into communion with God and with each other.

3. I believe that both traditions would see the church as always in need of reform, that is, greater growth in holiness, in order for it to be a more effective witness to the saving grace of Christ.

4. Based on the fact that God wills the salvation of all (see 1 Tim 2:4), the Catholic tradition sees holiness as available to people of other faiths, to all who through no fault of their own do not know the gospel of Christ or his church but who seek God with a sincere heart, and, "moved by grace, try in their actions to do his will as they know it through the dictates of their conscience" (*LG*, par. 16). The Wesleyan/Holiness tradition would seem to be in accord with this based on the hymn "The Church's Jubilee" as reported in Stafford's text.

POINTS OF RESONANCE AND DIFFERENCE: WHAT THIS MEANS ECUMENICALLY

1. There is certainly total agreement between the Wesleyan/
   Holiness tradition and the Catholic tradition in the claim
   that the dynamic of Christian unity is inspired by the
   Holy Spirit in the human heart—the Catholic tradition
   would also say, in Christian churches and ecclesial communities.

2. Based on the objective holiness given through the sacra-
   ment of baptism, the Catholic tradition sees other
   Christians as incorporated into the death/resurrection of
   Christ and so joined to them as members of his body.

3. It seems to me that the Wesleyan/Holiness tradition
   stresses more individual or personal holiness as the impe-
   tus for unity rather than the communal bond of holiness
   based on baptism.

4. In the Catholic tradition the movement for the restoration
   of Christian unity proceeds, under the guidance of the
   Holy Spirit, from the foundation of a real, though imperfect, ecclesial communion linking Christian churches and
   ecclesial communities with the Catholic Church. Besides
   baptism other bonds of communion include faith, hope,
   love, Lord's Supper, sacred scripture, presence of the Holy
   Spirit, life of holiness, and so on. About bonds linking
   Eastern Christians with the Catholic Church see *Unitatis
   redintegratio,* pars. 14–18; for Western Christians see the
   same document, pars. 20–23. These bonds are invested
   with objective holiness.

5. In view of points 2, 3, and 4 in the text immediately
   above there would seem to be a difference of perspective
   between the Wesleyan/Holiness tradition and that of the
   Catholic Church. While the latter prizes holiness of
   heart, seeing it as God's gift, this holiness is known to
   God alone. It constitutes an invisible *communio sancto-
   rum.* The holiness of the ecumenical movement has an

ecclesial character that possesses at one and the same time both invisible and visible realities and pushes the churches forward to the goal of visible and full communion.

DIALOGUE 2

THE HERMENEUTICS OF RECONCILIATION IN WORSHIP: A DIALOGUE BETWEEN HOLINESS AND EASTERN ORTHODOX TRADITIONS

THE HOLINESS PERSPECTIVE ON RECONCILING LOVE IN WORSHIP

Gilbert W. Stafford

Worship in those churches that are outgrowths of the nineteenth-century Holiness movement is understood to be a celebration with the opportunity for spontaneity and personal exuberance, of the gift of reconciliation between us and God. It is the occasion for this reconciling love to be visibly and extemporaneously expressed among believers. It is the time when the various dimensions of the individual believer's life can be consecrated to the God who is able to bring them all together so that one can serve the purposes of God with wholeness of heart. The benediction of 2 Thessalonians 5:23–24 is well known by worshippers in these churches: "May the God of peace himself sanctify you entirely; and may your spirit and soul and body be kept sound and blameless at the coming of our Lord Jesus Christ. The one who calls you is faithful, and he will do this."

The view is that it is not enough for people to function as formal members of a Christian church, to affirm with their minds the historic understandings of the faith, and to go through the liturgical actions of Christian worship. While such are part and parcel of the life of the Christian community, they are insufficient. The question is whether one knows in one's heart what the reconciling love of God means. This is in the tradition of John Wesley, whose journal entry about the events of May 24, 1738, gives his well-known testimony:

> In the evening, I went very unwillingly to a society in Aldersgate Street, where one was reading Luther's Preface to the Epistle to the Romans. About a quarter before nine, while he was describing the change which God works in the heart through faith in Christ, I felt my heart strangely warmed. I felt I did trust in Christ, Christ alone for salvation; and an assurance was given me that he had taken away *my* sins, even *mine,* and saved *me* from the law of sin and death."[1]

As one early twentieth-century Holiness songwriter expressed it: (1) "When I read how my Savior was nailed to the cross / For the sins of the world to atone / O I feel so unworthy such suff'ring and loss / For I know in my heart what it means." (2) "When the Gospel is preached in the name of the Lord / By the Spirit sent down from above / My soul thrills with joy at the sound of his word / For I know in my heart what it means." (3) "When the sweet songs of Zion are floating above / And the saints all rejoice in the Lord / I am happy in Jesus and lost in his love / For I know in my heart what it means." (4) "And when others proclaim that salvation is free / When they tell of the soul-cleansing blood / I too, can rejoice, for he sanctified me / And I know in my heart what it means." Refrain: "I know in my heart what it means / Salvation, that word so divine / His Spirit has witnessed to mine / And I know in my heart what it means" (D. Otis Teasley, "I Know in My Heart What It Means").

If one does *not* know in one's heart what it means, worship is understood to be the occasion when it can happen. Liturgically this often takes place at the end of a service when the altar call (a holdover from the American camp meeting tradition) is given. If one *does* know in one's heart what it means, one may give a spontaneous, verbal testimony, or one may witness by lifting a hand as songs of the faith are being sung. This is a different liturgical practice from what is found in Pentecostal and Charismatic services, where both hands are raised in praise and adoration to God. In the Holiness tradition, the one hand stretched forth is a liturgical testimony that the historical and intellectual content of the faith has struck a chord in one's own heart. By doing so, one affirms that the faith content being sung about is claimed as one's own personal experience.

In Holiness thought, personal experience is not to determine the conceptual content of the faith; rather, the historic deposit of the faith is to determine the nature of one's personal experience. Worship is the time when personal hallelujahs of experience resonate with the historic content of the faith.

We see a dramatic example of this in Charles Wesley's "And Can It Be That I Should Gain?" In the first stanza the worshipper stands in amazement at God's grace: "Amazing love! how can it be That Thou, my God, shouldst die for me?" The second stanza is a recital of the incarnation: "He left His Father's throne above...Emptied Himself of all but love, And bled for Adam's helpless race!" The third, then, is a personal hallelujah regarding the experience of this liberating grace: "Long my imprisoned spirit lay fast bound in sins and nature's night. Thine eye diffused a quickening ray; I woke—the dungeon flamed with light! My chains fell off, my heart was free, I rose, went forth, and followed Thee." The fourth stanza rejoices in the new status resulting from so great a salvation: "No condemnation now I dread...And clothed in righteousness divine, Bold I approach th'eternal throne."

This psalm of Christian redemption expresses the essence of the Wesleyan/Holiness worship tradition:

- amazement at God's grace;
- the retelling of the story of God's grace;
- the personal experience of God's grace;
- testimony about the experience of God's grace; and
- rejoicing in the new status that grace gives.

To the degree that any of these is missing, Wesleyan/Holiness worship is not living up to its historic standard.

To a very great extent, the founding of the Church of the Nazarene under the leadership of Phineas F. Bresee, a respected Methodist pastor in Iowa and later in southern California, was the result of a "liturgical philosophy" that differed from the one prevailing in the established church of his day. According to Carl Bangs, Nazarene worship emerged with the three following principles. First, their gatherings were expected to be occasions for personal and corporate joy. "The members came rejoicing in the sense of sins forgiven, of hearts freed from the recurring selfishness of the 'carnal nature,' and of fresh 'anointings' by the Holy Spirit that renewed and deepened the way of holiness. They came to the services expectantly, welcoming the company of kindred spirits and hoping that the service would not be barren of spiritual victories."

Second, while they "respected traditional forms of worship and sometimes drew on them, they were interested primarily in the spiritual vitality that had produced those historic forms. Bresee, noted for his mastery of ritual, was not ritualistic. He regarded the fashionable formality in the old churches as stifling to the life that once had enlivened the forms."

And third, "they believed that spiritual worship in such a basic, primary sense would issue in the salvation of sinners and the sanctification of believers. A public invitation to seekers of forgiveness and purity was always appropriate and nearly always took place. Meetings were described less in terms of attendance or program than in terms of seekers responding to Gospel promises. It was expected that people would seek God wherever Christians gathered."[2]

What we see in this characterization of Nazarene worship is true of Holiness worship in general:

- Worship is the gathering of those who have a personal walk with the Lord.

- Worship is not to be measured by external order but by the internal reordering of lives according to the image of Christ.

- Worship is time for transformation from the life of sin to the life of salvation, from the life of struggle as a Christian to one of victory, from the heaviness and frustrations of life to the peace and joy of the Lord.

Holiness worship at its best is a time for the heartfelt experience of the reconciling love of God in Christ. It is a time for this love to issue forth in reconciliation among believers, and between different classes and races of people. This emphasis is expressed in the openness of Holiness churches to the socially marginalized. It is seen in their historic acceptance of women in pastoral leadership. It is seen in the founding impulses of the Wesleyan Methodist Church and the Free Methodist Church, regarding their antislavery stance and the insistence that all church pews would be free.

WHAT THIS MEANS TO THOSE OUTSIDE THE COMMUNITY OF FAITH

What all this means in relation to those outside the community of faith is that worship is intended to be a time of openness to all regardless of social or spiritual status. Worship is intended as a corporate offer of salvation, sanctification, and reconciliation between people, classes, and races. But beyond this, worship is understood as being that time when believers are transformed to such an extent that they become agents of Christ in the world. This is understood in terms of their own personal quality of life, in terms of their willingness to effect change in unjust social structures, and in terms of service to people, especially those on the margins of society.

WHAT THIS MEANS ECUMENICALLY

Wesleyan/Holiness worship has the potential of providing a context for the Christian community as a whole to grow in its appreciation of the sacramental character of hymn singing, preaching, testimony, and decision making in the midst of community. Holiness churches lift up the reality of experiencing the grace of God through singing. Something divine can happen to us personally as we sing together. The community of faith can become aware that then and there God is speaking to them in fresh and transforming ways. Often Holiness people use phrases of songs as a kind of sacramental sign over their lives. In a recent publication of my own local congregation, an article about a retired couple who had spent their lives in public school administration and teaching ended like this: "A line from a favorite heritage song expresses the life commitment of Jan and Jerry Elston: 'I'll put my whole heart in His service, and do all He asketh of me.'" That song had become a sacramental experience for them.

The same is true of preaching. Holiness preaching is more than instruction; it is more than commentary on a text. It calls for personal response and transformation. It is intended to issue in a here and now change of heart and life.

The same is true regarding testimony and response to the altar call. As a testimony is given and as persons respond to the Spirit by going forward to the altar rail to pray, the grace of God is often experienced by the congregation as being visibly at work in the ones testifying and in the decisional movement to pray at the altar rails.

These dimensions of body life have been so highlighted in Holiness churches that they possibly may enrich the whole church's understanding of the potentially sacramental character of singing, preaching, testimony, and decisional responses.

NOTES

1. *John Wesley,* ed. Albert C. Outler (New York: Oxford University Press, 1964), 66.

2. Carl Bangs, *Phineas F. Bresee: His Life in Methodism, the Holiness Movement, and the Church of the Nazarene* (Kansas City: Beacon Hill Press, 1995), 231.

THE HERMENEUTICS OF RECONCILIATION: PERSPECTIVES FROM THE ORTHODOX LITURGICAL EXPERIENCE

John H. Erickson

To speak of Orthodox Christianity without speaking of Orthodox worship would be difficult, if not impossible. As has been pointed out so often, for the Orthodox Christian, orthodoxy does not mean simply adherence to right doctrine, to the letter of a dogma or ideology, as may be implied when one speaks of Lutheran or Freudian or Marxist orthodoxy. While the *doxa* that lies at the root of the word *orthodoxy* can mean "opinion" or "teaching," it also means "glory," a meaning picked up in the Slavonic word for orthodoxy, *Pravoslavie*. For the Orthodox Christian, orthodoxy preeminently means rendering glory, right worship, to the one to whom all glory, honor, and worship are due.

The central importance of worship for Orthodox church life can be demonstrated in many ways. For example, worship historically has been a primary vehicle for mission and evangelization. When Sts. Cyril and Methodius went from Constantinople to the Slavs of Moravia, they brought with them an alphabet which in principle made possible the translation of any texts whatsoever into the language of the people. But the texts that they translated were primarily liturgical. Their translations of scripture, for example, were in the form of lectionaries designed for liturgical use. So central was liturgy deemed to be that, according to the *Life* of Cyril, the saint's first activities included teaching his new disciples "the whole ecclesiastical office: matins, the hours, vespers, compline and the liturgy."[1] A century later, when a delegation of pagan Slavs came to Constantinople from Kiev on behalf of their prince, Vladimir, they were taken to services in the great Church of Haghia Sophia. Earlier they had found the worship of the Muslims to be abominable, that of the Germans to be "lacking in beauty," but in Haghia Sophia, "We knew not whether we were in heaven or on earth. For on earth there is no such splendor or such beauty, and we are at a loss how to describe it. We only know that God dwells there."[2]

For Orthodox Christians over the centuries, liturgy has formed their sense of Christian identity and maintained it not only when great temples like Haghia Sophia were fully functioning but also in times of marginalization and overt persecution. It has also served as a fundamental—if not *the* fundamental—point of reference in matters of faith, church order, and ethics. Contrary to the view of many Orthodox Christians themselves, Orthodox liturgy *has* experienced historical development. It is not static, utterly unchanged and unchanging. Nevertheless, the Orthodox liturgical tradition as a whole has been quite conservative. It has borne witness to the church's identity and continuity through the ages without major disruptions or revolutions. This has helped make it an independent and authoritative criterion in doctrinal and disciplinary matters to a degree unmatched in the Christian West, where liturgical rites more often have been viewed as external signs subject to regulation and easy modification by competent church authority, be that a Roman congregation, a worship committee, or an individual presider. The Orthodox East, having known its share of heretical patriarchs and emperors and pseudo-councils, regularly subjected the claims of individual officeholders to the test of liturgy, the central expression of the life of the whole body of Christ. While blessed by institutional continuity, the Orthodox East did not equate this with institutional infallibility. False institutional security was regularly challenged by the charismatic indiscipline of great monastic saints like Maximus the Confessor, who appealed to the Holy Spirit as the ultimate criterion of truth. Yet, monastic claims to spiritual authority, if they were not to be dismissed as examples of centrifugal and sectarian

"Messalianism," also were subject to the test of the church's liturgical ethos. As Fr. John Meyendorff has observed, "The prophetic or charismatic role of the Orthodox monks was seen as legitimate only in the context of sacramental liturgical communion, which itself presupposed the existence of an institutional hierarchy."[3]

In principle, then, Orthodox worship is the meeting place of institution and event, office and charism, word and spirit, where these are not simply juxtaposed but rather are experienced as one and inseparable. In principle, therefore, Orthodox worship should serve as the key for understanding Orthodoxy itself. It should provide insights into fundamental issues of faith and order that go beyond their formulation, for example, in the dogmas and canons of the ecumenical councils. Yet, the ethos of Orthodox worship is not easy to penetrate. Liturgy presents hermeneutical problems that those accustomed to wrestling primarily with authoritative texts seldom encounter. One cannot "read" liturgical services in the same way that one reads the Bible or the Augsburg Confession or the works of Marx or Freud.

These observations hold true for liturgy in general, even for the liturgy of Super Bowl Sunday, but they hold true especially for Orthodox liturgy, which is singularly intricate. If gathered in one place, the service books requisite for its execution in the course of the liturgical year would fill several bookshelves. Those acquainted with popular books on Orthodoxy, such as Bishop Kallistos Ware's excellent presentation of *The Orthodox Way,* or even with more esoteric works like Vladimir Lossky's *Mystical Theology of the Orthodox Church,* may suspect that, if worship is the key to Orthodoxy, then the key is much more complex than the mysteries it claims to open. Some years ago I took an elderly aunt to her first Orthodox Divine Liturgy. Shortly thereafter I overheard her describing the experience to a friend. Her first observation was: "It was different"— which in Midwestern English is the phrase one might use, for example, to describe one's first encounter with escargot. She then went on to add: "Well, there sure was a lot of ritual." Now I had spared my aunt the complications of the previous evening's "all-night vigil," in fact a service of slightly under two hours combining vespers, matins, and the first hour. I had seen to it that she had a chair (something not to be taken for granted in an Orthodox church). The service itself had been sung entirely in English (also something not to be taken for granted), and I had provided a running commentary on the service, noting structural affinities with the Lutheran eucharistic liturgy with which she had some passing familiarity. Still, I could understand her discomfort. The atmosphere of an Orthodox church is unlike that of most other Christian traditions. The many icons, the elaborate vestments, the clouds of incense, the postures and gestures of clergy and faithful, the melodies of the endless chants—for many Christians, all this is indeed "different." Here my aunt was certainly correct. But what makes Orthodox worship different is not simply the fact that there is "a lot of ritual." The difference lies also in the goal and object of this ritual: to communicate the most basic truths of the Christian faith through "right worship."

Jaroslav Pelikan neatly summarizes the goal of "right worship":

> From its beginning the Orthodox Christian liturgy has sought to emphasize simultaneously two opposite poles of faith: God's distance and majesty, and God's nearness and accessibility. God the Almighty is transcendent over heaven and earth and humanity—indeed transcendent over all the language, including the language of Orthodox liturgy and doctrine, with which mortals seek to describe the awesome mystery of the Holy One. At the same time, the Holy One is near and accessible to us through the ultimate mystery of the Incarnation of the Son of God, "God the Word," in the birth, life, death, and resurrection of Jesus Christ, and therefore through the "mysteries" (the Orthodox term for "sacraments") celebrated by the Church in its liturgy.[4]

Orthodox worship does indeed convey a sense of the transcendent majesty of the Holy One. Through the measured cadence of the many litanies, with their incessant *Kyrie eleisons;* through the strains of short hymns and acclamations, often thrice repeated, which cry out "Holy God, Holy Mighty, Holy Immortal: Have mercy on us!"; through prayers that praise God for his majesty without lecturing him unduly about what has appeared in the morning's headlines; through all the accoutrements of the temple and its ministers, worshippers enter into the rhythm and beauty of the heavenly liturgy, joining the cherubim and seraphim in their never-ending songs of praise. At the same time, this heavenly liturgy is wonderfully tangible, accessible, and inclusive. It does not just convey information about divine matters for those whose intellectual gifts and superior education enable them to "understand" what is going on and being said. It appeals to all the senses, making it readily accessible to children and others who otherwise might be marginalized. It says to each one, in ways beyond counting, that the Transcendent One is near, that the Holy One wants us to participate in his holiness, that the Immortal One invites us to share in his eternal life. A young child once explained to me why he liked to go to church. "We usually get something," he said. And that certainly is true: fruit at Transfiguration, holy water at Epiphany, palms and pussy willows on Palm Sunday, an egg at Easter, sweet-smelling oil on the forehead at nearly every vigil, something sweet to taste at the Eucharist. No doubt that child's explanations will become more sophisticated when he is an adult, but what he has experienced of Orthodoxy as a child, through all that ritual, at least is not something that he will subsequently have to unlearn. "Taste and see that the Lord is good"—these psalm verses sung during communion at the Lenten Liturgy of the Presanctified Gifts are as true for him now as they will be when he grows up.

As Pelikan's remarks suggest, Orthodox worship communicates the very substance of Orthodox theology. In and through right worship, the biblical message of God's reconciling love, which the dogmas of the ancient councils simply sought to safeguard, comes alive. The most obvious aspects of this message involve Christology, pneumatology, and the other classic issues in Christian doctrine. But this message also has important ecclesiological implications. Orthodox worship implies the presence of Orthodox worshippers, with all their diverse gifts, formed by the power of the Holy Spirit as one body of Christ. It is the worship of the church, of a community of faith, not just of an ad hoc gathering of individuals, much less of a single individual. A friend, now institutionalized, used to have a recurrent nightmare. He was in the midst of a hierarchical liturgy performing all the roles himself—bishop, attendant subdeacons and altar boys, deacon, college of presbyters, choir director and choir (SATB), reader, congregation. In short, he dreamed of an impossibility. Orthodox worship in the absence of icons, incense, and all the other ritual paraphernalia is hard to imagine, though it can be done. But Orthodox worship without a diversity of roles and ministries within the one ecclesial body is simply inconceivable. No doubt the role of the clergy in Orthodox worship is particularly conspicuous, with cantors and choir close behind. But it would be a mistake to label this worship as "clerical." One consequence of having a stable liturgy with "a lot of ritual" is that everyone (with the possible exception of ecumenical visitors) knows the rules. Everyone knows his or her proper place and task. Everyone feels at home. A middle-aged gentleman, perhaps the president of the parish council, presides at the candle stand. A lady rushes in, perhaps slightly late, with an armful of flowers that she arranges around the icons. A young mother exits without embarrassment to quiet her crying baby. An old man hobbles around snuffing out spent candles. And if the priest starts to sing the wrong troparion, very possibly the choir will quickly drown him out with the right one. Notably absent is the sense of confusion and alienation that so often results when a hapless congregation is left to the tender mercies of an inventive presider.

Orthodox worship both reflects and reinforces the solidarity of the faithful, clergy and laity together. It forms and manifests their identity as a community, where each one feels at home. A danger arises, however, when Orthodoxy comes to be perceived and experienced as a tribal religion—or indeed as a collection of tribal religions, for an Orthodox Christian "at home" with his own people, comfortable in his own particular cultural expression of Orthodoxy, may well find other expressions of Orthodoxy as different as any non-Orthodox would. How can this danger be averted? How can a given community of Orthodox Christians of whatever ethnic flavor truly become a community of faith, and therefore a community capable of recognizing other communities of the same faith? Historically, at least for the Chalcedonian Eastern Orthodox, the liturgy has provided a common point of reference, a test for integrity and authenticity. But if liturgy is truly to fulfill this function, it cannot be reduced to a collection of inherited rites to be slavishly followed with no concern for distinguishing between what is truly essential and what is historically and culturally relative. The theological content of liturgy, and not just its external forms, must be explored in depth. Is the same Spirit in fact at work, ever forming anew, in each new cultural context, the same one body of Christ? This is a question that Orthodox Christians need to ask not only of their own worship but also of that of other Christians. Quite possibly we will find that worship, even when "different," unites us in deeper ways than we hitherto have recognized.

NOTES

1. *VC* 15.2, cited by Francis Dvornik, *Byzantine Missions among the Slavs* (New Brunswick, NJ: Rutgers University Press, 1970), 107.

2. *The Russian Primary Chronicle: Laurentian Text,* ed. and trans. Samuel H. Cross and Olgerd P. Sherbowitz-Wetzor (Cambridge, MA: Medieval Academy, 1953), 95–96.

3. John Meyendorff, *The Byzantine Legacy in the Orthodox Church* (Crestwood, NY: SVS Press, 1982), 122–23.

4. Jaroslav Pelikan, "Orthodox Christianity," in *World Religions in America: An Introduction,* ed. Jacob Neusner (Louisville, KY: Westminster John Knox Press, 1994), 139–40.

RESPONSE

Gilbert W. Stafford

I very much appreciate the clarity with which Professor Erickson has discussed the Orthodox liturgical experience. In accordance with our agreed procedure, I shall respond at three levels.

RESONANCE

In light of the fact that my esteemed colleague describes his own tradition, he, of course, is the authority in this dialogue, as to what his tradition is. My role, therefore, is not to determine whether I agree with what he says about Orthodox liturgy. My role, as I see it, is to identify points at which what he says about the Orthodox liturgy evokes a Wesleyan/Holiness Amen. The following are examples of such Amens.

Erickson writes, "Worship historically has been a primary vehicle for mission and evangelization." Although we represent different liturgical traditions, the fact of the matter is that the North American Holiness churches, coming as they do out of a camp-meeting tradition, have always seen worship as the opportunity to set forth the gospel of converting and sanctifying grace in the firm hope that yet more persons would respond in faith to the gospel. The so-called altar call at the conclusion of services is the liturgical form this perspective takes in the Holiness tradition.

"Orthodox worship is the meeting place of institution and event, office and charism, word and spirit, where these are not simply juxtaposed but rather are experienced as one and inseparable." In Holiness worship the same is true with its emphasis on the whole people of God in worship. No sharp distinction is made between clergy and laity. The laity lead in prayer, enter into a common sensitivity to the leadership of the Holy Spirit as to the direction the service should go, assume responsibility for what goes on, and participate as the priesthood of all believers. I was interested in a subsequent point in the paper where reference is made to the responsibility of all participants for the service. Erickson says that "if the priest starts to sing the wrong troparion, very possibly the choir will quickly drown him out with the right one." I have seen this same dynamic especially in African American worship where the congregation not only sanctions audibly what the preacher and other leaders are saying or singing, but also lets them know when they need to do better, with such audible comments as "Come on, now, and preach."

In Holiness churches, worship is understood as the common focal point for both our institutional responsibilities and our spiritual development. What happens in worship often influences what we do in our institutional life. It is not uncommon for institutional decisions to be formulated, reversed, or revised as a result of common worship.

"Orthodox worship should serve as the key for understanding Orthodoxy itself." This may be a truism about all of our traditions. In my own church, which has no official confessional statements, we often say, "If you want to know what we believe, listen to our songs."

"Orthodox worship does indeed convey a sense of the transcendent majesty of the Holy One." One sees this in Wesley hymns such as "Rejoice, the Lord is King! Your Lord and King Adore!" Holiness worship at its best is a time when the congregation is in joyous awe of the transcendent God who does marvelous works of grace in our lives. This may be expressed in the spontaneous responses of the people as they listen to the message, sing, and participate in prayer. The unprogrammed expressions either of one's joy in the presence of the transcendent God who has done a mighty work in us, or of one's sorrow for sin against this holy God, is common. Regarding our joy in God's presence, my particular church sings with words like "It is joy unspeakable and full of glory, O the half has never yet been told!" and "I will sing hallelujah, for there's joy in the Lord, And He fills my heart with rapture as I rest on His Word."

"Quite possibly we will find that worship, even when 'different,' unites us in deeper ways than we hitherto have recognized." This is a position with which I very much resonate. In the worship of God, God is able to come in Self-presentation and do for us and in us that which not only is beyond our comprehension but also beyond our "best" and our "worst" liturgies. I am reminded of Ephesians 3:20–21: "Now to him who by the power at work within us is able to accomplish abundantly far more than all we can ask or imagine, to him be glory in the church and in Christ Jesus to all generations, forever and ever. Amen."

DIFFERENCES

Although the differences between our two liturgical traditions are vast, my purpose is not to identify all of the specifics, but to identify general perspectives in my colleague's paper with which my tradition would differ.

We would differ about the importance of "icons, incense, and all other ritual paraphernalia." Erickson says that it is hard to imagine Orthodox worship in the absence of such, though it can be done. I do not disagree that such is the case for Orthodox worship, but my tradition would hold that in order for worship to be truly Christian it in no way requires "ritual paraphernalia."

In addition, we differ with Orthodoxy in relation to the main point of this paragraph, namely, that "Orthodox worship without a diversity of roles and ministries within the one ecclesial body is simply inconceivable." If this means that worship is inconceivable whenever the congregation consists only of ordained clergy or only of laity, we would disagree. It is not the presence of these two components that makes for authentically Christian worship, but the gathering of any group of believers in the name of Christ.

LACK OF UNDERSTANDING

I need more information about the sentence: "Yet, monastic claims to spiritual authority, if they were not to be dismissed as examples of centrifugal and sectarian 'Messalianism,' also were subject to the test of the church's liturgical ethos." What is "centrifugal and sectarian 'Messalianism'"?

Another sentence that I am not sure I understand is: "One cannot 'read' liturgical services in the same way that one reads the Bible or the Augsburg Confession or the works of Marx or Freud." Is this remark about liturgical services a reference to their mystical character? If so, does this mean that there is no mystical character to the Bible, for instance?

RESPONSE

John H. Erickson

Professor Stafford and I were given a complex task. In an initial round of short papers, we were to introduce the most salient characteristics of the worship of our respective traditions to an ecumenical audience; we were to do this with special attention to the "hermeneutics of reconciliation" (whatever that may mean); and, appropriate to the topic of this study group, we were to tease out some ecclesiological implications. Then we were to exchange papers and respond, noting points of resonance (something rings a bell), dissonance (something sets off an alarm), and what might be called non-sonance (I just don't catch what you are saying). Finally, we were to pursue these points through dialogue and discussion. In the following paragraphs I shall respond to Stafford's initial paper, noting points of resonance, dissonance, and non-sonance, but I shall also use the occasion to carry our dialogue further by clarifying certain points in my initial paper that may have been misunderstood and by calling attention to certain new issues that seem to be emerging in Stafford's response to my initial paper.

As I tried to suggest in my initial paper, and as anyone familiar with Orthodox worship will attest, this worship is a kinesthetic experience. It appeals not just to the mind, but to all the senses—sight (e.g., through icons), hearing (e.g., through singing), smell (e.g., through use of incense), taste (e.g., through bread and wine both eucharistic and noneucharistic), and touch (e.g., through anointing with oil at a festal vigil). Certain points made by Stafford and my own limited experience of the Wesleyan/ Holiness tradition of worship (chiefly in African American contexts) suggest that this is true in some measure in that tradition also. His paper repeatedly emphasized the centrality—indeed the sacramentality—of singing in the Wesleyan/Holiness tradition and also called attention to the affective quality of Holiness preaching, which makes it "more than instruction." Holiness worship certainly does appeal to the ear, but it also appeals to at least some of the other senses, such as touch (e.g., the gesture of the raised hand mentioned by Stafford) and sight (e.g., the beautiful choir robes and "Sunday best" clothes so often encountered in African American contexts). If that is the case, it strikes me as mildly inconsistent for Stafford's tradition to "hold that in order for worship to be truly Christian it in no way requires 'ritual paraphernalia.'" The point of the "ritual paraphernalia" in Orthodox worship is to engage the entire human person, not just the mind or the disembodied "spirit." In and through the abundant use of material elements in its worship, Orthodoxy affirms that the whole cosmos is called to sanctification and "deification," that is, participation in divine life.

Stafford's initial paper twice called attention to worship as an occasion of a twofold reconciliation. In worship we celebrate "the gift of reconciliation between us and God" and experience "the reconciling love of God in Christ." At the same time, worship is "a time for this love to issue forth in reconciliation among believers." With this the Orthodox tradition in worship certainly resonates. In worship we experience the reconciliation of humankind with God, the reconciliation of earth with heaven that was accomplished when the transcendent God became immanent, accessible, and tangible through the mystery of the incarnation. In worship we also experience reconciliation with one another. This is most obvious when we become one body through sharing in the one Eucharist; but as I emphasized in my initial paper, the inclusive character of Orthodox worship is revealed in other ways as well. For example, by appealing to all the senses Orthodox worship is readily accessible to children and others who might be marginalized by a more verbal and intellectual approach. (In the Orthodox Church, it should be noted, infants and children are not excluded from receiving the Eucharist.)

At another point, Stafford's paper initially prompted a strong sense of resonance, but this gave way to some fears of nonsonance or even of dissonance: "In Holiness thought, personal experience is not to determine the conceptual content of the faith; rather, the historic deposit of the faith is to determine the nature of one's personal experience." So far the Orthodox would certainly agree. At this point, as an Orthodox theologian I would have expected some consideration of the ways in which worship has helped assure the diachronic identity of the church's apostolic faith. In what follows, however, Stafford does not specify how "the historic deposit of the faith" is maintained intact from age to age, whether through worship or some other means. He affirms that "worship is the time when personal hallelujahs of experience resonate with the historical content of the faith," and in the next paragraph he gives an example of this "personal hallelujah." But here the substance of the faith seems to be taken for granted, and, perhaps as a result, issues relating to its historical continuity and consistency are not broached.

We begin to touch on some major areas of dissonance in matters of "faith and order." For the Orthodox, continuity of the apostolic faith in all its fullness is inseparable from the historical continuity of the church as a structured community. But this structured community is not simply an institution. It is a sacramental organism whose nature and essential characteristics are revealed most fully when the faithful, with their diverse gifts, are gathered in worship, formed by the power of the Holy Spirit as the one body of Christ. Within this one worshipping body, there are diverse roles and ministries, reflecting a diversity of gifts. As I tried to emphasize in my paper, neither worship nor the church can be a one-man show. But how is the diachronic and synchronic identity of the church to be maintained? How is a given worshipping community to maintain continuity in the confession and living out of the apostolic faith and unity both internally and with other communities? Here the Orthodox would look first of all to the structuring ministry provided by the bishop assisted by the presbyters.

In his response to my paper, Stafford indicated two points on which he wished some clarification or word of explanation.

First, what is "centrifugal and sectarian 'Messalianism'"? In the Byzantine East, "Messalian" was a pejorative term applied to self-styled charismatics or illuminists who downplayed or rejected the church's sacramental life in the name of direct religious experience. Orthodox theologians sometimes have criticized Western Christianity, and particularly Roman Catholicism, for neglecting pneumatology and, as a consequence, for unduly emphasizing institution over event, office over charism. At the same time, for the Orthodox East the Holy Spirit is not a centrifugal but rather a centripetal force, forming one body of Christ out of what otherwise would be a collection of heterogeneous individuals.

Second, what did I mean when I remarked that "one cannot 'read' liturgical services in the same way that one reads the Bible or the Augsburg Confession or the works of Marx or Freud"? Here I wished only to indicate that one cannot transfer to liturgy hermeneutical principles intended for authoritative *texts*. Liturgy conveys meaning in a radically different way.

This leads me to one final observation. While at several points Stafford emphasized the extemporaneous and personal character of Holiness worship, from my own limited experience—but also from a number of passing comments in Stafford's paper and his response to mine—I have come to be rather impressed by the surprising number of ritualized gestures, actions, and exclamations, from the raised hand to the altar call to the Amen or the "Come on, now, and preach!" As I indicated in my own paper, I am accustomed to worship with "a lot of ritual," and I value this ritual because it allows worship to become a communal act in which everyone feels at home because everyone knows the rules. Given this background, I believe that I can recognize ritual when I see it. And I find a lot more ritual in Holiness worship, particularly in its African American manifestations, than Stafford's paper might suggest. Indeed, it may be that the great power of worship in this tradition comes precisely from its ritual quality.

DIALOGUE 3

APOSTOLICITY: A DIALOGUE
BETWEEN THE ROMAN CATHOLIC
TRADITION AND THE STONE-CAMPBELL
RESTORATION TRADITION

THE NATURE OF THE APOSTOLICITY OF THE CHURCH: PERSPECTIVES FROM CHURCHES OF CHRIST

Douglas A. Foster

CONTEXT

Churches of Christ make up one part of the Stone-Campbell Restoration Movement that originated in the nineteenth century.[1] Though not shaped exclusively by the American frontier, the movement drank deeply from the wells of the democratic and primitivist thought that permeated the early republic.[2] The roots of the restorationist/primitivist ideas of Churches of Christ have multiple origins, each shaping the group in distinctive ways—the Renaissance notion of *ad fontes* that fueled parts of the Protestant Reformation; the Anabaptist vision of a return to simple pre-Constantinian Christianity; the Puritan quest for a restitution of the primitive church purified from the corruptions of the medieval establishment; Enlightenment assumptions about human ability to discern the evident facts of religion and all reality. All were foundational in the creation of the movement's identity.

A strong ahistorical ethos characterized the America of the nineteenth century, an attitude that, ironically, led most of these restorationists to deny any influence from the past on their beliefs and actions. "The past," said Barton W. Stone, "is to be consigned to the rubbish heap upon which Christ died." The task they set for themselves was, like that of the Renaissance humanists, to leap over the corruptions that had overtaken the visible church for centuries and re-create the pure apostolic church of the first century. The Stone-Campbell Movement formulated its own precise vision of what that "New Testament church" would look like. Though other restorationist groups saw the goal in different ways, all were agreed that the quest to "go back" to the true apostolic church was essential.[3]

The restorationist theology of Churches of Christ is important for this discussion, then, partly because it represents a major stream of thinking in American Christianity, the implications of which have determined the basic understandings of the nature of the church and of apostolicity for many groups.

EARLY DEVELOPMENT

The early leaders of the Stone-Campbell Restoration Movement held to the universal Protestant understanding that relatively soon after the founding of the church a falling away from true apostolic teaching and practice had taken place. In line with Protestant thinking, they interpreted passages like 1 Timothy 4:1–3 to mean the apostasy of the Roman Church; but in these verses they also saw the Protestant denominations/institutions that perpetuated numerous departures from simple apostolic Christianity. They believed that, once freed from the shackles of the creeds and denominational hierarchies, anyone could read the New Testament and understand the simplicity of true Christianity. Following democratized Enlightenment understandings popular in the United States, they insisted that the facts were plain, and that human reason was capable of discerning them.

Most restorationist groups in the past had seen separation from "apostate" believers as essential to their enterprise. In contrast, many leaders of the Stone-Campbell Movement (and others in the American context) saw the restoration of the primitive apostolic church as the means of achieving the apostolic *unity* of Christians.[4] When the doctrinal corruptions and human additions that divided believers—particularly denominational creeds and structures—were dropped as terms of communion, Christians in every locality would flow together as one.

The precise appearance of that restored apostolic church developed over several decades, beginning with a document written in 1809 by a former Scottish Presbyterian minister named Thomas Campbell. Called "The Declaration and Address of the Christian Association of Washington County, Washington, Pennsylvania," it was designed as a call to all Christians to join the quest for the primitive purity and unity of the church. Among Campbell's points were these:

> Nothing ought to be inculcated upon Christians as articles of faith; nor required of them as terms of communion, but what is expressly taught and enjoined upon them in the word of God...expressly enjoined by the authority of our Lord Jesus Christ and his apostles upon the New Testament Church; either in express terms or by approved precedent.
>
> [No] human authority [has] power to impose new commands or ordinances upon the Church, which our Lord Jesus Christ has not enjoined. Nothing ought to be received into the faith or worship of the Church, or be made a term of communion among Christians, that is not as old as the New Testament.
>
> [N]ecessary to the highest state of perfection and purity of the church upon earth is...that her ministers...keep close by the observance of all Divine ordinances, after the example of the primitive church, exhibited in the New Testament; without any additions whatsoever of human opinions or inventions of men.[5]

Eventually Thomas Campbell's oldest son, Alexander, became the chief leader of the movement. The younger Campbell first attempted a precise articulation of the beliefs and practices of the apostolic church in a series of articles written between 1824 and 1830 and published in his journal the *Christian Baptist*. In the series, titled "A Restoration of the Ancient Order of Things," Campbell discussed such items of faith as the weekly Sunday observance of the Lord's Supper as a simple memorial, a plurality of bishops and deacons in every congregation, strict congregational polity, purging worship and speech of unscriptural words and ideas, and exercising discipline on church members as marks of the apostolic church.

Alexander Campbell's most complete exposition of apostolicity, however, is found in his 1835 book *The Christian System,* the closest thing to a systematic theology in the early movement. Many of the earlier emphases from the *Christian Baptist* articles reappear, but the bulk of the volume focuses on the matter of baptism (immersion) of believers for salvation. In his exposition of the doctrine Campbell stresses the apostolic witness of the New Testament documents. Interestingly he does not confine himself to that evidence, but quotes extensively from the church fathers and from Reformation leaders and creeds to demonstrate that baptism has always been understood as a salvific act, the place where God saves the submissive believer.[6] This doctrine of baptism became in the minds of many both in and out of the movement its most distinctive characteristic and the centerpiece of restoring the apostolic church.[7]

Roman Catholic scholar Richard Tristano describes this understanding of baptism as "a *via media* between the evangelical Protestant and Roman Catholic views on the subject." Because he taught that a real change of state is effected by the act of baptism, Campbell and others in the movement were often accused of denying the Reformation concept of justification by faith alone and of promoting the "papist" idea of baptismal regeneration. This was in spite of his insistence on the immersion only of believing penitents.[8]

Restoration of both the ancient Gospel and the ancient order early became the focus for the movement's leaders. Walter Scott, the movement's most successful evangelist in the 1830s, believed that he had restored the apostolic plan of salvation while preaching in Northeast Ohio in 1827. Faith, repentance, baptism, remission of sins, and the gift of the Holy Spirit became the "five finger exercise" that encapsulated the stages taught by the apostles through which one progresses for salvation.[9]

LATER DEVELOPMENT

These ideas were recapitulated often in the later movement. Two examples stand out in the late nineteenth and early twentieth centuries. In 1889 John F. Rowe published a volume titled *A History of Reformatory Movements Resulting in a Restoration of the Apostolic Church.* The volume proved very popular among the churches and was revised and expanded through at least nine editions. Rowe begins with a description of the church's apostasy in organization and teaching by the end of the second century. With a brief overview of European religio-political events through Pope Gregory X, he concludes his first chapter:

> These are strange developments of church affairs, compared with the origin of Christianity and primitive Gospel simplicity. The facts we glean and scrap [*sic*] from the Dark Ages, are the full fruitage of the workings of the "mystery of iniquity" alluded to by the Apostle Paul....That there was a remnant of the true worshipers of God found here and there through the Dark Ages, such as the Nestorians, is a pleasing fact well established in history; but that nearly all traces of the primitive order of things, as established by the apostles of Jesus Christ, are lost sight of in the raging conflicts of rival princes and aspiring ecclesiastics...are facts patent and intelligible to all readers of history. We wish the people of this generation, as well as the people of succeeding generations, to know the reasons why we stand apart from all denominations, Papal and Protestant, and why we propose to stand only on apostolic ground.[10]

Rowe spends most of the rest of the book tracing the history of specific departures from apostolic faith (including such items as holy water, monastic vows, purgatory, mariology, and the invocation of saints) and the attempt—but ultimate failure—of all reformatory movements prior to that of the Campbells and Barton W. Stone. While applauding the efforts of pioneers like Martin Luther, Rowe insisted that not one "effected a restoration of the apostolic order of things, either in doctrine or practice."[11]

Another example of this approach to apostolicity among Churches of Christ is a short book by James C. Creel published in 1902. In the *Plea to Restore the Apostolic Church,* Creel asserts that the apostolic church was built by Christ through his divinely inspired and commissioned apostles. That church was, in the beginning, exactly what Christ wanted it to be in eight essential areas: its faith, doctrine, organization, government, unity, terms of fellowship, terms of admission, and worship. He then specified what that meant in each area.

> The faith of the Apostolic Church was faith in the Christ, its divine founder. The doctrine of the Apostolic Church was the doctrine of the Christ, which was preached and taught by the inspired apostles and inspired teachers, who preached and taught all things whatsoever commanded by the Christ. [Its] organization consisted solely in the organization of the local congregation or local church. There was no aggregating of any number of local churches of Christ into some ecclesiastical organization in the days of the apostles. [Its] government was wholly congregational....Each local congregation was composed of "saints," "bishops" or "elders" or "pastors," and deacons. The unity of the Apostolic Church consisted in the spiritual oneness of all those in Christ,...in the faith in the Christ and in the doctrine taught by the Christ through the inspired apostles. The terms of fellowship of the Apostolic Church were these: (1) Faith in the Christ, (2) obedience to him in all things. Whatever is a Gospel condition of salvation, or entrance into the body of Christ, the Apostolic Church, that and that only, should be made a test of Christian fellowship. Its terms of admission are simple and plain. They are these: Faith in the Christ, repentance, confession of the Christ, baptism. The worship of the Apostolic Church is the simple worship of the Father in spirit and in truth, through the Christ....The primitive disciples of Christ met upon the first day of the week for worship in prayer, praise, reading the Scriptures, exhortation, teaching, fellowship and the partaking of the Lord's Supper.[12]

For Creel, the task of being apostolic, of restoring the apostolic church, was a complete return, wherever there had been a falling away, to original apostolic teaching found in its entirety in the New Testament.

TWENTIETH CENTURY

The idea of an early and radical break with the true apostolic church and the necessity of returning to the beliefs and practices of the primitive age by reproducing those found in the pages of the New Testament continued to dominate the thinking of Churches of Christ throughout the twentieth century. There are, however, two significant variations. The first reflects a particular kind of successionism most clearly seen in the thought of the nineteenth-century Landmark Baptists. The idea was that there had been a remnant of the true church in all ages that can be identified by the persecution of its members from the hand of the "apostate" Roman church and later Protestant churches. A classic example of the Landmark Baptist "Trail of Blood" historiography is a pamphlet of that name published in 1931 by J. M. Carroll.[13] The same effort to show a succession of apostolic Christians and churches through the ages is found in early histories of Churches of Christ as well. The most overt example is a book by evangelist E. M. Borden titled *The Crimson Trail: A Story of Trials, Hardships and Persecutions of Christians throughout the Early Centuries*. The author traces the existence of apostolic Christians from the second century to the Reformation. Though such information is not essential to the restoration of the primitive church today, Borden insists, the promise of Jesus that the gates of hell would not prevail against his church indicates that it continued to exist through the ages. The effort to document that unbroken connection with the first century was important.[14]

A second variation, of more recent occurrence in Churches of Christ, is the development of a historical consciousness by some of its more articulate scholars and writers both in the pulpit and classroom. The successionism of the "Trail of Blood" historiography is transformed into a sensitive and nuanced reading that clearly shows the historical roots of the group's beliefs and practices. Instead of repudiating or denying any connection with the past, these scholars and leaders are calling for members of Churches of Christ to recognize their inability to avoid the human reality of change and development.[15]

CONCLUSION

Churches of Christ represent, though with some unique stances, the stream of Christian thought that recognizes a break in the historical link to the apostolic church. The only way to be apostolic is to reestablish the teaching, church order, and practices of the apostles.[16] In sharp contrast to ideas of apostolic succession like those held by Roman Catholics, no unbroken chain of authoritative teachers or bishops from the present back to Christ is necessary. In fact, in light of the belief in an early departure from apostolic teaching by the great church, such overt evidence of a continuous connection would be damning rather than confirming. Only by reconnecting with the pure apostolic teaching found in its completeness in the New Testament writings—which are clear and understandable to all honest hearts—can one claim apostolicity. Only by casting aside the "rubbish of the ages" and throwing oneself into the simple beliefs and practices of the apostles can a church legitimately declare itself to be apostolic in belief and practice.

The differences between the successionist and restorationist understandings of apostolicity are real. Yet, there may be more room for discussion than some are willing to admit. I am reminded of the words of Fred Norris in his 1992 book, *The Apostolic Faith: Protestants and Roman Catholics.* Norris, a patristics scholar and professor who is a member of the Independent Christian Churches, states:

> The clearest mark of apostolicity is the New Testament itself. Conservative Protestants and Roman Catholics share Scripture together. The New Testament has been both a norm of faith and practice as well as a launching pad for remarkable speculative flights among Evangelicals and Catholics. Roman Catholics have had periods of deep biblical renewal. In fact, it is the Tradition of the Church that has declared Scripture to be the touchstone of Christian faith,

for many the norm of faith and practice. Today a number of Protestant Evangelicals are beginning to see the faithful function of Tradition in the life of the Church. If my observations are correct such is a mark of the present era.[17]

NOTES

1. The other major churches from that movement are the Christian Churches and Churches of Christ, often referred to as independent Christian Churches, and the Christian Church (Disciples of Christ).

2. Nathan O. Hatch, *The Democratization of American Christianity* (New Haven: Yale University Press, 1989); Richard T. Hughes and C. Leonard Allen, *Illusions of Innocence: Protestant Primitivism in America, 1630–1875* (Chicago: University of Chicago Press, 1988).

3. Douglas A. Foster, "Restoration: God's Finished Work, Our Never-Ending Task," *Wineskins* 1 (January/February 1993): 13–15.

4. For non-Stone-Campbell restorationist ideas, see, for example, James O'Kelly's "Plan of Christian Union," in W. E. MacClenny, *The Life of Rev. James O'Kelly and the Early History of the Christian Church in the South,* 2nd ed. (Indianapolis: Religious Book Service, 1950), 248–53.

5. Thomas Campbell, *Declaration and Address of the Christian Association of Washington County, Washington, Pennsylvania* (Washington, PA: Brown and Sample, 1809; repr., St. Louis: Mission Messenger, 1978), 46–48.

6. Alexander Campbell, *The Christian System in Reference to the Union of Christians, and the Restoration of Primitive Christianity, as Plead in the Current Reformation,* 3rd ed. (Pittsburgh: Forrester & Campbell, 1840; repr., Nashville: Gospel Advocate Co., 1980), 189–200.

7. See Campbell's "Apostolic Traditions," *Millennial Harbinger* (August 1858): 446–52, in which the entire discussion

focuses on the essentiality of the immersion of penitent believers for the remission of sins and entrance into the kingdom.

8. Richard M. Tristano, *The Origins of the Restoration Movement: An Intellectual History* (Atlanta: Glenmary Research Center, 1988), 90–92.

9. For an expanded study of apostolicity in the early movement, see Susan G. Higgins, "Apostolicity and the Restoration Movement Churches" (paper prepared for the American-Born Churches Consultation, Dallas, TX, March 1991).

10. John F. Rowe, *A History of Reformatory Movements Resulting in a Restoration of the Apostolic Church,* 9th ed. (Cincinnati: F. L. Rowe, 1913), 10–11.

11. Ibid., 37.

12. James C. Creel, *The Plea to Restore the Apostolic Church* (Cincinnati: Standard Publishing Company, 1902), 25–31. See also J. W. Shepherd, *The Church, the Falling Away, and the Restoration: A History of the Church from Pentecost to Our Own Times* (Cincinnati: F. L. Rowe, 1929).

13. J. M. Carroll, *The Trail of Blood: Following the Christians Down Through the Centuries; or, The History of Baptist Churches from the Time of Christ, Their Founder, to the Present Day* (Lexington, KY: Ashland Avenue Baptist Church, 1931).

14. E. M. Borden, *The Crimson Trail: A Story of Trials, Hardships and Persecutions of Christians throughout the Early Centuries* (Austin, TX: Firm Foundation, 1900).

15. Richard T. Hughes and C. Leonard Allen, *Discovering Our Roots: The Ancestry of Churches of Christ* (Abilene, TX: ACU Press, 1988).

16. See Donald Dayton, "Reflections on Apostolicity in the North American Context," in *Apostolic Faith in America,* ed. Thaddeus D. Horgan (Grand Rapids, MI: William B. Eerdmans, 1988), 31–33.

17. Frederick W. Norris, *The Apostolic Faith: Protestants and Roman Catholics* (Collegeville, MN: Liturgical Press, 1992), 128–29.

IRENAEUS ON APOSTOLICITY

John T. Ford, CSC

In light of the statement in the Epistle to the Ephesians (2:20) that the church is "built upon the foundation of the apostles and prophets, Christ Jesus himself being the cornerstone," it is not surprising that "all churches claim to be apostolic in the broad sense of the word."[1] Nonetheless, the history of the ecumenical movement in the twentieth century offers numerous examples of disagreement among churches precisely over what it means to say that the church is apostolic.

For example, from the time of the Reformation until the Second Vatican Council, Roman Catholic theologians customarily emphasized "three major elements...as distinctive of the true Church":

> [1] the apostolic origin, i.e., the Church was founded on the Apostles and, especially by the Apostles; [2] the apostolic doctrine, i.e., the continuity of the Christian faith throughout history, or also the identity of the faith of the 16th century with that preached by the Twelve; [3] finally, the apostolic succession, i.e., the uninterrupted train of legitimate pastors who link the early Church with that of the modern epoch.[2]

These three interconnected dimensions of apostolicity—origin, doctrine, and succession—have also been the source of apparently irresolvable disagreements among Western Christians since the Reformation. Nonetheless, there is seemingly "a broad sense" in which most Christians accept these "three major elements": first, the premise of apostolic origin, that the church was founded by the apostles; second, the compatibility of the faith of the present-day church with that of the apostles; and third, the duty of contemporary Christians to witness to the gospel preached by the apostles.

Yet, even granted a broad basis for ecumenical agreement about apostolicity, each of these three elements requires closer scrutiny: (1) In what sense is the church founded *on* and *by* the apostles? (2) Is there really *identity* between the faith of the church today and that of the apostles? (3) What is the importance of an *uninterrupted train* of pastors starting with the apostolic age and continuing to the present?

In addition, since Roman Catholic theologizing about apostolicity has been decidedly influenced by Counter-Reformation polemics, one also needs to ask to what extent the melding of these three elements is the result of theological controversy. In reply, it should first be noted that the weaving together of these three strands—origin, doctrine, succession—into a theology of apostolicity did not begin at the time of the Reformation, but in a far earlier polemical situation—in which leaders of the early church fought a number of religious movements now collectively known as Gnosticism.

IRENAEUS OF LYONS

In the church's campaign against Gnosticism, one of the major crusaders was Irenaeus of Lyons. In spite of his importance as a leader in the early church, comparatively little biographical information is available. The date of his birth is uncertain; the middle decades of the second century (140–60) are a reasonable estimate. His birthplace seems to have been in Asia Minor, since he mentions that he had heard the preaching of St. Polycarp, bishop of Smyrna. After emigrating to Gaul (France), he became a presbyter of the Church of Lyons (Lugdunum in Roman times). In 177 or 178, Irenaeus was sent as an emissary to Rome, where he presented a letter concerning the dangers of Montanism to Pope Eleutherius (ca. 175–89) on behalf of the Christians of Lyons.

On his return to Lyons, he was apparently chosen to succeed the martyred Pothinus, though "Irenaeus himself nowhere lays claim to being a bishop."[3] Irenaeus reappears briefly at the end of the second century in an irenic role interceding with Pope Victor (ca. 188–98) on behalf of the Asiatic bishops during the Easter controversy. "The date of Irenaeus' death is unknown, although convention places it ca. 202 to correspond with the renewed persecution under Septimus Severus. However, the texts which mention Irenaeus' martyrdom are late and uncertain."[4]

If biographical details about the life of Irenaeus are meager, even that minimal information might not have survived had it not been for his writings against Gnosticism. Yet, of what was once a larger corpus, only two complete works, both originally written in Greek, are extant. First, his short apologetic treatise, *Epideixis* or *Proof of the Apostolic Teaching,* whose existence was previously known through a reference in Eusebius's *Ecclesiastical History,* was rediscovered in an Armenian translation in 1904.

Second, his major work, *The Detection and Overthrow of the False Gnosis,* commonly known as *Adversus Haereses* and probably written between 180 and 190, has been preserved in its entirety only in a somewhat awkward Latin translation. *Adversus Haereses* is divided into five books: the first book is a presentation of Gnostic teachings in preparation for their fourfold refutation in the remainder of the work: book 2 is a refutation of Gnosticism on the basis of reason; the anti-Gnostic argumentation of book 3 is based on apostolic teaching and tradition; the refutation of Gnosticism in book 4 relies on the sayings of the Lord; the polemics in book 5 are based on the apostolic epistles.[5]

While recognizing his monumental achievement in such an extensive theological project, one must acknowledge that the thought of Irenaeus has a number of definite limitations—in part, due to his polemical purpose; in part, explicable by the inchoate state of Christian theology; and in part, due to a theological methodology quite different from what is customary today.

First, although his thought is pervasively biblical—indeed, he cites much of the New Testament—sometimes his interpretations are overly literal, perhaps the result of his effort to refute opponents whose scriptural interpretation was variously cosmological, mythical, or even numerical—interpretations that Irenaeus considered totally arbitrary.[6] Yet, at other times, his scriptural exegesis is decidedly allegorical, in fact similar in method to that of his opponents: "Even in Irenaeus, we occasionally find ideas which look to us as though they would be more comfortable in a gnostic setting."[7]

Simultaneously, Irenaeus's theology in *Adversus Haereses* is avowedly polemical: "Irenaeus identified certain views as incompatible with Christian truth and declared those who held them to be beyond Christian fellowship."[8] This polemical attitude, however, contrasts with his irenic attitude in the Easter controversy, when he recognized that "Diversity of opinion on important theological issues has existed in the Christian Church from the very beginning."[9] Seemingly Irenaeus was tolerant of what he considered legitimate diversity within the church, even though vigorously opposed to those whom he judged to be harming the church through a "pretended but false gnosis."

Yet, in spite of the historical problems, textual difficulties, and hermeneutical issues encountered in his writings, "As a witness to Apostolic tradition and a champion of the inspiration of both the OT and the NT, Irenaeus is one of the most important writers of the early Church."[10]

GNOSTICISM

Who were these Gnostics whom Irenaeus attacked so zealously? Patristic writers often described Gnosticism as the work of the devil, instigated by Simon Magus, "the first gnostic."[11] In contrast, modern authors usually see Gnosticism as encompassing a variety of groups, whose adherents commonly believed that salvation could be attained through *gnosis:* a special knowledge of the divine that was reserved for an elite. This esoteric doctrine was taught by the apostles only to a select few—or, according to some Gnostics, the *gnosis* was even unknown to the apostles but only revealed to the Gnostic leaders and those whom they initiated into the divine mysteries.

Precisely because church leaders like Irenaeus considered Gnosticism a major threat to sound doctrine, their refutation was energetic, eventually resulting not only in the practical eradication of the "heresy" but also in the destruction of most Gnostic documents. Until the discovery of a Gnostic library at Nag Hammadi in Egypt in 1945,[12] most information about Gnosticism was secondhand, stemming from its most vocal opponents.

Although this discovery of Gnostic documents is considered "one of the most important manuscript finds of the [twentieth] century, comparable in that respect to the discovery of the Dead Sea Scrolls,"[13] these original documents in Coptic translation have, if anything, made the theological situation even more debated. On the one hand, there is "a lack of significant overlapping in material and detail" between the Nag Hammadi documents and patristic writings; on the other hand, there are a few instances in which the Nag Hammadi documents correspond with what Irenaeus presented in *Adversus Haereses*.[14]

Under the broad umbrella of Gnosticism are elements of Jewish apocalyptic and sapiential speculation, Oriental mythology, Eastern religious myths, Greek philosophy, as well as Christian beliefs.[15] Not surprisingly, "Scholars have been sharply divided over what factor was most influential in giving rise to gnosticism."[16]

> Scholars currently engaged in the study of gnosticism fall into two main camps. Most of the North Americans and Germans...think that the earliest mythological roots of gnosticism developed alongside early Christianity in a heterodox syncretistic Jewish environment. But a fair number of British and French scholars continue to defend the patristic view that gnosticism emerges from Christian circles.[17]

In any case, beyond the bewildering "details of gnostic mythological systems, cultic practices, ethical injunctions, appropriation of religious and philosophical symbols, and sectarian organization"[18] is the central attraction of gnosis. "To have this knowledge is already to be saved."[19] In other words, at the heart of the Christian controversy with Gnosticism are rival claims about the nature of revelation and its intended recipients: gnosis is "not available to everyone, but it is intended only for those capable of being saved by it."[20]

The restriction of revelation and thus of salvation to an elite was tied to Gnostic anthropology, which postulated three different types of human beings:

1. *pneumatics* who possess a spark of the divine, but who must await the final separation of the divine element from matter so that it can return to the realm of the divine;

2. *psychics* who have souls and, though not capable of knowledge, are capable of faith;

3. *hylics* who are merely matter and whose only destiny is corruption.

As strange as this Gnostic anthropology may seem to modern minds, it had a fundamental religious appeal:

> [M]any scholars think that the primary audience of gnostic speculation was the growing class of literate bureaucrats and their families in the urban areas of the Greco-Roman world. Such persons did not belong to the aristocratic elite, with its literary and philosophic heritage; rather, they were intellectually and perhaps even physically dislocated from their ancestral religious roots. Gnosis makes them the true elite.[21]

But Gnosticism was not only a matter of status appeal; theologically speaking, "This doctrine of the three classes of human beings is part of an attempt, breath-taking in its extent, to account for the coexistence of evil and an all-powerful, all-good God."[22]

For present purposes, however, it should suffice to note that the gnosis was immediately revealed through the historical Jesus to his apostles, who in turn were responsible for communicating it to others:

> But since this revelation was intended only for the spiritual [pneumatic], by whom alone it could be understood, it was often hidden under allegory or in a numerical code. As the psychics could not penetrate to the spiritual meaning, some of the revelations made to the disciples by Jesus were kept secret from them.[23]

Simultaneously, Gnosticism presented a corresponding view of apostolicity: First, in regard to doctrine, *gnosis* was perfect knowledge of the divine that is salvific in itself and available only to those initiated into the Gnostic mysteries. Second, the origin of this *gnosis* was the historical Jesus who taught his apostles this salvific knowledge. Third, the apostles passed on this *gnosis* to select individuals capable of receiving it; ordinary persons could at best attain a superficial understanding of the scriptures—whose secret meaning was intelligible only to those endowed with "a spark of the divine."[24]

ADVERSUS HAERESES

In his major work, Irenaeus undertook the formidable task of "unmasking and refuting the false *gnosis*"—by a multipronged attack that covered topics ranging from cosmology to Christology, from anthropology to apostolicity. In the latter instance, the challenge confronting Irenaeus was how to combat adversaries whose claims not only contradicted but also paralleled his own.

In broad terms, both Irenaeus and his principal opponents claimed that their respective doctrines represented the authentic teaching of Christ; in addition to their differences about the content of this teaching, they also disputed whether this doctrine was universally available or knowable only by select initiates. Second, both Irenaeus and many of his opponents claimed apostolic origin for their teaching; for Irenaeus, apostolic teaching was public; for his adversaries, the *gnosis* was secret. Third, for Irenaeus, the transmission of apostolic teaching was guarded and guaranteed by a public line of ecclesiastical officeholders; for the Gnostics, the true doctrine was passed on by charismatic teachers, who purportedly had privileged access to divine knowledge.

In other words, both Irenaeus and the Gnostics claimed an apostolicity of doctrine-origin-transmission. Since the Gnostic presentation of apostolic doctrine-origin-transmission sometimes relied on the same scriptural sources as did Irenaeus, he was faced with the difficult task of refuting the secret Gnostic teachings while simultaneously preserving and defending the public apostolic doctrine-origin-transmission within the church.

As regards *apostolic origin,* Irenaeus emphasized that "the Lord of all gave his Apostles the power [to preach] the Gospel and it is through them that we know the Truth, namely, the Teaching of the Son of God."[25] Accordingly, "we have learned the plan of our salvation from none other than those through whom the Gospel has come down to us; this Gospel which they once preached and which they later transmitted by the will of God in the Scriptures, would become the foundation and column of our faith" (3.1.1).

Implicit in this statement is the fact that Jesus did not personally commit his message to writing; rather he communicated it verbally to his followers. Nonetheless, the transmission of the gospel did not rely merely on the apostles' memory of the words and deeds of Jesus:

> For after our Lord was raised from the dead, the Apostles were imbued with power from on high through the coming of the Holy Spirit; they were filled with all [gifts] and had perfect knowledge *(perfectam agnitionem)*. Then the Apostles went forth to the ends of the earth proclaiming the good news and announcing heavenly peace to all people, who one and all thus had the Gospel of God. (3.1.1)

Although this passage relates the direct oral transmission of the gospel by Jesus to the apostles, it also indicates that the apostles had "perfect knowledge"—evidently a counterclaim directed at those Gnostics who claimed that there was a secret revelation unknown even to the apostles.

Irenaeus then pointed out that the gospel was subsequently committed to writing by the four evangelists. In contrast, the Gnostics appealed to the wisdom of the perfect (cf. 1 Cor 2:6) over the written word. Thus, in Irenaeus's view, the Gnostics did not hesitate to preach their own opinions, thereby corrupting the rule of truth *(Regulam veritatis deprauans)* (3.2.1).

Second, when Irenaeus appealed to the *apostolic tradition,* "which is preserved in the churches through the succession of presbyters," the Gnostics replied that they had found the genuine truth and so claimed that they were not only wiser than the presbyters but even wiser than the apostles (3.2.2). Thus, in response to the Gnostic claim of apostolic origin and doctrine, Irenaeus pointed out that the Gnostics lacked apostolic tradition: "those who desire to see the truth can find in every church the Tradition of the Apostles manifested to all throughout the world" (3.3.1).

For Irenaeus, the best way to resolve any dispute about *what* the genuine apostolic teaching is and where it is to be found is by answering the question, *who* was your teacher? Accordingly, Irenaeus linked apostolic tradition with apostolic succession: "And we can list those whom the Apostles appointed as bishops of the churches and their successions *(successiones)* down to the present: these [bishops] never taught nor ever even knew anything that resembled the delirium of the Gnostics" (3.3.1).

In particular, if the apostles had known the "hidden mysteries" *(recondita mysteria),* which were purportedly taught to the "perfect" (Gnostic initiates), assuredly the apostles would have taught such mysteries to those to whom they entrusted the leadership of the churches. For the apostles wanted their successors *(successores)* to be perfect and blameless, since these successors were given the apostles' place as teachers *(locum magisterii).* If such teaching was faithfully communicated, it would redound to the great benefit of the church; correspondingly, any failure in teaching sound doctrine would be the greatest of calamities (3.3.1).

In order to show that the gospel had been transmitted in the same fashion in all the apostolically established churches—and simultaneously to prove that none of these churches knew, much less taught, the secret doctrines of the Gnostics—Irenaeus mentioned that it would be possible to examine the teaching that had been passed down from the apostles to their successors in all of these apostolic churches. Such a listing was presumably possible for Irenaeus but not particularly feasible—since he promptly excused himself from such a task and contented himself with commenting on the apostolic lineage of three churches: Rome— whose succession he treated at length; Smyrna—whose bishop, Polycarp, he knew personally; and Ephesus—"where John lived until the time of Trajan" (AD 98–117).

For present purposes, one can prescind from a discussion of the special significance given the Roman succession, in order to focus on what is seemingly Irenaeus's major line of argument in regard to apostolicity: it is easy to find the truth in the church, because the apostles, as it were, placed the total riches of truth in a deposit *(depositorium),* from which anyone who wishes may draw the drink of life (3.4.1).

Accordingly, one should avoid the Gnostics, but love with greatest affection the things of the church and to learn the tradition of truth *(ueritatis Traditionem)* (3.4.1).

Why? If there would be a dispute about a mere question of detail, would it not be necessary to have recourse to the most ancient of the churches, where the apostles lived, and from them learn what is truly certain and really clear in regard to the matter at issue? And if the apostles had not left us scriptures, would it not be necessary to follow the order of tradition that they transmitted to those to whom they entrusted the churches? (3.4.1).

For Irenaeus, this possibility was not merely hypothetical, but actual: "Such is the manner of assent of many nations of barbarians, who believe in Christ, and have salvation written—not with paper or ink—by the Spirit in their hearts and so carefully preserve the ancient Tradition" (3.4.2). These illiterate people may seem barbarians in their language, thought, customs, and manner of living, but "through faith, they are very wise and please God, because they live in complete justice, chastity, and wisdom" (3.4.2).

In contrast, the Gnostics can claim neither apostolic succession nor apostolic tradition: before Valentinus, there were no Valentinians; before Marcion, no Marcionites; none of these doctrines originated with the apostles, but only with the "initiators and inventors of these Gnostic perversities" (3.4.3).

Thus for Irenaeus, the Church alone has preserved the genuine apostolic tradition. This tradition comes from Jesus Christ, who is the Truth and who taught the gospel to his disciples. Irenaeus concluded his argument about apostolic tradition with an appeal to the honesty and integrity of the apostles: Would the apostles have fabricated doctrines as the Gnostics claimed? Definitely not: the apostles were sent to point out the way to the lost, to give light to the blind, to heal the sick—certainly the apostles would not have substituted their own opinions for the teachings of Christ; rather they proclaimed the truth that they had received.

THEOLOGICAL REFLECTIONS

Irenaeus's treatment of apostolicity is historically important, because the apostolic *origin* of Christianity was still a matter of living memory: writers like Irenaeus could still trace an "uninterrupted train" of bishops in a local church back to a particular apostle. Yet, the second century was also a time of tremendous challenges for the growing church.

On the one hand, Gnosticism was a heresy that was particularly threatening to the doctrinal core of Christianity. On the other hand,

> the gnostics, as creative theologians in their own right, often contributed to Christological, trinitarian and cosmological teachings. They were occasionally the first to raise such problems for discussion, and they caused the larger church to take a stand on a variety of subjects. Their activity in this regard was of positive value for the development of Christian doctrine.[26]

Yet, such an evaluation is retrospective; *Adversus Haereses* is marked by its polemical purpose: many passages include, at least implicitly, references to various Gnostic beliefs and leave a modern reader wondering how much Irenaeus's anti-Gnostic polemics may have influenced his theological positions. A second major challenge in reading Irenaeus is the fact that his was a pioneering effort. While he "is considered by many to be the first systematic theologian,"[27] he was faced with the herculean task of devising theological terminology and designing a doctrinal system. In such a task, he was not always consistent; for example, in his polemics, he seems to have been willing to adopt arguments and terminology that advanced this campaign—whether or not a given argument really aligned with the rest of his theology.[28]

Nonetheless, the broad outline of his teaching about apostolicity seems clear. The doctrine of the church can be traced back to Jesus Christ, who personally taught his apostles who subsequently received "perfect knowledge" through the Holy Spirit. Considered in terms of apostolic origin, his difficulty in defending this position is that the Gnostics made a similar claim: "He agrees with the gnostics that Jesus gave true teaching (which he calls the 'rule of truth') to his apostles, directing them to pass it on to their successors."[29]

Accordingly, Irenaeus needed to raise the issue of authoritative interpretation: at its origin, the gospel was unwritten, and among some (barbarian) peoples existed only in oral form. Thus, Irenaeus seems to have allowed for a *sensus fidelium* that would enable even illiterate Christians to distinguish between authentic apostolic doctrine and the delirium presented by the Gnostic teachers. It should be noted, however, that his suggestion of a lay witness to apostolic doctrine does not align well with what seems to have been Irenaeus's main argument: apostolic tradition, whether in oral form or in the written gospels, always needs authoritative interpretation—and who better than the apostles and their successors are able to do this?

Then, to substantiate his claim that the church's doctrine is genuinely apostolic, Irenaeus linked the doctrine passed down through apostolic tradition with apostolic succession: first, the link is historically verifiable, since it was still at this time historically possible to trace each apostolically established church back to its apostolic founder(s); second, this link with apostolic history is spiritually grounded, since each apostolic successor received a *charisma veritatis,* which enabled him to know and to teach the truth traditioned from the apostles. "In his view, there is no secret succession or tradition; the tradition is guarded by a public, known succession to the apostles; hence, the importance he attaches to the episcopal succession lists."[30]

Irenaeus's linking of the biblical message and apostolic tradition, of historical succession and hierarchical charism seemed to be an effective weapon against Gnosticism. His trio of apostolic origin-doctrine-succession eventually became a staple of Catholic theological thought: "In his view, the preservation, without adulteration, of the faith received from the apostles in opposition to novelties involved a close association of apostolic tradition *(paradosis)* with apostolic succession."[31]

Nonetheless, without detracting from the remarkable theological achievement of Irenaeus, one must also acknowledge some limitations in his teaching about apostolicity:

In regard to *origin,* while "few Christians would deny that the church is apostolic in the sense that it is built upon the foundation of the original apostles (to the extent that it proclaims their message and performs the same essential tasks),"[32] church history provides insufficient data to enable us to trace the lineage of most episcopal sees back to one of the original Twelve. Thus, the historical side of Irenaeus's argument is no longer as immediately convincing as it presumably was in his day. Further complicating this question of apostolic origin is the fact that others beside the Twelve and the "Apostle born out of due time" are called "apostles" in the New Testament. Thus, one might well ask anew: what does it mean to say that the church is "built upon the foundation of the apostles"?

In regard to *doctrine,* Irenaeus's argument works best if apostolic teaching is considered a deposit *(depositorium)* or rule of truth *(Regula veritatis),* which can be literally passed from generation to generation. Such an understanding of "the objective, unchanging nature of truth"[33] worked well in Irenaeus's polemics against the Gnostics. Elsewhere, however, Irenaeus seems to have allowed more doctrinal flexibility than speaking of apostolic doctrine as a "deposit" or "rule of truth" would suggest; for example, at the time of the Easter Controversy, he advocated allowing different observances—practices that implicitly at least were based on divergent theologies. Thus, Irenaeus's emphasis on the "unity of faith" should not necessarily be understood as precluding a plurality of practices and variety of doctrinal expressions.[34]

In regard to *succession,* while the threefold structure of bishop-presbyter-deacon had become dominant, if not universal, by the time of Irenaeus, such was not the case earlier, when some local churches were governed by presbyters, or possibly by a group of bishops. If it is not historically clear *when* and *why* the threefold clerical structure became accepted, it is evident that an episcopally structured church—where bishops are the successors of the apostles—is key to Irenaeus's argument. Yet the assumption that apostolic succession is an automatic warrant for apostolic doctrine is problematic, as the Arian controversy would illustrate in the centuries following Irenaeus.[35] Thus, Irenaeus's anti-Gnostic argument that linked apostolic tradition to apostolic succession does not imply that apostolic succession is the *sole* criterion for apostolic doctrine.

Underlying this controversy is a perennial contention within the church about the interpretation of the gospel: on the one hand are those who propose a personal, charismatic, even subjective understanding of the gospel; on the other hand are those who maintain an institutional, historical, and objective interpretation of the gospel. Perhaps the ecumenical challenge today is to find ways in which these two interpretive trends can be reconciled.

Insofar as Irenaeus's argument from "apostolicity" was formulated by the need to refute Gnostic claims, to what extent was his position akin to erecting a massive fortification against his adversaries? With better theological building materials available today, it is possible to construct a trimmer and more flexible structuralization of apostolicity.

NOTES

1. Peter Staples, "Apostolicity," in *Dictionary of the Ecumenical Movement,* ed. Nicholas Lossky et al. (Geneva: WCC Publications; Grand Rapids, MI: William B. Eerdmans, 1991), 44.

2. Gustave Thils, "Apostolicity," in *New Catholic Encyclopedia* (New York: McGraw-Hill, 1967), 1:700; the numbers in brackets have been added.

3. Denis Minns, *Irenaeus* (Washington, DC: Georgetown University Press, 1994), 2. Mary Ann Donovan, *One Right Reading? A Guide to Irenaeus* (Collegeville, MN: Liturgical Press, 1997), 9, states: "Irenaeus functioned as a bishop but he was chary in the use of the title."

4. Mary Ann Donovan, "Irenaeus," in *The Anchor Bible Dictionary,* ed. David Noel Freedman (New York: Doubleday, 1992), 3:457.

5. Donovan, *One Right Reading?*, provides both a concise summary (14–17) and an extended analysis (9–170) of *Adversus Haereses.*

6. Ibid., 14. Donovan observes: "The Bible known to Irenaeus included the Jewish Scriptures, the four Gospels, a collection of Paul's letters, Acts, Revelation, 1 Peter and 1 John."

7. Minns, *Irenaeus,* 12.

8. Ibid., 11.

9. Ibid., 12.

10. Hermigild Dressler, "St. Irenaeus," in *New Catholic Encyclopedia,* 7:632.

11. Kurt Rudolph, "Gnosticism," in *Anchor Bible Dictionary,* 2:1035.

12. *The Nag Hammadi Library in English,* translated by members of the Coptic Gnostic Library Project of the Institute for Antiquity and Christianity, James M. Robinson, director (San Francisco: Harper & Row, 1977).

13. Birger Pearson, "Nag Hammadi," in *Anchor Bible Dictionary,* 4:991.

14. Donovan, "Irenaeus," 458.

15. Rudolph, "Gnosticism," 1035–37.

16. Pheme Perkins, "Gnosticism," in *The New Jerome Biblical Commentary,* ed. Raymond E. Brown, Joseph A. Fitzmyer, and Roland Murphy (Englewood Cliffs, NJ: Prentice-Hall, 1990), 1353 §76.

17. Pheme Perkins, review of *Gnostic Truth and Christian Heresy,* by Alastair H. B. Logan, Theological Studies 58 (1997): 356.

18. Perkins, "Gnosticism," 1351 §65.

19. Minns, *Irenaeus,* 14.

20. George W. MacRae, "Gnosticism," in *New Catholic Encyclopedia,* 6:526.

21. Perkins, "Gnosticism," 1351:68.

22. Minns, *Irenaeus,* 15.

23. Ibid., 18.

24. According to some Gnostics, only Gnostic initiates (not even the apostles) were privileged recipients of the *gnosis.*

25. *Adversus Haereses,* bk. 3, preface; hereafter, *Adversus Haereses* will be cited within the text according to the divisions of Massuet, as given by Migne; for example, the reference (4.10.1) indicates book 4, chapter 10, paragraph 1. All translations are

mine from the Latin text given in Irénée de Lyon, *Contre les hérésies: Mise en lumière et refutation de la prétendu "connaissance,"* Livre III, prepared by F. Sagnard for the series *Sources Chrétiennes* (Paris: Cerf; Lyon: Emmanuel Vitte, 1952). A list of other editions of Irenaeus is given by Donovan, *One Right Reading?*, 178–79.

26. Rudolph, "Gnosticism," 1035.

27. Donovan, "Irenaeus," 457.

28. In contrast, some Gnostic positions seem systematically more elaborate than the counterpositions of Irenaeus.

29. Donovan, "Irenaeus," 460.

30. Ibid.

31. Klaus Schatz, *Papal Primacy: From Its Origins to the Present* (Collegeville, MN: Liturgical Press, 1996), 8.

32. Staples, "Apostolicity," 45.

33. Donovan, *One Right Reading?*, 12.

34. In addition, one needs to ask what were Irenaeus's model of revelation and his understanding of doctrine and its development.

35. In addition, there is a hint that Irenaeus envisioned a role for the laity—a type of *sensus fidelium*—in preserving the doctrine of Christ.

RESPONSE

Douglas A. Foster

Unlike John Ford's pairing of John Henry Newman and Alexander Campbell in his response to my apostolicity paper, I am unable to compare Irenaeus to a contemporary of the American Stone-Campbell Restoration Movement. Yet, there are relevant responses from Churches of Christ that address the issues John has identified as central to Irenaeus and Roman Catholic theology concerning the nature of the apostolicity of the church, particularly apostolic succession.

First, Churches of Christ would agree fully with Irenaeus's efforts to establish the essentiality of apostolic origin and transmission for any doctrine or practice. For example, Robert Milligan, author of the *Scheme of Redemption,* one of the most influential expositions of Christian doctrine in the Stone-Campbell movement, emphasized the role of the apostles as foundation of the church.

> The gift of plenary inspiration…was necessary in order to enable [the apostles] to understand aright the oracles and teachings of the Old Testament, to reveal fully and infallibly the remaining mysteries of the Scheme of Redemption, and to give to the church such a code of laws and regulations as would, in all ages and under all circumstances, be to her a perfect rule of faith and practice.[1]

We will not linger on this point of resonance.

The difficulties arise when dealing with the matter of apostolic succession. As stated in my paper in the March meeting, there is a kind of successionism found in some places in Churches of Christ. Sometimes labeled Landmarkism after the Baptist movement that promoted this idea, it asserts that a remnant of the true church has existed in all ages, identified chiefly by the persecution its members received at the hand of the "apostate" Roman church and later Protestant churches. Such a reading of history is often known as the "Trail of Blood."[2] Yet, any notion of an "uninterrupted train of legitimate pastors who link the early Church with that of the modern epoch" as the basis for determining true doctrine and practice is strenuously rejected.

From Alexander Campbell to contemporary theologians, Churches of Christ have insisted, along with all Protestants, that the idea of apostolic succession as developed by Roman Catholicism is (1) a significant change from the original idea set forth by Irenaeus, and (2) at best unnecessary for the maintenance of pure doctrine and practice in the church, and at worst detrimental to it.

Everett Ferguson, in his article on "Apostolic Succession" in the *Encyclopedia of Early Christianity,* for example, explains:

> A person could go to the churches founded by the apostles, Irenaeus contended, and determine what was taught in those churches by the succession of teachers since the days of the apostles. The constancy of this teaching was guaranteed by its public nature; any change could have been detected, since the teaching was open. The accuracy of the teaching in each church was confirmed by its agreement with what was taught in other churches. One and the same faith had been taught in all the churches since the time of the apostles.
>
> To be in the succession was not itself sufficient to guarantee correct doctrine....The succession pertained to faith and life rather than to the transmission of special gifts. The "gift of truth" (*charisma veritatis*) received with the office of teaching [Irenaeus, *Haer.* 4.26.2] was not a gift guaranteeing that what was taught would be true, but was the truth itself as a gift. Each holder of the teaching chair in the church received the apostolic doctrine as a deposit to be faithfully transmitted to the church. Apostolic succession as formulated by Irenaeus was from one holder of the teaching chair in the church to the next and not from ordainer to ordained, as it became....Churches were apostolic that agreed in the same faith, even if not founded by apostles.[3]

The notion of the special passing on of a supernatural guarantee of truth was rather crudely attacked by Alexander Campbell in an 1843 article in his journal the *Millennial Harbinger*.

> What charm of grace is in the idea of succession! Still, no one can describe what does succeed. What is it descends from the fingers of one consecrated through a line of 250 Popes, to him touched by his hands? The electricity of heavenly grace, methinks, could not have been kept in such crazy, flawy, earthenware Bishops....It is well said, that the grace of ordinances is not in him that does administer them, neither a fortiori, can it be in official succession. Authority is not a flood nor a stream of celestial grace to be conveyed through a long series of men touched by human hands.
>
> And if it were, is it not essential to the satisfaction of all conscientious persons that the succession be Divinely prescribed—infallibly preserved, and registered, to the full assurance of all who desire to participate in the holy ordinances? But where is such a precept—where is such a roll of lineage, and where are the infallible registers of the facts of such a succession? No living man can furnish the Divine precept—exhibit the roll of succession, or name its safe keepers.[4]

In his paper, John himself states, "the assumption that apostolic succession is an automatic warrant for apostolic doctrine is problematic, as the Arian controversy would illustrate in the centuries following Irenaeus." Obviously the succession is not in itself sufficient to guarantee true doctrine.

One of the areas of strongest dissonance concerns Irenaeus's attempt to refute the Gnostics by portraying them as ultraelitists who see themselves as the only legitimate interpreters of the scriptures and Christianity. The *gnosis* was not for everyone, only those capable of being saved. Ironically, the position taken at least in embryo by Irenaeus and developed into the Catholic doctrine of apostolic succession might also be interpreted as a kind of dangerous elitism. A select cadre was created in the bishops who alone possess the ability to interpret correctly scripture and the Christian faith. By virtue of a purported supernatural superintendency, these bishops are the essential key to the continuation of true apostolic Christianity. The terminology John uses to describe the Gnostic teachers partially fits that notion of the authority of bishops, with the exception of the secret nature of their teaching: "ordinary persons could at best attain a superficial understanding of the scriptures—whose secret meaning was intelligible only to those endowed with a 'spark of the divine.'"

What, then, is the standard of apostolic teaching and practice? Those in Churches of Christ would insist that God's superintendency rests not in any individual or individuals, but in the written word itself. The Bible alone, specifically the New Testament, is sufficient for supplying anyone with the ability to understand it, all apostolic teaching concerning the gospel and the church. Apostolic teaching is to be found in its entirety in the New Testament. No apostolic succession as delineated by Irenaeus or the later church is needed. The following excerpts reflect the historical position taken by Churches of Christ.

> The early Christians, in confessing their faith in Christ, accepted the whole revelation of God…as their absolute and only authority. The teaching of inspired men was to them what the New Testament is to us, till their teaching was recorded and the necessity for oral inspiration ceased.
>
> The all-sufficiency of the Holy Scriptures is thus expressed by the inspired apostle: "Every scripture inspired of God is also profitable for teaching, for reproof, for correction, for instruction which is in righteousness: so the man of God may be complete, furnished completely unto every good work" (2 Tim 3:16, 17).
>
> Since the Bible furnishes all this, it would be difficult to conceive of any want it does not supply. It leaves no room for a human creed or any other authority in matters of faith. Hence it is a fact, conceded by all biblical students, that the apostolic church accepted the word of God as its absolute and only authority in all religious affairs.[5]

> There is not a spiritual idea in the whole human race that is not drawn from the Bible. As soon will the philosopher find an independent sunbeam in nature, as the theologian a spiritual conception in man, independent of the *One Best Book*.

The words and sentences of the Bible are to be translated, interpreted, and understood according to the same code of laws and principles of interpretation by which other ancient writings are translated and understood; for, when God spoke to humans in their own language, he spoke as one person converses with another—in the fair, stipulated, and well-established meaning of the terms. This is essential to the character of the Bible as a revelation from God; otherwise it would be no revelation, but would always require a class of inspired persons to unfold and reveal its true sense to humankind.

Every one, then, who opens the Book of God, with one aim, with one ardent desire—intent only to know the will of God—to such a person the knowledge of God is easy; for the Bible is framed to illuminate such, and only such, with the salutary knowledge of things celestial and divine.[6]

[T]he apostles could have no successors in office.... The fact is that in, and by, and through their writings they themselves still live and preside over the whole Church of God, according to the promise of Christ given to them in Matthew xix, 28, and in the same sense it is that Christ himself will be with them, even to the end of the world (Matthew xxviii, 20). And hence we conclude that the twenty-seven Canonical Books of the New Testament are the only proper successors of the Apostles of Christ now on earth.[7]

In the nature of the case, the apostles had an unrepeatable ministry. With their passing, no one else could give the testimony that they could. Their witness to the life, teachings, and resurrection of Jesus made them the foundation of the church (Eph 2:20). When the apostle James was killed (Acts 12:2), no successor for him was chosen because James still held his office. Judas had renounced his apostleship and fallen away from his ministry (Acts 1:20, 25). Death in the case of James, by way of contrast, did not end his testimony to the resurrection; in fact, his death as a martyr to his faith only enhanced his witness to the resurrection. Hence, he continues to fulfill his apostolic function as the foundation on which the church exists. The authority of the apostles remains after their death in the authority of their testimony.

The church today has the same "apostles of Christ" as the first-century church had, the Twelve and Paul. They are still the foundation of Christian faith and the basis for the life of the church. One could speak of successors to the apostles in their work as missionaries, but there can be no "apostolic succession" in their function as foundation of the church.

[T]he church still has the same apostles and prophets as in the first century, for their words of testimony and revelation preserved in scripture form the foundation of the church's message and faith.[8]

In his discussion of Irenaeus on apostolicity, John himself raises, albeit briefly and tantalizingly, all the questions that had arisen in my mind as I read his description of the apostolic origin–apostolic doctrine–apostolic succession argument against the Gnostics. The Quartodeciman or Easter Controversy seems to pose serious problems for the notion of apostolic transmission and apostolic succession. Both the Asian and Roman practices could claim apostolic foundation. Yet, the differences in practice produced early tensions in the case of Anicetus and Polycarp (ca. 154) and led to threatened schism between Victor and Polycrates (ca. 189); the Council of Nicaea finally anathematized the Quartodeciman practice in 325. The fact that Irenaeus seems to minimize the differences between these groups of Christians may lend weight to John's suggestion that his construction of the idea of apostolic succession may have been more another tool to use against the Gnostics than a universal principle of faith. More investigation is needed here.

Already mentioned is the problem John raises of rightly ordained bishops who perverted apostolic doctrine. I am not familiar with how Roman Catholic theology deals with such breaches, and believe this also needs elaboration and discussion in light of its implications for the doctrine of apostolic succession and its role of superintending Christian truth.

In the context of Faith and Order, the implications for the doctrine of apostolic succession for ecumenism are most pressing. For Roman Catholicism, is it possible for churches not in the historic episcopal succession to be truly apostolic? Does agreeing on the same basic faith make a church apostolic? Vatican II's Decree on Ecumenism certainly recognizes the existence of legitimate Christianity outside the Roman Catholic Church. The question remains, however, what role does apostolic succession play in legitimating the "true church of Christ," its beliefs and practices? These are not new questions, as seen in the dialogues carried on for many years between Catholics and churches not in the historic episcopal succession. But John has raised them and the others mentioned above in a very helpful way in his look at Irenaeus.

NOTES

1. Robert Milligan, *Exposition and Defense of the Scheme of Redemption as It Is Revealed and Taught in the Holy Scriptures* (Cincinnati: R. W. Carroll, 1869; repr., Nashville: Gospel Advocate Company, 1977), 297.

2. J. M. Carroll, *The Trail of Blood: Following the Christians Down through the Centuries; or, The History of Baptist Churches from the Time of Christ, Their Founder, to the Present Day* (Lexington, KY: Ashland Avenue Baptist Church, 1931); E. M. Borden, *The Crimson Trail: A Story of Trials, Hardships and Persecutions of Christians throughout the Early Centuries* (Austin, TX: Firm Foundation, 1900).

3. Everett Ferguson, ed., *Encyclopedia of Early Christianity* (New York: Garland Publishing Company, 1990), s.v. "Apostolic Succession," by Everett Ferguson.

4. Alexander Campbell, "Anglican and Roman Bishops Have No Divine Right to Ordain," *Millennial Harbinger* n.s. 7 (May 1843): 224–25.

5. J. W. Shepherd, *The Church, the Falling Away, and the Restoration* (Nashville: Gospel Advocate Company, 1929), 42–43.

6. Alexander Campbell, *The Christian System in Reference to the Union of Christians, and the Restoration of Primitive Christianity, as Plead in the Current Reformation,* 3rd ed. (Pittsburgh: Forrester & Campbell, 1840; repr., Joplin, MO: College Press, 1989), 3–5.

7. Milligan, *Scheme of Redemption,* 297.

8. Everett Ferguson, *The Church of Christ: A Biblical Ecclesiology for Today* (Grand Rapids, MI: William B. Eerdmans, 1996), 306, 310.

RESPONSE

John T. Ford, CSC

At almost the same time that Alexander Campbell (1788–1866) was presenting his ideas about apostolicity as part of advancing church unity on the American frontier, on the other side of the Atlantic, John Henry Newman (1801–90), then a cleric of the Church of England and a fellow of Oriel College, Oxford, published the first of the *Tracts for the Times* (1833) that called upon the Anglican clergy to support their bishops in restoring the Church of England to its apostolic heritage.

Tract Number One—"Thoughts on the Ministerial Commission," written by Newman, though published anonymously—envisioned the reform of the church as dependent on the episcopacy, because,

> If we trace back the power of ordination from hand to hand, of course we shall come to the apostles at last. We know we do, as a plain historical fact; and therefore all we who have been ordained clergy in the very form of our ordination acknowledged the doctrine of the Apostolical Succession.[1]

In other words, Newman's clarion call for reform in the Church of England was based upon the premise of its apostolicity.

Although the establishmentarian ambiance of Oxford University and the religious needs of the expanding American frontier were vastly different, some basic concerns of Campbell and Newman are surprisingly similar. Not only did Restorationist ideas—particularly, the need for a purification of the church from accumulated corruptions and the need to address the relationship of reason and religion—resonate with Tractarian ideals, but both

Restorationists and Tractarians considered it essential to return to the teachings and practices of the apostolic church. Yet, while recognizing their similarities in purpose and sometimes even in evangelical strategy—Newman, in a manner similar to American circuit riders, rode about the British countryside on horseback to distribute the *Tracts*—one must also note that Restorationist and Tractarian views about apostolicity diverge in at least three significant ways: (1) their interpretation of scripture: a basic hermeneutical difference; (2) their evaluation of creedal statements: a basic confessional difference; and (3) their understanding of history: a basic historical difference.

HERMENEUTICAL DIFFERENCE

In contrast to Restorationist claims that the New Testament writings are "clear and understandable to all honest hearts," Newman felt that differences in scriptural interpretation have led to the fragmentation of Christianity. To counteract the endless diversity of "private interpretation," Newman became persuaded that scripture must be interpreted according to the apostolic tradition that continues to live in the church like a "living Apostle":

> [T]here is nothing which the Church has defined or shall define but what an Apostle, if asked, would have been fully able to answer and would have answered, as the Church has answered, the one answering by inspiration, the other from its gift of infallibility; and that the Church never will be able to answer, or has been able to answer, what the Apostles could not answer, e.g. whether the earth is stationary or not, or whether a republic is or is not better than a monarchy. The differences between them being that an Apostle could answer questions at once, but the Church answers them intermittently, in times & seasons, often delaying and postponing, according as she is guided by her Divine Instructor; and secondly and on the other hand, that the Church does in fact make answers which the Apostles did not make, and in one sense did not know, though they would have known

them, i.e. made present to their consciousness, and made those answers, had the questions been asked.[2]

In other words, one fundamental difference between Newman and Restorationism lies in their different ways of interpreting scripture; for Restorationists, individual Christians, equipped with their God-given reason, can come to a genuine understanding of scripture; for Newman, an individual must rely on the church, which is enlightened and guided by the Holy Spirit to interpret scripture and tradition correctly. While, historically speaking, these hermeneutical avenues have often gone in opposite directions, ideally at least, they could come to identical conclusions. In any case, neither of these approaches is immune from human deficiencies: personal interpretations of scripture can be overly individualistic and ecclesiastical interpretations can be unduly authoritarian. In effect, church unity can be harmed both by excessive individualism and by overbearing authoritarianism.

CONFESSIONAL DIFFERENCE

While Restorationists considered creeds to be divisive, Newman believed dogmas to be essential for reforming the church. As he later commented on the principles that underpinned his leadership of the Oxford Movement: "First was the principle of dogma: my battle was with liberalism; by liberalism I mean the anti-dogmatic principle and its development."[3] Indeed, commitment to dogma was a lifelong concern for Newman that went back to his adolescent conversion:

> From the age of fifteen, dogma has been the fundamental principle of my religion; I know no other religion; I cannot enter into the idea of any other sort of religion; religion, as a mere sentiment, is to me a dream and a mockery. As well can there be filial love without the fact of a father, as devotion without the fact of a Supreme Being.[4]

Not only was this dogmatic principle part of his adolescent conversion, it was a central element in his efforts at combating what he considered "false liberty of thought":

> Liberalism then is the mistake of subjecting to human judgment those revealed doctrines which are in their nature beyond and independent of it, and of claiming to determine on intrinsic grounds the truth and value of propositions which rest for their reception simply on the external authority of the Divine Word.[5]

While, at first sight, Newman's insistence on the dogmatic principle stands in sharp contrast to the noncreedal stance of Restorationists, both share a commitment to church unity. In the Restorationist tradition, on the one hand, any dogmatization of the gospel works against the unity of the church. To Newman, on the other hand, the lack of dogma is destructive of unity: Christians must have a common belief if they are to worship together. Nonetheless, perhaps there is some common ground insofar as Newman's statements that seemingly absolutize "dogma" were balanced by some of his later writings, where he made an eloquent case for the need to interpret dogma as minimalistically as possible.[6]

HISTORICAL DIFFERENCE

Whereas Restorationists believed that the early church fell away from the apostolic teaching and thus needed to be restored to its pristine condition, Newman did not find such a radical break. Early in his academic career, Newman began reading the patristic writings in chronological order and detected a basic continuity in the living apostolic tradition as it developed in response to the threat of heresy from within the church and continual attacks from outside.

In contrast to those Protestants who have postulated a fundamental rupture in the life of the church that could be mended only by restoring the church to its pristine purity and unity, Newman detected lines of continuity in the midst of diverse developments and in spite of periodic distortions. Thus, for Newman, it is not a matter of *restoring* the apostolic church, but of continually *reforming* and *renewing* the present-day successor of the apostolic church.

Accordingly, Newman in his pioneering work, *An Essay on the Development of Christian Doctrine* (1845), a book whose writing led him from Anglicanism to Roman Catholicism, tried to show how the apostolic church has *developed* through the course of history.[7] Yet, as Ian Ker has observed:

> In the *Essay* Newman is not attempting to "prove" anything, in the strict sense of that word. Rather, he is concerned with two pictures he has before his mind's eye, that of the modern Roman Catholic Church and that of the early church.[8]

Just as Newman imaged the continuation of the apostolic tradition as comparable to the presence of a living apostle, he dramatized the continuity of the patristic church:

> Did St. Athanasius or St. Ambrose come suddenly to life, it cannot be doubted what communion he would take to be his own. All surely will agree that these Fathers, with whatever opinions of their own, whatever protests, if we will, would find themselves more at home with such men as St. Bernard or St. Ignatius Loyola,...than with the teachers or with the members of any other creed.[9]

In other words, while Newman acknowledged the existence of many developments from the time of the early church to modern times, underlying the plethora of changes over the course of centuries was a basic continuity from the apostolic and patristic church to the Roman Catholic Church of the present.

Thus, the basic ecclesiological questions of Campbell and Newman were different: for Campbell, the question was, how can the church of the present be *restored* to its original unity? In contrast, for Newman, the essential question was, how can the church of the apostles and fathers be *recognized* among the various competing churches today?

IMPLICATIONS

In historical retrospective, there are some unexpected parallels between the ecclesiological visions and ecclesiastical options of Campbell and Newman: on a personal note, perhaps their similarities stem partially from the fact that both were evangelicals, even though their understanding of the gospel ultimately led them in quite different directions.

Nonetheless, while their denominational options went in different directions, there seems to be a commonality, which, while recognizable today, probably would not have been so easily acknowledged during their lifetimes. Yet in historical retrospect, this commonality gives rise to the question whether their obvious divergences might be ecumenically reconcilable by their religious heirs today.

(1) Central to any resolution of these differences is the perennial question of the interpretation of scripture: where Protestants once claimed to rely on *sola scriptura,* today there seems to be a greater willingness to acknowledge that scripture is always interpreted within a particular ecclesial tradition. Simultaneously, where Roman Catholics in the past sometimes emphasized tradition and magisterium to the apparent neglect of scripture, the Second Vatican Council envisioned tradition, scripture, and magisterium as "so linked and joined together that one cannot stand without the others."[10] Nonetheless, if there is a basic ecumenical convergence about the relationship of scripture and tradition, much dialogue is still needed about the role of magisterium in interpreting scripture.[11]

(2) Similarly, while there initially appears to be no evident convergence between churches that are professedly noncreedal and those that espouse a "dogmatic principle," again there may be a basic commonality underlying these denominational stances; on the one hand, do not nondoctrinal churches really profess more implicit doctrine than they explicitly acknowledge? On the other hand, does not Roman Catholicism allow for greater latitude in interpreting doctrinal pronouncements than may be evident at first sight? In any case, further dialogue is needed about how

apostolic doctrine functions—both in theory and in practice—in the Restorationist and Catholic traditions.

(3) Perhaps the most anomalous difference between Campbell and Newman is their different reading of history. While one might initially presume that "facts speak for themselves," one must recognize that facts are often aligned to theological assumptions. On the Restorationist side is the claim that there is a basic break between the apostolic church and its historical successors—a break that can be mended only by *restoring* the church of the present to its primordial purity. Nonetheless, at least a few in the Restorationist tradition—those who find a "Trail of Blood" leading back to apostolic times—recognize the need for linking the ecclesial present with the apostolic past.

On the Catholic side is a vision of the church as developing through the course of history, as if "writing straight with crooked lines"; in this view, there is a continual need for *renewing* or *reforming* the church so that it is more clearly like the church of the apostles and martyrs. Rather surprisingly, these co-issues of doctrinal development and ecclesiological historiography have received comparatively little attention in recent ecumenical dialogue.

Latent in these hermeneutical, confessional, and historical differences are assumptions about the apostolic nature of the church itself. For example, is the church in every age really capable of *restoring* itself to apostolic purity? If so, how will this restoration come about? And who will lead this restoration? Similarly, if the church is historically constituted in apostolic succession, how will necessary *renewal* take place? And how can one ensure that those officially responsible for renewal will be willing to be agents of authentic reform? In other words, concern about apostolicity inevitably raises questions about the nature of the church, its leaders, and their authority.

Finally, both Campbell and Newman, as religious leaders of the nineteenth century, were inevitably limited by the current theological assumptions of their day concerning revelation, scripture, and tradition. A century-plus later, many of these assumptions have notably changed, and so there is a new—indeed promising—ecumenical opportunity to reconsider the implications of apostolicity, which deeply concerned both Campbell and

Newman. Newman at least anticipated such a reconsideration: "In a higher world, it is otherwise, but here below to live is to change, and to be perfect is to have changed often."[12]

NOTES

1. "Tract Number One," cited in Marvin R. O'Connell, *The Oxford Conspirators: A History of the Oxford Movement 1833–45* (London: Macmillan, 1969), 146.

2. John Henry Newman, "Letter to Flanagan" (February 15, 1868), in *The Theological Papers of John Henry Newman on Biblical Inspiration and on Infallibility,* selected, edited, and introduced by J. Derek Holmes (Oxford: Clarendon Press, 1979), 158.

3. John Henry Cardinal Newman, *Apologia Pro Vita Sua,* ed. David J. DeLaura (1864; New York: W. W. Norton, 1968), 50.

4. *Apologia,* 51; after reading Newman's description of his conversion, some Evangelicals claimed that it was quite different from their own.

5. *Apologia,* 218. Given the varying meanings of "liberalism," in the nineteenth century as well as at present, three aspects of Newman's understanding of, and consequent opposition to, liberalism should be noted: First, Newman opposed the rationalistic bias of liberalism: "No religious tenet is important, unless reasons show it be so" (222). Second, Newman rejected the subjectivism of liberalism: "No theological doctrine is any thing more than an opinion which happens to be held by bodies of men" (223). Third, Newman attacked the liberal bastion of private judgment: "There is a right of Private Judgment: that is, there is no existing authority on earth competent to interfere with the liberty of individuals in reasoning and judging for themselves about the Bible and its contents, as they severally please" (223).

6. Newman's most extensive treatment of the interpretation of dogma is found in his "Letter to His Grace the Duke of Norfolk" in *Newman and Gladstone: The Vatican Decrees,* with an introduction by Alvan S. Ryan (Notre Dame: University of Notre Dame Press, 1962).

7. Newman dated the preface of the first edition October 6, 1845, a few days before his entrance into the Roman Catholic Church; a second edition with some slight variations was published in 1846; Newman prepared a third edition in 1878, with major revisions that have the effect of making his essay less a hypothesis and more of a thesis. Most modern editions of *Development* reproduce the third (1878) edition; the 1845 original is available in a modern edition with an introduction by J. M. Cameron (Penguin Books, 1974).

8. Ian Ker, *The Achievement of John Henry Newman* (Notre Dame: University of Notre Dame Press, 1990), 113.

9. John Henry Newman, *An Essay on the Development of Christian Doctrine* (London, New York, and Bombay: Longmans, Green, 1900), 97–98.

10. Vatican Council II, Dogmatic Constitution on Divine Revelation, *Dei Verbum (DV),* chap. 2, par. 10. Quotations from the documents of the Second Vatican Council in the present chapter are from the Vatican website, http://www.vatican.va/archive/hist_councils/ii_vatican_council/

11. Stephen V. Sprinkle, *Disciples and Theology: Understanding the Faith of a People in Covenant* (St. Louis: Chalice Press, 1998), 56, points out a Restorationist magisterium: "The Disciples do not have bishops; they have editors."

12. Newman, *Development,* 40.

DIALOGUE 4

THE ROLE OF CREEDS AND CONFESSIONS: A DIALOGUE AMONG REFORMED, METHODIST, AND QUAKER TRADITIONS

CONFESSING THE FAITH IN THE REFORMED TRADITION

Joseph D. Small

The Reformed tradition is the most diffuse of the ecclesial streams to have emerged from the sixteenth-century Reformation in Europe. It was so from the outset: Zurich and Zwingli on the one hand, Geneva and Calvin on the other. From these related yet distinct origins, the Reformed tradition has found ecclesial expression in presbyterian and congregational forms of governance, liturgical and free church worship, a high view of baptism, the Eucharist, and sacramental minimalism, doctrinal precision, and individualistic convictions.

In North America, churches with Reformed ancestry cover a broad range, and most embody some form of the tensions that have been present from the outset. Tendencies are detectable, however. Churches with Dutch and Scottish roots find Calvin congenial, for example, the Christian Reformed Church, the Reformed Church in America, and the Presbyterian Church (USA). Churches with English roots are more Zwinglian, such as the United Church of Christ. Other churches with Reformed antecedents are no longer self-consciously or identifiably Reformed, for example, Baptist churches and churches of the Stone-Campbell Movement.

The fragmentation of the Reformed tradition, so unlike the relative cohesion of Lutherans, Anglicans, and Methodists, has several causes. One of these is the conviction, shared by Calvin and Zwingli, that the one holy catholic and apostolic church finds appropriately diverse expression in local contexts. Calvin has a high view of the unity of the church, acknowledging that "the

church universal is a multitude gathered from all nations...,
agrees on the one truth of divine doctrine, and is bound by the
bond of the same religion." Yet, he also recognizes that the church
"is divided and dispersed in separate places....Under it thus are
included individual churches, disposed in towns and villages
according to human need, so that each rightly has the name and
authority of the church."[1] The dispersion of the church is more
than geographical; human need calls for the freedom of churches
to express convictions differently without fracturing unity in
word and sacrament.

The freedom and necessity to express the faith locally has
always led Reformed churches to be confession-making churches.
In different times and various contexts they have believed it necessary to give present testimony to their faith and action. In the
sixteenth century alone more than sixty confessions were produced by Reformed churches. The World Alliance of Reformed
Churches has published a representative collection of more than
twenty-five Reformed confessions from the twentieth century.
The great variety of Reformed confessions is not an accident of
history and geography, however. Reformed emphasis on the sovereignty of God leads to acute awareness of the dangers of idolatry, including the idolatry of creeds. Thus, Reformed churches
rarely identify a particular historic confession as the authoritative
expression of Christian faith.

Representative of the Reformed stance toward confessions is
the statement of Zurich's Heinrich Bullinger at the signing of the
First Helvetic Confession:

> We wish in no way to prescribe for all churches through
> these articles a single rule of faith. For we acknowledge no
> other rule of faith than Holy Scripture....We grant to every-
> one the freedom to use his own expressions which are suit-
> able for his church and will make use of this freedom
> ourselves, at the same time defending the true sense of this
> Confession against distortions.[2]

Although there have been times when a Reformed church has
required allegiance to a single confession—often the
Westminster Confession of Faith—Westminster itself attests that

"[a]ll synods or councils…may err, and many have erred; therefore they are not to be made the rule of faith or practice, but to be used as a help in both."[3]

Typically, Reformed aversion to "a single rule of faith" has not led to the avoidance of confessional statements, for it has been coupled with "freedom to use expressions which are suitable to particular churches." Thus, alongside Westminster's acknowledgment of confessional error and its relegation of confessions to subordinate status is its conviction that "[f]or the better government and further edification of the Church, there ought to be such assemblies as are commonly called synods or councils: and it belongs to the overseers and other rulers of the particular churches…to appoint such assemblies; and to convene together in them, as often as they shall judge it expedient for the good of the church."[4] Distrust of a single confession, coupled with freedom to express the truth of the gospel in various ways, focused in the particular needs of churches in different contexts, leads to the continuing Reformed practice of confession-making.

The Reformed tradition understands the formulation of confessions as part of the mandate of proclamation entrusted to the church. Thus, churches belonging to the Reformed family have been inclined to state their deepest convictions in every generation. All of this is stated succinctly in the Presbyterian Church (USA)'s Confession of 1967. The preface begins with the conviction that "[t]he church confesses its faith when it bears a present witness to God's grace in Jesus Christ." The need for *present* witness has always been a feature of ecclesial existence, for "[i]n every age, the church has expressed its witness in words and deeds as the need of the time required….No one type of confession is exclusively valid, no one statement is irreformable."[5]

So far, so good: churches of the Reformed tradition in North America share a basic stance toward confession of faith. Their commonality embraces diverse ways of living with confessions, however. The churches grant authority to different confessions and have different understandings of the nature of confessional authority.

It is tempting to characterize the diverse positions of Reformed churches by labels such as "weak" and "strong," or "fluid" and "rigid." But these designations would reveal more about Reformed intramurals than about distinctive understandings of the place of confessions in the church. Nevertheless, it is possible to locate confessions of faith nearer or farther from the center of ecclesial faith and life. While all Reformed churches are clear that confessions are subordinate standards, they vary in the placement of those standards within the faith-formation praxis of the church.

The United Church of Christ identifies the faith that unites it and to which it bears witness as

> that faith in God which the Scriptures of the Old and New Testaments set forth, which the ancient Church expressed in the ecumenical creeds, to which our own spiritual fathers gave utterance in the evangelical confessions of the Reformation, and which we are in duty bound to express in the words of our time as God Himself gives us light.[6]

Specific confessions are not identified as authoritative, however. Instead, identification with the Christian tradition provides a backdrop for the church's responsibility in each generation to make the faith its own. The UCC has developed a contemporary statement of faith (in three versions: 1959, 1977, 1981), but it is not a standard or objective authority in the church. Instead, it is to be regarded "as a testimony, and not as a test of faith."[7] What Roger Shinn says of this statement of faith may be taken to characterize the UCC stance toward creeds and confessions generally: "Whatever authority it has is the authority of an honest testimony, whose persuasiveness depends on its contents."[8] UCC ordination vows only reference the creeds, confessions, and church statements within the broader category of the shared heritage of the universal church.[9]

The Reformed Church in America, in typical Reformed fashion, declares the primacy of the scriptures in the faith and practice of the church. The RCA also affirms the importance of the church's confessions as both response and distinctive witness to the truth of scripture. "They have authority among us as faithful expressions of the Word, and have usefulness among us in so far as they are relevant witnesses thereto."[10] The acknowledged confessional *Standards* of the RCA are the ancient ecumenical creeds together with three confessions from the sixteenth and seventeenth centuries: the Belgic Confession of Faith, the Heidelberg Catechism with its Compendium, and the Canons of the Synod of Dort. Stress is placed on the role of confessions as faithful witnesses to God's Word in the Scriptures. Although the RCA has produced a contemporary statement of faith, "Our Song of Hope," the statement has not been added to the church's *Standards*. Instead, it is endorsed as "a statement of the church's faith for use in its ministry of witness, teaching, and worship."[11] RCA ordination liturgies couple scripture and confessions, but they make a clear distinction between present scriptural authority and past confessional testimony. Ordinands are asked if they believe that the scriptures are the word of God, and if they accept "the *Standards* as historic and faithful witnesses to the Word of God."[12]

For most of its history, the Presbyterian Church (USA) and its antecedents held to the seventeenth-century Westminster Confession of Faith and Catechisms as the sole confessional standard. The development of a new confession—the Confession of 1967 (C67)—represented more than the displacement of older standards or the addition of another in a string of Reformed confessions. Together with the adoption of C67, the Presbyterian Church adopted a collection of authoritative confessions, thereby making explicit its conviction that there is no single rule of faith. *The Book of Confessions* includes two creeds from the early centuries of the church (the Nicene Creed and the Apostles' Creed); six confessional statements from the sixteenth and seventeenth centuries (the Scots Confession, the Heidelberg Catechism, the Second Helvetic Confession, and the Westminster Confession of Faith together with the Larger and Shorter Catechisms); and three twentieth-century confessions (the Theological Declaration of Barmen, the Confession of 1967, and A Brief Statement of Faith). In adopting these creeds and confessions, the PCUSA "acknowledges itself aided in understanding the Gospel by the testimony of the church from earlier ages and from many lands."[13]

The Presbyterian collection of creeds and confessions is not a museum of past faith or a bow in the direction of doctrinal diversity. The church's *Book of Order* states, "In these confessional statements the church declares to its members and to the world who and what it is, what it believes, and what it resolves to do."[14] Instead of general statements concerning the confessions' relationship to scripture or their historical significance, the church is explicit about the centrality of the confessions: "They guide the church in its study and interpretation of the Scriptures; they summarize the essence of Christian tradition; they direct the church in maintaining sound doctrines; they equip the church for its work of proclamation."[15] Presbyterian seriousness about the place of confessions in the church's faith and life is evident in the questions asked of candidates for all the ordered ministries of the church— Minister of the Word and Sacrament, Elders, and Deacons. Following profession of belief in one God, Father, Son, and Holy Spirit, and acceptance of the scriptures as the unique and authoritative witness to Jesus Christ, candidates are asked:

> Do you sincerely receive and adopt the essential tenets of the Reformed faith as expressed in the confessions of our church as authentic and reliable expositions of what Scripture leads us to believe and do, and will you be instructed and led by those confessions as you lead the people of God?
> Will you fulfill your office in obedience to Jesus Christ, under the authority of scripture, and be continually guided by our confessions?[16]

The place of confession in the United Church of Christ, the Reformed Church in America, and the Presbyterian Church (USA) illustrates the cohesion and diffusion of the Reformed tradition. The three churches share a set of convictions: the scriptures are the supreme rule of faith and practice, confessions of faith are subordinate standards, no single confession of faith is adequate, and the church is responsible to confess its faith anew in every time and place. Clearly, however, the three churches hold differing convictions regarding the centrality of confessions in the formation of faith and life.

Reformed churches do not understand a "development of doctrine" in which ecclesial apprehension of the gospel's truth becomes fuller in succeeding ages. Neither do Reformed churches identify a particular period with purer understanding of the gospel, whether the "New Testament church," third-century liturgical life, fourth-century creedal formulations, or the sixteenth-century Reformation. Instead, Reformed churches understand themselves to be participants in a continuous theological and doctrinal conversation that endures through time and space. Perhaps a set of images will be useful.

Reformed churches do not perceive the history of doctrine as a line stretching from the past toward the future, with the contemporary church at its head. In this image, the present church would benefit from the formulations of those who have gone before while advancing beyond them. The church of the past would provide the foundation of wisdom necessary for the present church to build upon previous insights. Gathering up the voices of the past, the church could now articulate a fuller expression of faith and faithfulness.

Reformed churches do not see the history of doctrine as a broken line of detours and wrong turns. In this image the present church would have to leap back over most of those in the line in order to reach an authoritative point in the past. An ideal moment (or moments) would provide a model to which the present church must conform. Most voices of the past would be expressions of error; only by heeding the true word of the faithful moment could the church restore its own fidelity.

Reformed churches regard the history of doctrine as a circle in which believers from every time and place carry on a continuous conversation. The colloquy occurs through Christ, the circle's center. In this image, the contemporary church brings its own insights into an ongoing discussion with those who have gone before. All voices are necessary to the conversation; ancient voices are not privileged because of their proximity to the beginnings, nor are contemporary voices privileged because they have access to the intellectual tools of modernity.

Although Reformed churches share this basic orientation to the relationship between Christian past and present, it is clear that they also differ in their understanding of the relationship's dynamics. If the theological and doctrinal history of the church catholic is a continuous conversation, the various Reformed churches have different understandings of the nature of the conversation and different evaluations of the conversation partners.

For the United Church of Christ, others in the circles are esteemed forebears to whom is owed respectful attention. However, the words of these forebears do not carry determinative authority. Indeed, those who have gone before are answerable to the present community of faith—just as it is answerable to them; what forebears have to say will be received insofar as its substance is persuasive. This does not mean that the present church possesses the fullness of truth or that it has nothing to learn from the past. It does mean that the contemporary church has the responsibility to judge what its forebears have to offer. The emphasis is clearly placed on the freedom and responsibility to make present witness to the gospel. If the past is helpful in making contemporary confession, its aid is accepted gratefully. If the past is not helpful, its words cannot constrict the church's proclamation of its faith.

The Reformed Church in America participates in the conversation with a more modest understanding of its own voice. It pays particular attention to early creedal statements and certain Reformation-era voices, even though it is aware of their limitations. It is hesitant to consider its own words on a par with the magisterial voices of its *Standards,* however. In all this the Reformed Church in America is aware that all voices in the conversation are inadequate expressions of the word of God, which must be allowed full voice in the judgment of all other voices. Thus, as the RCA is acutely aware of the danger of confessional idolatry, no voice is accorded supreme authority.

The Presbyterian Church (USA) understands itself to play an active role in the conversation, both as listener and as speaker. It gives voice to its own convictions in the Confession of 1967 and A Brief Statement of Faith (1991). Yet, the church is attentive to voices from other times and places, considering itself answerable to those voices. While the contemporary church may and should question those who have gone before, it must first be questioned by them. Only then will the church's temptation to historical arrogance be subjected to the primary authority of the word of God.

It may be helpful to delve deeper into the confessional stance of the Presbyterian Church (USA). The PCUSA is highly attentive to its confessional heritage. It has explored its confessional basis in a General Assembly statement, "The Confessional Nature of the Church" (1986), and has articulated criteria for changes in the *Book of Confessions* (1997). It encourages study of the confessions by presbyteries, sessions, and adult education groups. Many of its debates on issues such as the ordination of gay and lesbian persons take place with reference to the confessions. What, precisely, is the role of the confessions in the church's continuous theological table talk?

The eleven creedal statements in the *Book of Confessions* are not the only voices in the ongoing conversation. Individuals also participate, from Clement of Alexandria to Jürgen Moltmann. Yet, the confessions have an authority that individuals do not, precisely because they are the voice of the church, the articulated convictions of the community of faith in various times and places. The creeds and confessions were adopted by councils of the church, whether by an ecumenical council or the assembly of a particular church. As the voice of the church, adopted by the Presbyterian Church (USA), the confessions have a prior claim on individual conviction. That is to say, we are answerable to the confessions before they are answerable to us.

The confessions are not freestanding authorities. The *Book of Order* makes it clear that confessional statements are subordinate standards "subject to the authority of Jesus Christ, the Word of God, as the Scriptures bear witness to him."[17] This serves to locate confessional authority, however, not to diminish it. The *Book of Order* is also clear that while confessions are subordinate standards, "they are, nonetheless, standards. They are not lightly drawn up or subscribed to, nor may they be ignored or dismissed."[18]

But why these eleven? Presbyterians do not limit their attention to the creedal statements of the *Book of Confessions*. The church continues to confess its faith in statements that are not included among its confessional standards. "A Declaration of Faith," written in the early 1970s, has been commended to the church for use in education and liturgy, and the church will soon approve two contemporary catechisms. The church also listens to voices from the past that are not part of the *Book of Confessions*. A new translation of the French [Gallican] Confession of 1559 has been prepared and will be published with an introduction and study guide for educational use by the church. So why do the particular eleven documents compose the church's confessional standards? The church is clear that the contents of the *Book of Confessions* are the result of ecclesiastical judgment. The church chose these confessions and not others. Yet, the church's judgment is not arbitrary or capricious. The eleven creeds and confessions were chosen by the church as expressions of its faith and witness, and expressions of the doctrinal standards by which its faith and witness are formed. The *Book of Order* states that "[i]n its confessions, the Presbyterian Church (U.S.A.) gives witness to the faith of the Church catholic...identifies with the affirmations of the Protestant Reformation...[and] expresses the faith of the Reformed tradition....Thus, the creeds and confessions of this church reflect a particular stance within the history of God's people. They are the result of prayer, thought, and experience within a living tradition."[19]

NOTES

1. John Calvin, *Institutes of the Christian Religion,* ed. John T. McNeill, trans. Ford Lewis Battles (Philadelphia: Westminster, 1960), 4.1.9, 1023.

2. Philip Schaff, *Creeds of Christendom* (New York: Harper & Bros., 1877), 1:389–90.

3. The Westminster Confession of Faith, XXXIII. Presbyterian Church (USA), in *The Book of Confessions* (Louisville: Office of the General Assembly, Presbyterian Church [USA], 1997), 6.175, p. 162.

4. Ibid., 6.173.

5. Presbyterian Church (USA), "Confession of 1967," *The Book of Confessions,* 9.03, 9.02, p. 261.

6. United Church of Christ, *Basis of Union,* in *The Shaping of the United Church of Christ,* by Louis H. Gunneman (New York: United Church Press, 1977), 208.

7. Ibid., IV. F., p. 211.

8. Roger Shinn, *Confessing Our Faith* (New York: Pilgrim Press, 1990), 12.

9. United Church of Christ, *Book of Worship* (Cleveland: United Church of Christ Office of Church Life, 1986), 406–8.

10. The Reformed Church in America, "General Synod Statement on Scripture, 1963," in *A Common Calling,* ed. Keith Nickle and Timothy Lull (Minneapolis: Augsburg, 1993), 26.

11. The Reformed Church in America, "General Synod (1978)," in *Reformed Witness Today: A Collection of Confessions and Statements of Faith Issued by Reformed Churches,* ed. Lukas Vischer (Bern: Evangelische Arbeitsstelle Oekumene Schweiz, 1982), 220.

12. The Reformed Church in America, *The Book of Church Order* (New York: Reformed Church Press, 2004), 122.

13. Presbyterian Church (USA), "Confession of 1967," in *Book of Confessions,* 9.04, p. 261.

14. Presbyterian Church (USA), *Book of Order* (Louisville, KY: Office of the General Assembly, Presbyterian Church [USA], 2002), G-2.0100a.

15. Ibid., G-2.0100b.

16. Ibid., G-14.0405 (3), (4).

17. Ibid., G-2.0200.

18. Ibid.

19. Ibid., G-2.0500b.

THE ROLE OF DOCTRINE AND CONFESSIONS IN THE UNITED METHODIST CHURCH

Ted A. Campbell

INTRODUCTION

The role of doctrine, creeds, and confessional statements has become an emotionally contested issue in the United Methodist Church in recent decades. The denomination's attempts to clarify its doctrinal and theological heritage through theological study commissions (1968–72 and 1984–88), new disciplinary statements on "Our Theological Task" (1972, revised in 1988), the process of study of the issue of baptism (1988–96), the processes of liturgical reform (ongoing) and hymnal revision (1984–88), and long-standing ecumenical dialogues have compelled the denomination as a whole to reconsider its corporately agreed-upon doctrinal inheritance. A sense of liberality in doctrinal issues, coupled with a contemporary concern to reassert historic teachings, has given a particularly emotional tone to these discussions.[1]

The United Methodist Church is grounded in two distinct Christian traditions, each of which brought its own doctrinal inheritance to the church. On the one hand was the Anglican tradition mediated to United Methodism by the Wesleys, with its inheritance of the Thirty-nine Articles of Religion, the *Book of Common Prayer,* episcopal polity, and its sixteenth-century *Homilies.* On the other hand was the tradition of German Reformed Pietism mediated to United Methodism by Philipp William Otterbein, with its inheritance of the Heidelberg Catechism, and a polity that was in its origins presbyterian, but developed a form of episcopacy (or at least superintendency) in the nineteenth century. A catalytic element in the formation of these religious movements (both for the Wesleys and for Otterbein) was the pervasive presence of what I and others have called a "religion of the heart," a turn toward the heart and the affections in spirituality that often carried a notable tendency to deemphasize corporate doctrinal consensus.[2]

The religious movements of the Wesleys and of Otterbein became churches in the period after the American Revolution: Otterbein was himself present in Baltimore in 1784 when Wesley's American societies constituted themselves as the Methodist Episcopal Church, and the congregations allied with Otterbein's church in Baltimore developed their own ecclesial structures through the decades of the late eighteenth and early nineteenth centuries. When these two traditions came together in 1968 to form the United Methodist Church, they brought two centuries of doctrinal development, which we might summarize roughly in the following schematic manner: (1) the inheritance of Anglican and German Reformed faith and worship presupposed by the Wesleys and Otterbein, respectively; (2) a trend toward doctrinal minimalism encouraged by the revivalism of the American frontier; (3) an even stronger trend toward doctrinal liberality encouraged by the influence of Protestant Liberalism very late in the nineteenth century and through the twentieth century; and (4) a countervailing trend to recover the importance of doctrinal consensus, growing in strength through the twentieth century.

This paper attempts to lay out some parameters for the understanding of the role of doctrine and confessions in the United Methodist Church, in preparation for our trilateral discussion with representatives of the Presbyterian Church (USA) and Friends General Conference. The paper (a) describes historic United Methodist doctrinal "standards" and discusses both their legal status and their status by customary use, (b) describes the manner in which the church's *Book of Discipline* enforces doctrinal standards, both for candidates for ordained ministry and for lay members, and (c) discusses in brief the content of Methodist doctrinal statements.

UNITED METHODIST DOCTRINAL "STANDARDS"

The United Methodist Church has a number of doctrinal statements, referred to in our *Book of Discipline* as "doctrinal standards." The UMC follows the pattern of its Methodist Episcopal predecessor denominations in identifying specific doctrinal statements as protected by Restrictive Rules in the denomination's constitution. The effect of the Restrictive Rules is that the denomination (represented by its General Conference) cannot alter the protected documents without altering the constitution itself, and, in fact, these documents have not been altered since they have been protected by Restrictive Rules. This degree of protection (which I have designated in the descriptions below as "constitutionally protected") offers a higher degree of doctrinal status to the documents named, but we must note in the text that follows which documents are in fact named as constitutionally protected.

THE ARTICLES OF RELIGION

The Articles of Religion are included in *Discipline* and are constitutionally protected. The United Methodist Church inherited from the Methodist Episcopal Church and its successors Twenty-five Articles of Religion, which John Wesley edited from the Thirty-nine Articles of the Church of England. In the pattern typical of Protestant doctrinal statements, the articles deal with issues of trinitarian theology and Christology, the grounds of religious authority, issues of human nature and salvation, and issues of sacramental theology and practice. Since 1812 the articles have been protected by a Restrictive Rule in the denomination's constitution in its *Disciplines* and have never been altered.

THE CONFESSION OF FAITH

The Confession of Faith is included in *Discipline* and is constitutionally protected. Otterbein's successors in the United Brethren in Christ adopted a brief doctrinal statement in 1816 that was subsequently revised numerous times. The Confession, like the Articles of Religion, deals with issues of trinitarian theology and Christology, grounds of religious authority, human nature and salvation, and sacramental theology and practice. This Confession of Faith was inherited by the United Methodist Church upon its union in 1968 and placed alongside the Articles of Religion. The denomination's new constitution protected the Confession of Faith in the same manner in which the Articles of Religion had been protected in the past.

At the time of union in 1968 it was felt that the Articles and Confession were "substantially" in harmony, but a Theological Study Commission was appointed by the Uniting Conference. Chaired by longtime ecumenist Albert C. Outler, the commission was given the task of reconciling the Articles and Confession into a single doctrinal statement for the denomination, but the commission elected instead to let the two historic documents stand and to create a new, contemporary theological statement (see "Statement of 'Our Theological Task'" below).

THE GENERAL RULES

The General Rules are included in *Discipline* and are constitutionally protected. The General Rules were drawn up by John Wesley in 1743 and functioned as a kind of contract by which members of early Methodist societies agreed to hold each other accountable for specific moral behaviors (under the three categories of "doing good of all kinds," "avoiding evil of all kinds," and "attending upon the ordinances of God"). These have been protected by a Restrictive Rule since 1812, and, up until 1939, all Methodist elders were required to read the General Rules to their congregations once annually. The prohibition against slaveholding and slave trade in the General Rules was the grounds for the most significant division in the Methodist Episcopal Church (1844), but because the General Rules are concerned with issues generally appropriate to eighteenth-century Britain (such as avoiding goods that have not paid import tariffs), they have not been consistently utilized by Methodists in recent years.

WESLEY'S STANDARD SERMONS

Wesley's Standard Sermons are constitutionally protected, but are not included in the *Discipline*. John Wesley's "Model Deed" for

Methodist chapels stipulated that preachers in the chapels could not express doctrine at variance with those expressed in the first four volumes of his *Sermons on Several Occasions* and in his *Explanatory Notes upon the New Testament* (see "Explanatory Notes upon the New Testament" below). This deed was utilized by British Methodists, who still regard the "Wesleyan Standards" (*Sermons* and *Notes*) as their formal doctrinal statements, and by early American Methodists at least until the time of the Christmas Conference (1784). One of the disputed points of American Methodist history is whether the founders of the Methodist Episcopal Church presupposed the Wesleyan Standards, which they failed to name in their earliest *Disciplines,* and whether the Restrictive Rules adopted in 1812 presupposed that the Wesleyan Standards were constitutionally protected along with the Articles of Religion and the General Rules.

Although Methodists had consistent reference to Wesley's *Sermons* through the nineteenth century, it is unclear whether they functioned as doctrinal standards. At the time of the adoption of "Our Theological Task" (6 below) in 1972, the denomination's Judicial Council ruled that the Wesleyan Standards *were* constitutionally protected. This decision was challenged by Richard P. Heitzenrater on the basis of historical scholarship[3] and defended by Thomas Oden.[4] At the time of the adoption of a revision of "Our Theological Task" in 1988, the General Conference adopted legislation clarifying that the Wesleyan Standards should be understood as part of the doctrinal standards protected by the Restrictive Rules of the constitution. Although the number of Wesley's sermons constituting a doctrinal standard has been disputed by British and American Methodists, the Sermons bear particular importance in laying out the distinctly Wesleyan understanding of the "Way of Salvation" that lies at the basis of Wesleyan spirituality.

WESLEY'S EXPLANATORY NOTES UPON THE NEW TESTAMENT

Wesley's New Testament *Notes* are constitutionally protected, but are not included in the *Discipline*. What has been said above about the Wesleyan Standards applies formally to Wesley's *Notes,* although it is relevant to consider that Wesley's *Notes* have been utilized far less frequently than the *Sermons* in Methodist theological reflection. This is because (1) Adam Clarke's *Commentary* replaced Wesley's *Notes* early in the nineteenth century as the favored biblical commentary used by Methodists, and (2) Wesley's biblical scholarship, though progressive and up-to-date for the eighteenth century, seems quite antiquated since the developments of mid-nineteenth-century biblical scholarship.

STATEMENT OF "OUR THEOLOGICAL TASK"

The Statement is included in the *Discipline* but is not constitutionally protected. The Theological Study Commission established by the 1968 Uniting Conference was to have produced a new and reconciled theological statement incorporating the teachings of the Articles of Religion and the Confession of Faith. The commission chose, instead, to leave the two historical doctrinal statements in place and to adopt, in addition to them, a contemporary theological statement, interpreting the Wesleyan tradition in the light of contemporary, including ecumenical, issues. Their new statement, which included the first official assertion of the so-called Wesleyan Quadrilateral—the use of scripture, tradition, reason, and experience in theological reflection—was adopted by the General Conference of 1972 with little opposition. But, in a surprise move, the Judicial Council determined that the new doctrinal statement was to be considered simple legislation, amenable by a simple majority of the General Conference, and not a constitutionally protected doctrinal statement as Outler and members of the commission had intended. This has proven to be a helpful theological document in Methodist theological reflection, and was revised by the General Conference of 1988 to make clear the primacy or priority of scripture among the elements of the Quadrilateral and to make clear Methodist commitment to ecumenical and apostolic faith underlying all of our doctrinal statements.

THE ROLE OF HYMNALS IN MEDIATING METHODIST DOCTRINE

All of the previously mentioned doctrinal statements have a degree of constitutional, or at least disciplinary, force within the

United Methodist Church. This and the next item do not, although I want to make the case that the *Hymnal* and the historic creeds included in Methodist *Hymnals* function in practice as *de facto* standards of commonly agreed-upon teaching or doctrine. Methodist *Hymnals* uniformly begin with the praise of the Trinity, recalling the worship underlying the ancient ecumenical creeds, and almost uniformly have a lengthy section on the "Christian life," which lays out the more distinctly Wesleyan spiritual tradition that focuses on the "way of salvation" from recognition of sin and repentance, to justification and "assurance of pardon," to sanctification and the quest for "Christian perfection." Thus, the *Hymnal* reinforces the faith taught in the Articles and Confessions, as well as the distinctly Wesleyan spirituality explicated in Wesley's *Standard Sermons*.

USE OF HISTORIC CREEDS

The Thirty-nine Articles of Religion of Wesley's Church of England formally sanctioned the use of the Apostles', Nicene, and Athanasian creeds. Wesley himself omitted this article in revising the Articles of Religion for the American Methodists, and in fact omitted the creed from the eucharistic rite in his revision of the Prayer Book, *The Sunday Service of the Methodists in North America* (1784).[5] With the exception of anathemas attached to the Athanasian Creed, Wesley's exclusions certainly do not indicate any objection to the doctrines of the creeds, but are significant nonetheless because they left Methodists without a formal affirmation of the historic creeds. As we shall note below, the Articles of Religion and the Confession of Faith utilize the language of the Nicene-Constantinopolitan Creed and of the Chalcedonian Definition of Faith, so there could be little doubt that the Methodists agreed with the content of the historic creeds.

Methodist *Hymnals* from the middle of the nineteenth century began to utilize the Apostles' Creed in worship, and it has become the customary creed recited in American Methodist churches, including the historically African American Methodist denominations (AME, AMEZ, and CME).[6] Only in the twentieth century (beginning with the 1964 *Hymnal*) have American

Methodists utilized the Nicene Creed in worship, and my own impression is that its use remains relatively rare. Perhaps the most explicit affirmation of Nicene Faith on the part of United Methodists comes in the denomination's formal acceptance of the *COCU Consensus.*[7] One can make the case that exposure to the ecumenical movement in the twentieth century has led the United Methodist Church and its predecessors to be more explicit than in the past about its commitment to historic Christian doctrine.

THE ROLE AND ENFORCEMENT OF DOCTRINE IN THE UMC

Given the inheritance of doctrinal standards listed above, we may now ask in what ways the United Methodist Church utilizes and enforces its stated doctrinal commitments. Put differently, to what extent is the United Methodist Church serious about its doctrinal commitments?

We must state in the first place, as is customary for Methodists to do, that the Methodist tradition in general allows wide latitude in doctrine and teaching. This comes as no coincidence, given the rise of our denominational traditions in the context of a "religion of the heart," and the prominence of various forms of Protestant Liberalism in our churches in recent decades. Wesley himself insisted on a "Catholic Spirit" that agrees in doctrinal "essentials" but allows for a wide range of difference on "opinions that do not strike at the root of Christianity."[8] He insisted on the content of the ancient creeds but did not insist that believers should subscribe to their precise words.[9] There is, I think, broad agreement that Methodism has historically embraced a considerable degree of latitude in "indifferent" matters; there remains, however, substantial disagreement on what constitutes the essential doctrines on which unity is imperative. Acknowledging this problem, though, we can describe some specific ways in which a degree of doctrinal unity is expected in the United Methodist Church.

DOCTRINE AND CHURCH MEMBERSHIP

Methodists have made few doctrinal requirements for church membership, but have consistently reserved the possibility of removing church members for "dissemination of doctrine contrary to the established standards of doctrine of the Church."[10] Through the beginning of the twentieth century, Methodist churches and churches of the United Brethren in Christ tradition practiced a form of catechumenate that they described as "probationary membership" in a local congregation. An individual was received temporarily and upon training and evidence of Christian conduct was later received as a full member of a congregation, but the focus was overwhelmingly on morality and spirituality rather than profession of doctrine.

In fact, it has been only in this century that Methodists have made more explicit doctrinal requirements for church membership. The ritual for reception of adult members in the *Hymnal* of 1935 included the question, "Do you receive and profess the Christian faith as contained in the New Testament of our Lord Jesus Christ?"[11] This doctrinally dubious question appeared at odds with the sixth Article of Religion, which asserts the unity of the Testaments, so the question was revised in the 1964 *Hymnal*, "Do you receive and profess the Christian faith as contained in the Scriptures of the Old and New Testaments?"[12] At the same time, the order for the baptism of adults added the question, "Do you believe in God the Father Almighty, maker of heaven and earth; and in Jesus Christ his only Son our Lord; and in the Holy Spirit, the Lord, the giver of life?"[13] These same questions remain in the current *Hymnal* (1988), although the profession of faith in the Trinity is set as three separate questions and allows the use of the whole of the three articles of the Apostles' Creed (said with the whole congregation) as a response.[14]

One could argue, then, that in this case as in the use of the historic creeds, ecumenical dialogue and contact have influenced the United Methodist Church to be more explicit about its doctrinal commitments. I would note again that although church members make a minimal profession of doctrine, they still remain liable to dismissal on grounds of teaching doctrines contrary to those of the denomination, although actual cases of dismissal on doctrinal grounds become increasingly few in the twentieth century.

DOCTRINAL PROFESSION AND METHODIST ORDINATION

Candidates for ordination in the United Methodist Church are examined on a variety of topics, including historic Christian doctrine and specific Wesleyan teachings. Although it would be difficult to demonstrate, I have the general impression that in the last two decades, Annual Conferences (the United Methodist synodal body that functions as a presbytery in presenting candidates for ordained ministry) have examined candidates with increasing attention to issues of doctrine and Wesleyan spirituality. Beyond these general examinations, all candidates for the presbyterate (the Methodist order of "elder") and the diaconate (we moved from a transitional diaconate to a permanent order of deacons in 1996) are asked the following questions before the Annual Conference:

- Have you studied the doctrines of our Church?
- Upon full examination do you believe them to be in accordance with the Holy Scriptures?

Candidates for the order of elder are asked the following additional question:

- Will you preach and maintain them?[15]

This is an interesting way to put the questions: the candidates are never directly asked if they themselves subscribe to "the doctrines of our Church," only if they have studied them, find them to be in accord with scripture, and (in the case of elders) will "preach and maintain" them. We may note, further, that "the doctrines of our Church" are not specified, although this presumably refers to the content of the constitutionally protected doctrinal standards named above.

As in the case of lay members of congregations, ordained ministers can be removed on the grounds of teaching doctrine contrary to the church's doctrinal standards,[16] but, again, there were increasingly few (but some) cases of removal on doctrinal grounds in the twentieth century.

THE DOUBLE CONTENT OF UNITED METHODIST DOCTRINE

It is impossible to summarize in this space the content of the varied doctrinal standards indicated above. But it is, I believe, possible to state in general that these doctrinal standards include two rather different sets of doctrines. They include, on the one hand, doctrines that define Christian (we might say, ecumenical) unity, and, on the other hand, doctrines that define the distinctive spirituality of the Methodist movement.

We have noted above that John Wesley himself distinguished between "essential doctrines" on which the church's unity hinges and "opinions" in indifferent matters on which latitude could be allowed. Earlier Wesleyan scholarship has cataloged a number of doctrines that Wesley identifies somehow as essential, but the resultant list is somewhat inchoate and not a list in any order that Wesley himself authorized. Colin Williams, for example, listed the following six doctrines as Wesleyan essentials: original sin, the deity of Christ, the atonement (saving work of Christ), justification by faith alone, and the work of the Holy Spirit (including assurance of pardon).[17]

I am convinced that closer attention to the contexts of Wesley's claims about essential doctrines reveals a rather clearly thought-out distinction between doctrines defining Christian unity in general and doctrines defining the more particular theology and spirituality of the Methodists. When writing his "Letter to a Roman Catholic" (1749), for example, Wesley focused on the doctrines of the Nicene-Constantinopolitan Creed: the doctrine of the Trinity, the deity of Christ as the Second Person of the Godhead, the work of the Holy Spirit, and the like.[18] When describing the distinctive teachings of the Methodists, by contrast, he gave an entirely different list of essentials, typically, repentance (as the work of "preventing" or prevenient grace), justification (often specifying assurance), and holiness.[19]

That is to say, Wesley understood doctrine in relation to the unity of particular communities. An examination of the Methodist doctrinal standards listed above (see pp. 130–135) shows a similar division of materials. Some of the doctrinal standards define the unity of the Christian community broadly (the Articles of Religion, the Confession of Faith, the historic creeds, and the initial section of Methodist *Hymnals* on the praise of the Trinity). Others define the much more particular inheritance of Wesleyan spirituality and theology focusing on the "way of salvation" and related doctrines about prevenient, justifying, and sanctifying grace (the General Rules, Wesley's *Standard Sermons,* and the organization and content of the "Christian Life" section of Methodist *Hymnals*).

This double set of doctrines results, I would argue, from Methodism's dual identity as a religious movement and then only later as a church. As a religious movement within the Church of England, Methodism had only to define its own distinctive teachings about the "way of salvation," hence, the oldest doctrinal material (the General Rules, 1743, the *Standard Sermons* from the 1740s and 1750s, and the original *Hymnal* codified in 1780) has to do with specifically Wesleyan spirituality. The more Methodism became a church separate from the Church of England (and this was a gradual process), the more it became necessary for Methodists to define the doctrines that define the unity of the broader Christian community, hence the Articles of Religion (1784), the Confession of Faith (1810s), the addition of sections of material in praise of the Trinity at the beginning of Methodist *Hymnals* from the middle of the nineteenth century,[20] and eventually the inclusion of the historic creeds (late nineteenth and early twentieth centuries).

CONCLUSION

Methodism's dual ecclesial character (ecclesial schizophrenia?) and its origins as a movement for the "religion of the heart" within the Church of England account for much of United Methodism's contemporary ambiguity on the role of doctrine and confessions. Some contemporary Methodists engaged in ecumenical dialogue, such as Geoffrey Wainwright, have suggested that Methodism remains a church incomplete apart from its location within ecumenical Christianity.[21] As obvious as this seems to me as a participant in ecumenical dialogue, United Methodists often act entirely on their own, for example, in constructing new understandings of ordained ministry. The Ecumenical Movement can help the United Methodist Church by helping us to clarify our relationship to the broad inheritance of catholic faith, and also by helping us to discern more clearly our distinct contemporary vocation within the catholic inheritance of faith.

NOTES

1. See William Abraham, *Waking from Doctrinal Amnesia: The Healing of Doctrine in the United Methodist Church* (Nashville: Abingdon Press, 1995).

2. Ted A. Campbell, *The Religion of the Heart: A Study of European Religious Life in the Seventeenth and Eighteenth Centuries* (Columbia: University of South Carolina Press, 1991).

3. Richard P. Heitzenrater, "'At Full Liberty': Doctrinal Standards in Early American Methodism," in *Mirror and Memory: Reflections on Early Methodism* (Nashville: Kingswood Books, 1989), 189–204.

4. Thomas Oden, *Doctrinal Standards in the Wesleyan Tradition* (Grand Rapids, MI: Francis Asbury Press, 1988).

5. See Nolan B. Harmon, ed., "The Creeds in American Methodism," s.v. "Confession of Faith," in *Encyclopedia of World Methodism* (Nashville: United Methodist Publishing House, 1974), 1:563.

6. An AME declaration on apostolic succession and religious formalism (1884) states, "we grant that the orderly repetition of the...Apostles' Creed...may conduce to the attainment" of spiritual worship (cited in *The Book of Discipline of the African Methodist Episcopal Church* [Nashville: General Conference, 1976], 31).

7. "The COCU Consensus," in *Growing Consensus: Church Dialogues in the United States, 1962–1991,* ed. Joseph A. Burgess and Jeffrey Gros, FSC, Ecumenical Documents V (New York: Paulist Press, 1995), 42.

8. The distinction between "doctrines" and "opinions" is drawn most clearly in the sermon on the "Catholic Spirit" (1749), where Wesley insists that although we may not share the same opinions or ways of worship as others, our hearts should nevertheless be right with God and with all our neighbors, and our "hands" should be extended to them (I–II). Wesley insists, however, that a "catholic spirit" is not to be confused with a "speculative Latitudinarianism," an "indifference to all opinions," or an "indifference to all congregations" (III:1–3). Wesley's sermon entitled "A Caution against Bigotry" (1750) maintains that we should not forbid the efforts of persons who do not have an outward connection with us, who are not of our "party," with whose opinions we differ, with whose practices we differ, who belong to a church we consider to be beset with error, or who hold bitter affections toward us, so long as their ministries bring forth good fruits (II–III).

9. John Wesley, "On the Trinity," par. 4, in *The Works of the Rev. John Wesley, A.M.,* ed. Thomas Jackson (London: J. Mason, 1829–31), 6:201; and in *The Works of John Wesley,* ed. Albert Outler et al. (Nashville: Abingdon; Oxford: Clarendon, 1975–2003), 2:377–78.

10. United Methodist Church, *Book of Discipline of the United Methodist Church* (Nashville: Methodist Publishing House, 1996), par. 2624.3.d, p. 656.

11. *Hymnal* of 1935, p. 543.

12. *Hymnal* of 1964, ritual section, no. 829.

13. Ibid., no. 828.

14. *Hymnal* of 1988, p. 35.

15. UMC, *Discipline,* par. 327, questions 8–10.

16. Ibid., par. 2624, item "f."

17. Colin Williams, *John Wesley's Theology Today* (Nashville: Abingdon Press, 1960), 16–17.

18. Wesley, "A Letter to a Roman Catholic," in *Works,* ed. Jackson, 10:80–86.

19. Wesley, "Principles of a Methodist farther Explained," VI:4–6, in *Works,* ed. Jackson, 8:472–75.

20. There was, of course, material in praise of the Trinity in the 1780 *Hymnal,* but the structure of the 1780 *Hymnal* focused on teachings about the way of salvation. It was not until the middle of the nineteenth century that Methodist *Hymnals* began to include explicit sections on the praise of the Trinity.

21. Geoffrey Wainwright, "Ecclesial Location and Ecumenical Vocation," in *The Future of the Wesleyan Theological Traditions,* ed. M. Douglas Meeks (Nashville: Abingdon Press, 1984), 93–129.

THE PLACE OF CREEDS AND CONFESSIONS AMONG FRIENDS (QUAKERS)

Ann K. Riggs

The topic for our consideration is "The Place of Creeds and Confessions among Friends (Quakers)." Using one hermeneutic on this topic, one could say that Friends General Conference Friends perceive creeds and confessions as, at best, adiaphora and, at worst, actual stumbling blocks to the true life of the church and to Christian unity, placing a burden beyond the necessary, and imposing styles of thought and language-use that are characteristic to some communities on communities to which these are alien.[1]

From another hermeneutical position, however, the phrasing of the topic as stated, "the place of creeds and confessions in the life of the church," opens a doorway to a quite different perspective. For Friends the *place,* the location, of authentic *creeds and confessions* is precisely *in the life,* in the living, *of the church,* the community of believers. In a characteristic Friends' phrase, the community of believers is called to have "lives that speak."[2] Or, we might say that, in Friends' view, in the church it is our lives that are to confess what we believe.[3]

METHOD

In the church, the confession of faith offered in the recitation of a creed can be seen as a speech act: a speech act of declaring the faith in its fullness for the first time in baptism; a speech act of responding in faith to the proclamation of the gospel in worship; a speech act of doxology. The Quaker notion of the life that speaks can be seen as an instance of a declaration of faith offered in acted speech. The lived acts of the faithful Friend are acted speeches that declare the faith, respond in faith to the gospel, and offer praise to God.[4]

To be more precise, but to avoid an extensive theoretical discussion, let us define *act speech* in terms of analogy to *speech act,* as that concept has come into theological discourse through Paul Ricoeur.[5] A *speech act,* performative speech, is speech that in its moment of speaking effects what it declares. In declaring the marriage vows, as for instance in the traditional Quaker vows— "In the presence of God and these our friends, I take thee, N., to be my husband/wife, promising with Divine assistance, to be a loving and faithful wife/husband to thee as long as we both shall live"—the covenanting act of marrying is achieved.

Yet, this act presupposes the "act speech" of the subsequent union of the couple. And the continuing declaration of the marriage vows is carried out through the acted speech of the lived acts of mutuality and union of the marriage partners.

The ever-changing reality of human lives is difficult to capture for study and theological reflection. However, Friends have a traditional form of literature that makes their lives available in a literary form, the Quaker *Journal.* Without taking up here the complex literary-critical questions of the relationship between the physically and psychologically lived experience of the writer and the experience presented in writing by the autobiographical author in the Quaker journal form,[6] we can read this literature as it offers itself. In the world of the journal, thoughts, feelings, and activities are presented as a flow of acted occurrences that bespeak the lived faith of the actor. To demonstrate, let us consider briefly two characteristic passages.

One of the best-known and best-loved passages to be found in Quaker literature is an entry from the *Journal* of early Friend George Fox. Fox had been engaged in a deep spiritual quest for understanding and insight. He records that his "inward sufferings were heavy." He cried out in prayer to the Lord. His prayer was answered in a series of new insights, which he records. "The Lord shewed me that the natures of those things which were hurtful without, were within in the hearts of wicked men....I saw an ocean of darkness and death, but an infinite ocean of light and love, flowed over the ocean of darkness. And in that also I saw the infinite love of God."[7]

What Fox saw, what he reported in the narrative of his own lived experience, consists in a highly compressed statement of core Christian faith. Sin is within our very hearts. To look at the vastness of sin is to behold "an ocean of darkness and death." There is, however, an ocean of love and light, which we may also "see," and which flows over the darkness. This latter ocean, unlike the dark one, is infinite. In seeing the ocean of light and love we see the infinite love of God for us.

Isaac Penington, another important early Friend, recorded a vivid experience of the Trinity in Meeting for Worship:

> I felt the presence and power of the Most High among them [i.e., the worshiping community] and words of truth from the Spirit of truth reaching my heart and conscience, opening my state as in the presence of the Lord. Yea, I did not only feel words and demonstrations from without, but I felt the dead quickened, the seed raised; insomuch as my heart, in the certainty of light and clearness of true sense, said: "This is he; this is he; there is no other; this is he whom I waited for and sought after from my childhood, who was always near me, and had often begotten life in my heart, but I knew him not distinctly, nor how to receive him or dwell in him."…I have met with my Saviour, and he hath not been present with me without his Salvation.[8]

In the passage a recollection of a lived experience of the Triune God is presented. Penington experiences the spirit of truth reaching his heart and probing his conscience. He meets the Saviour. He feels his deadened self raised to newness of life. The lived event occurs in the presence of and through the power of the First Person of the Trinity, who is in the midst of the assembled community.

Earlier publications of the Faith and Order Commission of the National Council of Churches of Christ in the United States of America have located their theological discussion in the specifically American context. Turning now to a longer exposition of the Nicene-Constantinopolitan elements confessed by lived speaking acts, let us look at the *Journal* of the eighteenth-century American Friend John Woolman.[9]

THE FAITH CONFESSED IN THE JOURNAL OF JOHN WOOLMAN

In a much-loved sequence of his *Journal,* Woolman presents a missionary visit he made in 1763 to a community of Native Americans some considerable distance west of his home in Mount Holly, New Jersey. After a time of sensing himself drawn to undertake this journey and considering this "leading" with other senior members of his Meeting community, Woolman set out on his pastoral visit, which is presented in intimate detail.

Our framework for the consideration of the fifteen-page passage, however, will not be the flow of the events. It will come, rather, from the structure of the Nicene-Constantinopolitan Creed, as it was reflected upon by the Faith and Order Commission in *Confessing One Faith: The Origins, Meaning and Use of the Nicene Creed, Grounds for a Common Witness.*[10] In the *Journal* pericope one can find instances of a large proportion of the doctrinal elements of the creed referred to or implied. None is contradicted.

> *We believe in one God, the Father, the Almighty, maker of heaven and earth, of all that is, seen and unseen.*

Confessing One Faith notes five key theological elements in the first article of the creed. The God of whom we are speaking is a God in whom we trust. This God is the one God, not one among many. God is loving parent of all. This God has the power needed to achieve the divine purposes of creation. This God is, in fact, the creator of all.

Woolman's trust in God presented in the *Journal* is profound. The journey he undertook to visit the Wyalusing community occurred at a time of high tension between the English settlers and the native peoples. The night before Woolman was to set out, and again during the trip, news reached Woolman and his party of native attacks on English settlements, the capture of forts, and open war with some groups. Woolman repeatedly struggled to maintain his sense of trust and confidence that in proceeding with his planned visit despite these hostilities, he was following the will of God for him. In the *Journal* he reports that "thoughts of the journey were often attended with an unusual sadness, in which times my heart was frequently turned to the Lord with inward breathings for his heavenly support, that I might not fail to follow him wheresoever he might lead me."[11]

Woolman's ability to continue his planned journey was rooted in his conviction that God is the one parent of all. He rejoices in the Lord's "fatherly care"[12] over him on the visit. Woolman's sense of the power of God to achieve the divine purposes of creation was intense and was closely linked with his conviction of the universality of God's providential care. "In this lonely journey," he wrote, "I did this day greatly bewail the spreading of a wrong spirit, believing that the prosperous, convenient situation of the English requires a constant attention to divine love and wisdom, to guide and support us in a way answerable to the will of that good gracious, and almighty Being who hath an equal regard to all mankind."[13]

In the *Journal* Woolman's affirmation of the value and meaningfulness of creation and creaturely life are evident. Traveling through the "mountain deserts" of the Pennsylvania mountains Woolman is awed by the roughness of the rock formations and the steepness of the hills. Part of the charm of Woolman's *Journal* lies in his inclusion of extensive homey detail of his own physical experience and that of others. He tells us that one night it rained so hard that the water came through the tents and wet the travelers and their baggage; that toward the end of the trip he caught a cold; that the canoe the party needed to use in crossing a particular river was leaky. Woolman is concerned for the native people because in changing the way they clothe themselves they have made themselves vulnerable to the demands and injustices of the fur trade. It disturbs him that the population of "wild beasts" on which the natives had depended for food is threatened by the expanding British settlements.

We believe in one Lord, Jesus Christ, the only Son of God, eternally begotten of the Father, Light from Light, true God from true God, begotten, not made, of one Being with the Father. Through him all things were made. For us and for our salvation he came down from heaven: by the power of the Holy Spirit became incarnate of the Virgin Mary and became human. For our sake he was crucified under Pontius Pilate; suffered death and was buried. On the third day he rose again in accordance with the scriptures; ascended into heaven and is seated at the right hand of the Father. Christ will come again to judge the living and the dead, and his kingdom will have no end.

In commenting on the Nicene-Constantinopolitan Creed, the authors of *Confessing One Faith* note that the second article presents the views of Jesus as Christ found in scripture, augmented by insights developed by the faith communities during the intervening centuries of lived experience. It was scripture and the experience of the early church, which have come down through the centuries to us in the form of a tradition, which gave rise to the emphases of the creed. Reflection on Jesus, as known in the scriptures and experienced in life by believers, indicated that he was so intimately connected with the Father that they must be of the same kind of being—in the way that light as it shines forth continues to be light. At the same time, Jesus was evidently a real human being who entered human life in the way that we do, lived a human life, and was killed. Reflection on Jesus' actions in our world, during his lifetime, and after his death indicated that for those who entrusted themselves to him he effected release from the sin that so entangles our actions. Reflection indicated that Jesus' power and activity were crowned and symbolized by his overcoming of death. Meditation on the memory and experience of Jesus indicated that in the life, death, and resurrection of Jesus, God was doing something different in reaching out in protective care of us.

The extensive detail of the second article of the creed is not as evident in the Woolman pericope as were the specifics of the first article. There are, however, several important christological passages that, considered together, give insight into Woolman's theological understanding of Jesus the Christ and its congruity with the creed's presentation.

Woolman reports on his preaching at a youth meeting shortly before he set off on his journey. There he was

> led to speak on that prayer of our Redeemer to his Father: "I prayed not that thou shouldest take them out of the world, but that thou shouldest keep them from evil" [John 17:9]. And in attending to the pure openings of Truth, [I] had to mention what he elsewhere said to his Father: "I know that thou hearest me at all times" [John 11:42], so that as some of his followers kept their places, as his prayer was granted, it followed necessarily that they were kept from evil.[14]

At one juncture Woolman questions himself as to his faithfulness to Christ:

> And here I was led to a close, laborious inquiry whether I, as an individual, kept clear from all things which tended to stir up or were connected with wars, either in this land or Africa, and my heart was deeply concerned that in future I might in all things keep steadily to the pure Truth and live and walk in the plainness and simplicity of a sincere follower of Christ.[15]

At a third place, Woolman describes what he feels in regard to the native people he has visited when his heart is "enlarged by the love of Christ": "I thought that the affectionate care of a good man for this only brother in affliction does not exceed what I then felt for that people."[16]

In these passages, Woolman demonstrates his knowledge of scripture and his sense that he understands Jesus in the same way that the scriptures do. He demonstrates, also, the traditional Friends preference for the fourth gospel. He refers to Jesus as the Redeemer. He compares "the love of Christ" to affectionate care for the stranger like that of a good man for his only brother in affliction. And he reveals that he understands a sincere follower of Christ, patterned after the Master, to be free from engagement with war and a lover of truth, plainness, and simplicity.

We believe in the Holy Spirit, the Lord, the giver of life, who proceeds from the Father. With the Father and Son he is worshipped

*and glorified. He has spoken through the Prophets. We believe in
one holy catholic and apostolic Church. We acknowledge one
baptism for the forgiveness of sins. We look for the resurrection of
the dead, and the life of the world to come. Amen.*

The commentators of *Confessing One Faith* note that the
creed's presentation of the third article is action oriented. The
Holy Spirit gives, proceeds, speaks. The creed's method here,
then, has some affinity to the method we have used to consider the
creedal elements in John Woolman's *Journal.*

A vivid sense of the immediacy and pervasive presence of the
Spirit informs much of Quaker thought. Woolman is clear in his
belief that the Holy Spirit is active in his own speaking and in his
hearers:

> In the afternoon, they coming together and my heart being
> filled with a heavenly care for their good, I spake to them
> awhile by interpreters, but none of them being perfect in the
> work. And I, feeling the current of love run strong, told the
> interpreters that I believed some of the people would under-
> stand me, and so proceeded, in which exercise I believe the
> Holy Ghost wrought on some hearts to edification, where all
> the words were not understood. I looked upon it as a time of
> divine favour, and my heart was tendered and thankful
> before the Lord.[17]

Woolman's visit to Wyalusing community had a specifically
ecumenical dimension, suggesting something of Woolman's
understanding of the unity, holiness, catholicity, and apostolicity
of the church and the action of the Spirit incorporating us into the
church's community. The meeting referred to in the above passage was not a Quaker meeting, but a Moravian one.

On the way to the village Woolman had met the Moravian
missionary David Zeisberger,[18] and Zeisberger was present there
when Woolman arrived. Woolman reports the concern that the
villagers had that there should be no "jarring or discord" because
of the presence of the two visitors. The villagers offered to hold
two different meetings, so that both missionaries could present
their thoughts. Woolman, instead, approached Zeisberger and

asked if he might have what Friends would call "the liberty of the meeting," the freedom to speak and participate in the life of the church community as moved by the Holy Spirit. This request was granted and the two worked together in a common evangelization effort.

Through the pages of the Wyalusing pericope Woolman admits on several occasions to his real fear for his life and his well-being on the journey. In so doing he also reveals his conviction that if he follows where the Spirit leads, he will be in a right relationship with God at the close of his earthly life. "I came to this place through much trouble," he writes. "Through the mercies of God I believed that if I died in the journey it would be well with me....The Lord alone was my helper, and I believed that if I went into captivity it would be for some good end."[19]

THE AUTHORITY OF PARTICULAR FORMULATIONS AND HERMENEUTICS OF THE FAITH AMONG FRIENDS

Among Friends, creedal formulations of the faith are not forbidden. One may find the formulations of the Nicene-Constantinopolitan Creed helpful to one's own articulation of the faith or not. The appropriateness and authority of any particular verbal articulation of or hermeneutical position upon the faith is not viewed, however, as a matter of indifference. Seventeenth-century Friend Robert Barclay, author of the most classically constructed theology the Society of Friends has produced, *An Apology for the True Christian Divinity, Being an Explanation and Vindication of the Principles and Doctrines of the People Called Quakers,* offers the characteristic norms for Friends' verbal and hermeneutical articulations. After one has been reached by the mysterious power of God and allowed oneself to be "knit and united" with the Christian community, "the knowledge and understanding of principles will not be wanting, but will grow up so much as is needful, as the natural fruit of this good root, and such a knowledge will not be barren nor unfruitful."[20] The test of a hermeneutic or a verbalization, then, is twofold. Does it grow out of conversion and Christian community life? What kind of fruit does it bear?

It may be argued, hoped, and believed that these tests are the same utilized in the solidification of the Nicene-Constantinopolitan Creed in the fourth century. The creed grew out of the lived experience of conversion to God and of Christian community. Its adequacy was further tested in its ability to bear fruit in offering a satisfying hermeneutic on the faith experience of those who came after.

Like any historical product, however, the fact that the creed can bear good fruit does not mean that it will. These formulations, good in themselves, can be used for evil as well, when they become the occasion for arrogance, brutality, and hatred.

The most deeply cherished sentence from the fifteen-page pericope of Woolman's journey to Wyalusing is undoubtedly the following. Friends who utilize quite different formulations of the faith view it with a common reverential awe: "Love was the first motion, and then a concern arose to spend some time with the Indians, that I might feel and understand their life and the spirit they live in, if haply I might receive some instruction from them, or they be in any degree helped forward by my following the leadings of Truth amongst them."[21] In Friends' understanding, any articulation or hermeneutic, if it becomes disconnected from the motion of love, loses its ability to bear the fruits worthy of truth.

NOTES

1. Dean Freiday brings out this possible articulation of Friends' self-understanding in "Apostolicity and OrthoChristianity" (in *Apostolic Faith in America,* ed. Thaddeus D. Horgan [Grand Rapids, MI: William B. Eerdmans for Commission on Faith and Order, National Council of Churches of Christ in the United States of America, 1988], 34–52) when he quotes John Punshon's remarks that "ecumenical services are a jolly good idea, and churches coming together is a very good idea, but I don't think that the practices of the largest of the Western churches should be taken as the standard for

everybody else." In "On the Nature and Centrality of the Concept of 'Practice' among Quakers" (*Quaker Religious Thought* 27, no. 4 [December 1995]: 33–37), Rupert Read argues that Quakerism is almost devoid of articulable faith content. British Friends engaged in ecumenical work have taken more positive views of the creeds. See especially Rex Ambler, *Creeds and the Search for Unity: A Quaker View* (London: Quaker Home Service for the Committee on Christian Relations of London Yearly Meeting of the Religious Society of Friends [Quakers], 1989) and his references to earlier and related work by British Friends. My own position is closer to Ambler's view than some other North American views.

2. See, for instance, Margaret Hope Bacon, *Let This Life Speak: The Legacy of Henry Joel Cadbury* (Philadelphia: University of Pennsylvania Press, 1987), and Marnie Clarke, ed., *Lives That Speak: Stories of Twentieth Century Quakers* (Philadelphia: Quaker Press of Friends General Conference, 2004).

3. Freiday brings this view out in "Apostolicity and OrthoChristianity," in *Apostolic Faith,* ed. Horgan, 45.

4. James F. White makes a related point when he claims that the true texts for the study of Friends' worship are Friends (*Protestant Worship: Traditions in Transition* [Louisville: Westminster/John Knox, 1989], 138).

5. Paul Ricoeur, *Interpretation Theory: Discourse and the Surplus of Meaning* (Fort Worth: Texas Christian University Press, 1976), esp. 14–19.

6. On Quaker journals, see Howard H. Brinton, *Quaker Journals: Varieties of Religious Experience Among Friends* (Wallingford, PA: Pendle Hill Publications, 1972); Thomas D. Hamm, "The Transformation of the American Quaker Narrative Style, 1850–1910," *Quaker Religious Thought* 26, no. 3 (November 1993): 39–57; and Edward Higgins, "John Woolman's *Journal:* Narrative as Quaker Values Transmission," *Quaker Religious Thought* 26, no. 3 (November 1993): 25–37.

7. Quoted in most, if not all, Friends' books of discipline and doctrine, e.g., Yearly Meeting of the Religious Society of Friends (Quakers) in Britain, *Quaker Faith and Practice: The Book of Discipline of the Yearly Meeting of the Religious Society of Friends (Quakers) in Britain* (Warwick: Warwick Printing Company for

Yearly Meeting of the Religious Society of Friends [Quakers] in Britain, 1995), par. 19.03.

8. Ibid., par. 19.14.

9. John Woolman, *The Journal and Major Essays of John Woolman,* ed. Phillips S. Moulton (Richmond, IN: Friends United Meeting, 1989).

10. Faith and Order Commission of the National Council of Churches of Christ in the United States of America, *Confessing One Faith: The Origins, Meaning and Use of the Nicene Creed, Grounds for a Common Witness* (Cincinnati: Forward Movement, 1988).

11. Woolman, *Journal,* 123.

12. Ibid., 134.

13. Ibid., 129.

14. Ibid., 123.

15. Ibid., 129.

16. Ibid., 134.

17. Ibid., 133.

18. Ibid., 132–34.

19. Ibid., 134.

20. Robert Barclay, *An Apology for the True Christian Divinity, Being an Explanation and Vindication of the Principles and Doctrines of the People Called Quakers* (Philadelphia: Friends Book Store, 1908), 340; *Barclay's Apology in Modern English,* ed. Dean Freiday (Newberg, OR: Barclay Press, 1967), 254–55.

21. Woolman, *Journal,* 127.

RESPONSE

Joseph D. Small

In this conversation with Ann Riggs of Friends General Conference and Ted Campbell of the United Methodist Church, I have to abandon all ambition of speaking for the Reformed tradition in general, confining my response to the perspective of the Presbyterian Church (USA). In a way, this is unfortunate because the conversation would be enriched by bringing into dialogue the Friends' conviction that "the *place,* the location, of authentic *creeds and confessions,* is precisely *in the life,* in the living, *of the Church,* the community of believers" (Riggs), and the United Church of Christ's conviction that Christians are called to express the faith in the present "as God gives the light." It would also be beneficial to explore the relationship between the ambiguous status given to the United Methodist statement of "Our Theological Task" and the Reformed Church of America's "Our Song of Hope." But, once we get beyond the realm of generality, I am not competent to do full justice to the whole of the Reformed tradition.

My desire to represent the Reformed tradition and not just my own church is, itself, typically Reformed. In North America, and in most other parts of the world, particular Reformed churches do not act ecumenically apart from other Reformed churches. Thus, the Lutheran-Reformed "Formula of Agreement" establishing full communion was a "bilateral" agreement with three distinct churches on one side. Although sometimes confusing to our dialogue partners (and to ourselves), Reformed churches generally commit themselves to an ecumenical solidarity that bears witness to Reformed ecumenical openness. (Debate on the Formula of

Agreement in the PCUSA's 172 presbyteries focused on Presbyterian hesitation about the UCC!)

RESONANCE

I appreciate the Friends' emphasis on confession of faith in the lives of the faithful. Ann's discussion of "act speech" may not use a traditional Quaker formulation, but it is particularly apt. It expresses a central Christian truth about the articulate power of Christian living. The first American Presbyterian General Assembly in 1789 adopted "Preliminary Principles" that remain in the *Book of Order.* Among these is the conviction that "Truth is in order to goodness" and that "the great touchstone of truth [is] its tendency to promote holiness." The section concludes with the assertion that "there is an inseparable connection between faith and practice, truth and duty. Otherwise, it would be of no consequence either to discover truth and embrace it."[1] It must be admitted, however, that there have been times in Presbyterian history that concern for doctrinal precision has left concern for holy and loving life in its wake. Even when holy living in the community of faith has been an explicit concern of the church, the tendency has been to stipulate holiness with doctrinal correctness!

I was a pastor in Westerville, Ohio, for eight years. A suburb of Columbus, Westerville was home to three large United Methodist churches: the Church of the Master, the Church of the Savior, and the Church of the Messiah. They represented the lineage of United Methodism: one had been a United Brethren congregation, one an Evangelical congregation, and one a Methodist congregation. All lived in the shadow of Otterbein College. I understand Ted's point that United Methodism brings together two traditions with two centuries of doctrinal development. This creates some tensions and ambiguities, yet these are consciously addressed by American Methodism. The Presbyterian Church continues to live with two "traditions"—English Independent Calvinism and Scots-Irish Presbyterian Calvinism. These separate traditions split in the eighteenth and nineteenth centuries into

New Side and Old Side, then New School and Old School. Contemporary American Presbyterianism continues to embody these different tendencies; one of the differences is the role and authority of creeds and confessions! Perhaps the United Methodist Church deals with its different traditions more openly, and thus more creatively, than Presbyterians.

The United Methodist Church's distinctions among (1) documents that are "constitutionally protected" and those that are not, (2) documents included in the *Book of Discipline* and those not included, (3) documents that are both protected and in the *Discipline,* and (4) documents that are one but not the other is confusing. Nevertheless, I understand and appreciate the necessity for making distinctions among various doctrinally significant statements. The Presbyterian *Book of Confessions* is "constitutionally protected" by a demanding, protracted process for amendment (adding, subtracting, or clarifying confessions). The PCUSA has adopted other doctrinal statements and positions that are not granted confessional status, but are nonetheless important and useful in the church's articulation of the faith.

I appreciated Ted's brief discussion of the distinction between doctrinal "essentials" and "opinions that do not strike at the root of Christianity," between "indifferent" matters and "essential" doctrines. The greater the quantity of confessional documents, the greater the confusion regarding what is central and what is not. The Presbyterian Church (USA) asks church officers (ministers of the word and sacrament, elders, and deacons) to "sincerely receive and adopt the essential tenets of the Reformed faith as expressed in the confessions of our church as authentic and reliable expositions of what Scripture leads us to believe and do." What are these "essential tenets"? They are nowhere identified!

DISSONANCE

While Presbyterians can appreciate the Friends' emphasis on "living the faith" as a way of "confessing the faith," we are puzzled by the assumption that "speaking the faith" is *adiaphora* at best and, more likely, a stumbling block. There is a long tradition in

American Protestantism that understands doctrine as divisive, for example, "Doctrine divides, mission unites." However, it is at least as true that "Mission divides, doctrine unites." All of the sharp debates and deep divisions in the recent history of the Presbyterian Church have occurred around the church's *action,* not its doctrine. This may be a sign of doctrinal indifference, but there is a growing conviction that the church's unity is to be found in its *articulated faith.* Perhaps this resonates with Ted's observation that within the UMC there is "a countervailing trend to recover the importance of doctrinal consensus, growing in strength through this century."

Both Ann and Ted identified the writings of particular persons who are exemplars and/or authorities. The *Journals* of Friends such as Fox and Penington and the *Standard Sermons* of Wesley seem to occupy a more prominent place than the writings of Calvin do for Presbyterians. Many Presbyterians pay attention to Calvin, finding his thought provocative and compelling. But none of Calvin's writings occupies a formal place in the church's standards. Neither does Calvin's work occupy a special place in the thought or piety of Presbyterian ministers and members. Calvin studies are alive and well, but this is a theological, not a doctrinal matter.

NON-SONANCE

In the end, it seems that Friends and Reformed are not talking about the same thing when discussing confessions of faith. Although it might be said that all Christians are called to confess their faith, *Confessions of Faith* are understood to be corporate acts of responsible church councils, whether ecumenical councils or assemblies of particular churches. While confessional churches do not dismiss the place of personal testimony, personal testimony and ecclesial confession are different acts. It might make more sense to acknowledge that we are talking about two different things, and then talk specifically about those two different things! In that way, we might learn more from one another.

CONVERGENCES?

Presbyterians are becoming more aware of what Calvin knew well: *lex orandi, lex credendi.* The intimate reciprocal relationship between what is prayed and what is believed, between liturgy and theology, seems to be integral to Methodist and, in a somewhat different way, Friends life and thought. Although Presbyterian hymnbooks and prayerbooks are optional in Presbyterian congregations, there is a concerted effort to promote the use of the *Presbyterian Hymnal* (1990), the *Psalter* (1993), and the *Book of Common Worship* (1993). Additionally, there is a growing use of the Daily Office, particularly among ministers. It would be beneficial to explore the formative relationship between liturgy and theology in each of the traditions, as well as the way in which theology shapes the worship of communities of faith.

Presbyterians are also becoming more aware of another thing that Calvin knew: *lex orandi, lex credendi, lex agendi.* The reciprocal relationships among worship, theology, and action seem integral to Friends thought in a particularly intriguing way. It may be that Friends patterns of life and thought could help to rescue Presbyterians from a self-imposed split between theology and mission, belief and action.

NOTE

1. Presbyterian Church (USA), *Book of Order* (Louisville: Office of the General Assembly, 1997), G-1.0303.

RESPONSE

Ted A. Campbell

INTRODUCTION

This paper responds to Joseph Small's "Confessing the Faith in the Reformed Tradition" and Ann Riggs's "The Place of Creeds and Confessions among Friends (Quakers)" from the perspective of a United Methodist participant in the NCCC Faith and Order Ecclesiology Group, based on my own paper entitled "The Role of Doctrine and Confessions in the United Methodist Church." The format follows an earlier format of our "Fordian" methodology involving identification of "points of resonance," "points of dissonance," and points of "non-sense."

POINTS OF RESONANCE

There are many points of resonance between Methodist and Reformed approaches to the role of creeds and confessions. Some of these are as follows:

- Our traditions clearly agree in placing *the primacy of scripture above all creeds* and in understanding creeds as having a role in confession of the faith limited by the possibility of error (and the need for reform) of all subapostolic statements of Christian faith. This is apparent from Wesley's own writings, from historic Methodist doctrinal standards (Articles of Religion and Confession of Faith), and from the contemporary UMC statement of "Our Theological Task," especially as the latter was revised in 1988.

160

- Our traditions also converge in the *pattern* of affirming (a) historic ecumenical faith as confessed in the Nicene and Apostles' creeds, (b) the broad heritage of Reformation faith, (c) our own respective families of tradition (Reformed and Wesleyan, respectively), and (d) some materials peculiar to specific denominations. There is a strong degree of similarity in the questions placed to ordinands in the PCUSA and in the UMC regarding their fidelity to our doctrinal statements. I wonder if Joe Small could clarify what doctrinal requirements exist for membership in the PCUSA. Is there any requirement of fidelity to specifically Reformed doctrinal statements?

- Further, it seems to me that if my paper had considered not only the UMC but the broader Wesleyan tradition, perhaps the family of Wesleyan churches represented in the World Methodist Council (parallel to the manner in which Joe Small's paper deals with the broader Reformed tradition), it might show *a similar range of attitudes toward historic doctrinal statements.* Undoubtedly, between the PCUSA and the UMC there exists a parallel spectrum of attitudes toward the contemporary reception of historic creeds, with vocal conservatives insisting on stronger enforcement of historic doctrinal standards and more progressive church leaders insisting on a more relaxed attitude (so to speak) toward corporate consensus in faith.

- Finally, it seems to me worth stating as a point of consonance that Wesleyan and Reformed traditions (both of which are represented in the United Methodist Church) largely agree in their confession of *the content of the apostolic faith,* specifically in our confession of faith in the Trinity, the two natures in one Person of Christ, the centrality or primacy of scripture, the nature of the church as embracing a community of faith marked by preaching, sacraments, discipline, and the like.

With respect to the Quaker traditions represented in Ann Riggs's paper, there would also be some points of consonance with historic Wesleyan faith:

- Since both the Quaker movement and the Wesleyan movements represented in their origins what I have described as a "religion of the heart," there is broad range of agreement on *the centrality of lived experience* as lying at the center of Christian faith. Perhaps it is worth stressing with Ann's paper that for Wesleyans "consensus" involves the fullness implied in *consentire,* "to feel" as well as "to think" or believe together.

- It follows from this that there would be a broad range of consonance between Wesleyans and Quakers on the *present activity of the Holy Spirit confessed in personal testimony.* Wesley's *Journals* and the diaries of other early Methodists could be placed alongside those of Fox and Penington and early Quakers in this regard.

- One further point might be made, although neither my paper nor Ann's paper alludes to this. We might find upon further investigation some evidence of a *pneumatological understanding of Christ* in both of our traditions. As problematic as this might appear from the perspective of other traditions of Christian teaching (like the Reformed tradition), it seems to me a rather natural outgrowth of the strongly pneumatological focus of early Quaker and Methodist movements.

POINTS OF DISSONANCE

What would be the points of dissonance between our churches or traditions, including points at which we may speak the same language but with apparently different meanings? With respect to the Reformed tradition, one important distinction between Reformed and Wesleyan traditions is reflected in the fact that the Fundamentalist-Liberal controversy of the latter part of the nineteenth century and the early twentieth century affected our churches in remarkably different ways. Whereas Presbyterians were strongly divided in this controversy, Methodists were only scarcely involved, and one of the significant outcomes of the controversy was that the Presbyterians ended up with a number of church-related colleges and seminaries reflecting the more conservative strand of Reformed faith. This was not the case among Methodists, almost all of whose denominational schools came eventually under the spell of liberalism, leaving only unofficial schools (such as Asbury College and Seminary) representing the more conservative strain of Wesleyanism. I do not quite know how to explain this, except to say that Methodism's pietistic ethos did not involve the level of corporate responsibility for teaching that was involved in the Reformed tradition.

With respect to the Society of Friends, perhaps the most obvious point of difference might be the way in which we differ over the meaning of "confessing the faith." As Ann has explained it, Friends typically confess the faith in their own narratives of religious experience. Although the Wesleyan tradition has historically emphasized the confession of one's own faith in personal testimony, both the Wesleyan and Reformed traditions also utilize historic forms of words as corporate confessions of faith (not simply as means of expressing one's own faith). One might argue that the Quakers extended the Reformation's suspicion of idolatry lying behind traditional religious expressions to the one form of religious expression in which Protestants had reveled, namely, the use of spoken and printed words. But the distinction between words that are owned corporately and words that are the expression of individual persons remains significant.

POINTS OF "NON-SENSE"

The remaining question has to do with points of "non-sense" or "non-sonance" between traditions. Methodist and Reformed folk have been conversing with each other for a long time and at points have managed to avoid simply talking past each other. In fact, the United Methodist Church incorporates vestigial remains of the

Reformed tradition from the former United Brethren in Christ denomination. Wesleyan and Reformed are aware of the major differences separating our traditions (issues about the doctrine of election and divine initiative, the possibility of "entire sanctification" in this life, issues of ecclesial polity, and so on) and have worked out some language to overcome these.

The situation is somewhat different with Quakers. It is simply difficult to tell if there is resonance, dissonance, "synonyms," or "homonyms" in language usage between the Reformed and Wesleyan traditions, on the one hand, and the Friends, on the other, because of the distinctive attitude of Friends toward corporate creedal statements. For this reason it is more difficult to develop a common language, beyond that of the Christian scriptures, by which we can describe our historic points of resonance, dissonance, and so forth. The same problematic relationship would prevail, it seems to me, between any of the churches utilizing doctrinal statements for consensus and those who don't (e.g., Churches of Christ).

CONCLUSIONS

One interesting result of this three-part dialogue is that it shows a somewhat different angle on our original intent of demonstrating forms of ecclesial unity between "older" Christian traditions long involved in the ecumenical movement, on the one hand, and "younger" traditions that typically originated in North America and have not been ecumenically active. The schema breaks down here, because all three traditions represented here have European and British origins, and in point of fact the Quakers originated a century before the Methodists.

However, the discussion shows the importance of dialogue between "creedal" and "noncreedal" traditions. We could make the case that "noncreedal" traditions, whatever their origins, have flourished in a distinctive way on this continent. Douglas Foster's papers have shown how examination of customary teachings expressed in hymns and significant theological writings of denominational leaders can point the way to a greater acknowledgment of common faith between "creedal" and "noncreedal" churches. Ann Riggs's paper offers another tool for dealing with this problematic issue. One outcome of our discussions, we may hope, will be the development of a kind of "toolkit" of approaches to relationships between creedal and noncreedal families of Christian tradition.

RESPONSE

Ann K. Riggs

As I prepare my response to Joseph Small's paper "Confessing the Faith in the Reformed Tradition" and Ted Campbell's "The Role of Doctrine and Confessions in The United Methodist Church," I have before me already the responses of my dialogue partners. While addressing the categories of resonances, dissonances, and non-sonances in regard to the original papers, it seems most useful to allow my own response to be shaped by Campbell's and Small's responses before me as well. I would concur with much that they have observed about the relationships of resonance and dissonance among our papers and our traditions. What follows are additions to their comments.

POINTS OF RESONANCE

First, I might note that Campbell's and Small's traditions are part of my own theological landscape. Members of my own extended family belong to the United Church of Christ and the PCUSA, and I hold two master's degrees from a United Methodist divinity school (and—not unusual for the present generation of Quaker theological scholars—a doctorate from a Roman Catholic institution).

Our communities, as well, have developed over time in familiarity and tension with one another. As Campbell rightly notes, historically the United Methodist Church, the Presbyterian Church (USA), and Friends General Conference are all communities developed in the Anglo-American Protestant milieu. Already in the 1670s, the Scots-Quaker theologian Robert Barclay engaged in a well-documented series of dialogues with the Scots-Presbyterian theologians at Aberdeen.[1] It is generally accepted that John Wesley was familiar with the Religious Society of Friends. My own assessment is that Quakerism and Methodism are both best understood as *via media* traditions, part of the continuing unfolding and development of the multivalent internal complexity of the Reformed-Catholic fusion of Anglicanism. Friends and Methodist communities have long been close to one another, and in the last century and a half some parts of the Quaker world have drawn closer and closer to Wesleyan life and thought. For instance, the Haggard School of Theology at Azusa Pacific University, in Azusa, California, a Wesleyan institution, has Quaker as well as Methodist roots and today serves both communities.

POINTS OF DISSONANCE

In taking up the original assignment on the place of creeds and confessions in the life of church, I took the assignment to mean the place of the Nicene-Constantinopolitan Creed and analogues in the life of church, where Small and Campbell took the assignment to include all doctrinal and normative theological articulations of their respective communities. The result may have suggested that Friends utilize no doctrinal books or normative theologies other than the narratives of the faith lives of heroic figures of our tradition. This is a miscommunication. Supplemental information at this point may be helpful.

Friends General Conference is an association of fourteen Yearly Meetings and regional groups not yet developed to the level of Yearly Meeting, plus six directly affiliated Monthly Meetings located in geographic areas at a great distance from other FGC meetings. The Yearly Meeting, equivalent to a diocese, bears responsibility for creating and enacting a doctrinal and juridical document called a *Book of Discipline* or *Faith and Practice*. The *Faith and Practice* books of the Religious Society of Friends throughout the world and over the three and a half centuries of the society's existence are similar to one another, but not identical. Distinctive local elements are cherished.

Three characteristics of Friends *Faith and Practice* books may be noted here. *Faith and Practice* volumes use an ancient theological method, familiar to historians of Christianity. Articulation of the faith is presented in the manner of the medieval *catenae.* Short blocks of text are arranged together, demonstrating continuity and development or pluriformity within continuity on a particular aspect of faith: for example, scripture or Christian unity or care of creation.

In Quaker books of discipline, "practice" and "faith" are related in a distinctive way. Practice is not presented as a sequela of faith. In our books of discipline, normative practice is presented as part of what we believe. "Faith-and-practice" would ordinarily be understood as a single unit. Numerous biblical passages that Friends see as displaying their understanding of the relationship between faith and practice might be adduced. One will be sufficient:

> This is the message we have heard from him and proclaim to you, that God is light and in him there is no darkness at all. If we say we have fellowship with him while we are walking in darkness, we lie and do not do what is true; but if we walk in the light as he himself is in the light, we have fellowship with one another, and the blood of Jesus his Son cleanses us from all sin. (1 John 1:5–7)

The passage brings into prominence the idea that truth is something one does. Our having fellowship with God is here presented in connection with our "walk," rather than with our "talk." "Walking in the light" is a favorite Quaker phrase. Here the related phrasing appears.

As Small and Campbell have noted, Friends emphasis on the truth-act relationship is at variance with the truth-words emphasis presented by them. It may be worth noting, however, that the passage from First John holds *koinonia* with God (and others) and speaking truth (rather than speaking falsehoods), and *koinonia* with God (and others) and doing truth together, rather than contrasting them as we have been doing in our discussion.

Third, FGC Friends are often viewed through the lens of our liberal social justice and peace concerns and activity. In itself this is not inaccurate. But another side of FGC, our extreme traditionalism and conservatism in some aspects of our ecclesial life, is less often evident to outsiders. Liturgist James White has remarked that the traditional unprogrammed worship style found in Friends General Conference may be contrasted to almost all other Western Christian liturgical traditions in being unchanged since the 1650s. Similarly one might note that John Woolman, whose life I have used to display our understanding of acted speech, was a contemporary of John Wesley and belonged to one of the several FGC Yearly Meetings that at the beginning of the eighteenth century were already well-established jurisdictions. My choice of Woolman for my presentation would not be considered antiquarian among FGC Friends. Among Friends, Woolman's life, his faith and his practice, are viewed as a living resource of wisdom, authentic practice, and faithful living.

The arenas in which continuity and change are evident within Friends General Conference seem to be different at some points from those most in flux within the United Methodist Church and the Presbyterian Church (USA). In a variety of ways, it is continuity of practice, in personal life, in social witness, in public worship, and in governance, which has served to maintain coherence over time for Friends General Conference Friends and has supported continuity in faith. Among Methodists and Reformed it appears to be rather continuity in articulation of faith that has maintained coherence over time and supported faithful practice.

In addition to *Faith and Practice* books and the lives of faithful women and men, the discursive theology of some leading Quakers is held in high regard for defining the authentic Quaker faith. Seventeenth-century Friends Margaret Fell Fox, Isaac Penington, Robert Barclay, and William Penn continue to draw readers and function as major resources for defining the faith. Twentieth-century figures include Thomas Kelly, Howard Brinton, and Rufus Jones.

POINTS OF NON-SONANCE

As Joe Small noted, a notable non-sonance exists between his Presbyterian paper and my own in the identification of some

personal lives and some individual theological thought as having significance for the entire community. I would suggest that
it is the very definition of the categories in which the personal
and the corporate are being discussed that is non-sonant
between the two and divergent between Campbell's paper and
my own, as well.

In a Quaker view scripture is, in part, a record of personal
lives and individual thought that have been understood to have
transpersonal significance. The biblical witness preserves
accounts of the personal lives of faithfulness and the theological
reflection of the patriarchs and matriarchs of the Genesis sagas,
Moses, Ruth, Esther, the Prophets, David, Mary, Peter, Paul, and
Jesus himself, because these are human beings whose lives and
thought have public significance for the entire Christian community and, Christians believe, for the whole world. The *Confessions*
of Augustine of Hippo, the *Ecclesiastical History* of Bede, the
behavior of Perpetua and Felicity in the course of their martyrdom, the sayings of the desert mothers and fathers, the guides to
religious experience of Ignatius of Loyola and Teresa of Avila
found in the *Exercises* and the *Interior Mansions,* the *Ethical
Discourses* of Symeon the New Theologian, the *Showings* of Julian
of Norwich, the *Summae theologiae* and *Contra gentiles* of Thomas
Aquinas are all personal statements of thought and life that,
within the traditioning process and by means of various forms of
formal ecclesial action, the community of Christian believers has
come to recognize as having transpersonal import.

Friends' view that the personal lives and thought of the eighteenth-century John Woolman, seventeenth-century George Fox,
and nineteenth-century Elizabeth Fry have transpersonal, corporate, and public significance seems to us a recognition that the
same processes that created the scriptures and the tradition continue among believing communities today. Similarly, John
Wesley's Aldersgate experience and John Calvin's *Institutes of the
Christian Religion* might be spoken of as personal life experience
and personal theological reflection that have come to have public,
transpersonal, and corporate significance.

It is not clear to me why both Campbell and Small speak out
of categories of "personal" as contrasted to "public and corporate"

that appear to leave no theologically coherent location for transpersonally, corporately, publicly significant personal thought and life. Such a category would seem to me to be the obvious heritage of all Christian communities, founded as they are in the public, corporate significance of the work of God effected in the personal human life of the man Jesus.

This non-sonance of categories may be indicative of one of the ways in which Quakerism does not fit easily within the boundaries of Protestantism. The role that the lives and faith of significant figures of the community's past play in Quakerism is perhaps more similar to the role of the saints in Catholic, Orthodox, and Anglican communities than to the role of the private individual in Reformed and Methodist traditions.

NOTE

1. Alexander Skene, ed., *A True and Faithful Accompt of the Most Material Passages of a Dispute Betwixt Some Students of Divinity (So Called) of the University of Aberdene and the People Called Quakers* (London: no publisher indicated, 1675).

DIALOGUE 5

CHRISTIAN INITIATION:
A DIALOGUE BETWEEN BAPTIST
AND ROMAN CATHOLIC TRADITIONS

INITIATION INTO THE CHURCH AND THE BAPTIST TRADITION

Paul E. Robertson

The Baptist way of "doing church" always makes discussions of "Baptist beliefs" difficult. Our aversion to creeds and our non-hierarchical structure can often leave us in a quandary in stating the Baptist position. I will attempt, however, to present a majority position in Baptist life that draws upon some historical confessions, some who have written to interpret Baptists, and my own observations.

Several limitations of this presentation should be noted. First, time and space limitations make it difficult to deal with many of the various subtleties of Baptist life. Second, I am interpreting Baptists from what may seem to be a narrow position of my own denomination, the Southern Baptist Convention, and its North American perspective. Third, my personal involvement in formal ecumenical conversations is fairly recent and limited in scope. Nonetheless, I will attempt to synthesize Baptist thought on this topic.

From my vantage point an understanding of "initiation" in the Baptist heritage involves looking at a matrix of interrelated factors. I have chosen for this presentation to think through our understanding of three of these factors: (1) the nature of the church, (2) salvation, and (3) the role of baptism. After discussing these areas, I will make some concluding remarks regarding implications for ecumenical dialogue.

THE BELIEVER'S CHURCH

The nature of the church has been of crucial importance for Baptists since their beginnings in the early seventeenth century. Some in fact have seen ecclesiology as defining the essence of the Baptist identity. For example, Winthrop Hudson and Norman Maring insisted that "the doctrine of the church is where Baptists began to diverge from other Protestants."[1] Though many may not see ecclesiology as the central Baptist distinctive, certainly most Baptists would see it as crucial to any discussion of initiation. The seventeenth-century world in which Baptists emerged was in a sense supercharged with authoritarianism. Early Baptists found themselves disagreeing with many other Protestants in the way in which the church is visibly expressed in the world. Religious authority traditionally had rested in the "official" church and focused on apostolic succession as a means of guaranteeing the perpetuity of the church. In agreement with other Reformation churches, Baptists feared that an institutional church could exhibit outwardly the four marks (one, holy, catholic, and apostolic) of the church and lack a vital relationship with Christ. The Reformers shifted to a focus on word and sacrament: the church is found where the Word is rightly proclaimed and the sacraments are rightly administered. Baptists, and some others as well, felt comfortable with the direction of the Reformers, but felt the need to go further. Thus, they suggested starting with a new emphasis: the true church is found where persons voluntarily stand in covenant relationship with God and one another. Our Baptist forebears argued that the church was not "parochial, diocesan, provincial, or national, but was congregational, gathered by an act of mutual confederation...expressed in a covenant."[2] Stewart Newman observed that Baptists and others such as the Anabaptists "insisted on the freedom and responsibility of the individual as being central in all matters of faith, beginning with human participation in revelation and becoming articulate in the voluntary aspects of association in church membership."[3]

John Smyth stated the emerging Baptist ecclesiological principle: "We say the Church of two or three faithful people Separated from the world and joyned together in true covenant, have both Christ, the covenant, and promises and the ministerial powre of Christ given to them."[4] On another occasion he would write "that the church of Christ is a company of the faithful; baptized after confession of sin and of faith, endowed with the power of Christ."[5] The *New Hampshire Confession* states: "[We believe t]hat a visible Church of Christ is a congregation of baptized believers, associated by covenant in the faith and fellowship of the Gospel."[6] A more recent statement reads: "A New Testament church of the Lord Jesus Christ is a local body of baptized believers who are associated by covenant in the faith and fellowship of the Gospel, observing the two ordinances of Christ, committed to His teachings, exercising the gifts, rights, and privileges invested in them by His Word, and seeking to extend the Gospel to the ends of the earth."[7] Miroslav Volf has recently suggested his understanding of the church: *"Where two or three are gathered in Christ's name, not only is Christ present among them, but a Christian church is there as well,* perhaps a bad church, a church that may well transgress against love and truth, but a church nonetheless."[8] He goes on to observe two conditions of the church. The first is the faith of the ones who assemble. Without faith there is no church. The second is that these faithful are an assembly of those who gather in the name of Christ. This implies a commitment to have their lives shaped by Jesus Christ. This is consistent with Baptist emphasis, as will be seen later.

In coming to their position, Baptists observe that *ekklesia* in the New Testament designates both the people of God in their totality and any local congregation of his people, with the local church usage being more numerous and at the forefront. Baptists understand that any local church is the embodiment of the "church" in any given locality. Though it may seem contradictory, there is one church, yet it is found in many places at the same time. We feel the same tension in seeking to understand that there is one Christ, but that he is present wherever two or three are gathered together in his name (Matt 18:20).

Of course the consensus among Baptists would not preclude that there is no New Testament emphasis on the universal church.[9] The concept of the universal church is in fact recognized in the concluding sentence of the *Baptist Faith and Message* article on the church: "The New Testament speaks also of the church as the body of Christ which includes all of the redeemed of all the ages."[10] Most major Baptist confessions make a similar affirmation—the universal church consists of all those in relationship to Christ as Savior.

A Baptist understanding of the church has implications in several interrelated areas. Paramount is that the church is to be an intentional faith community. All communities have boundaries. Key for Baptists is an understanding that for the early churches, membership, though surely not formalized as we practice today, was held in high esteem. Early believers understood themselves to be persons who had been personally incorporated into the larger community (Acts 8:14–17; 18:24–27; Rom 15:26–27). For Baptists, each local church is constituted of members who have made an intentional faith commitment to Christ.[11]

The "profession of faith" as the key initiatory rite is based on the Baptist conviction that church membership is only for those that make a conscious declaration of faith. Of course, the focus of this confession of faith is not on verbal assent to a set of theological beliefs. Rather, the focus is on professing that "Jesus is Lord." For Baptists, the confession is on the one hand personal, but on the other hand never intended to be solely an individual and private matter. Confession is an acknowledgment of one's own faith and of one's participation in the larger community of faith. Thus infants and young children are not included because "they are not able to bear testimony to personal conversion or express consciously chosen loyalty to Christ."[12] This is perceived as a logical outgrowth of the Puritan principle of "regenerate church membership." The church is to be a company of the redeemed; its membership consists only of those who give testimony of regeneration (Rom 6:4; 2 Cor 5:17; 1 John 5:4) evidenced by confession of faith in Jesus Christ. In Baptist life persons are qualified for church membership based on a confession of faith in Jesus Christ made public in baptism. This assures that persons are mature enough to engage responsibly in the affairs of church life.[13]

Baptists are nonconformists. William Estep, in discussing the beginnings of Baptists, stated that "they opted out of the Church of England, which had separated from the Roman Catholic Church in 1534; and like the Anabaptists before them, they organized local congregations of believers who were baptized upon their own profession of faith."[14] This view was affirmed by many English Baptist writers, including John Smyth, Thomas Helwys, Leonard Busher, and John Murton. This tradition is also seen in America in the writings of Roger Williams and John Clark. One contribution of Baptists in America was their role in the struggle for religious freedom and the resulting First Amendment to the Constitution.

As for infants and children, they are certainly to be nurtured spiritually in the context of the community of faith until such time as they are old enough to deal with spiritual matters,[15] mature enough to engage responsibly in the affairs of church, confess faith in Christ, make a commitment to the church, and be received into membership of the local church. The church does not determine faith, but nurtures it and later supports it. The church, for Baptists, would be remiss in its opportunity and responsibility if it failed to nurture children in their faith. But church membership is reserved until such time as one responding to the call of God voluntarily professes faith in Christ and desires to be a part of the intentional community of faith along with the covenantal responsibilities that this entails. For Baptists, this process is an attempt to live out the pure church ideal.[16] Though from the outside it may appear that the intent is to keep persons out, such is not the case. Just look at our intense emphasis on evangelism and church growth. Rather, our intent is to ensure, so far as humanly possible, that only true disciples of Christ are church members.

As Charles Deweese has observed, the early Baptist emphasis on regenerate church membership led them to four basic conclusions: (1) admission standards should be high, (2) believer's baptism is essential, (3) church members should consistently meet biblical standards for Christian belief and living, and (4) discipline should be administered for serious failures.[17]

A part of the Baptist heritage of attempting to live up to this ideal has been the use of church covenants, which are pledges based on the Bible, dealing mainly with the moral and spiritual commitments related to the life of faith in the context of an intentional faith community.[18] Unfortunately, from my perspective at least, covenants have received little emphasis in Baptist life in the mid- to late twentieth century. Though theoretically we still hold to the ideal of a regenerate church membership, practically there is a decreased emphasis. The use of the church covenant was an attempt to hold before Baptists that ideal at least visibly.

SALVATION BY GRACE

A second important concept to understand in the Baptist matrix of initiation is our emphasis on salvation by grace. Certainly we Baptists have disagreed among ourselves on some issues related to the concept of salvation, in particular the role of the human will.[19] Rather than pursue those areas, I will focus on the main points of agreement among Baptists and those issues that seem to be most relevant to a discussion on initiation.

Let me begin by citing from the *Baptist Faith and Message* article on salvation: "Regeneration, or the new birth, is a work of God's grace whereby believers become new creatures in Christ Jesus. It is a change of heart wrought by the Holy Spirit through conviction of sin, to which the sinner responds in repentance toward God and faith in the Lord Jesus Christ."[20] Several common emphases of Baptists are included here. First, Baptists agree that salvation comes by grace. Salvation is a gift of God. One does not deserve or earn God's grace (Eph 2:8–9). Human works or effort have no role in salvation. Salvation comes to us not because of what we have done, but in spite of what we have done (Eph 2:1, 8–9; Col 2:13; Titus 3:4–6; John 3:5–8). This emphasis was stated clearly in the *London Confession* of 1644: persons are "redeemed, quickened, and saved, not by themselves, neither by their own workes, lest any man should boast himselfe, but wholly and only by God of his free and mercie through Jesus Christ" (art. 5). This emphasis was repeated in the *Philadelphia Confession* (1742) and the influential *New Hampshire Confession* (1833).

At the same time, Baptists emphasize that salvation is received by faith. Baptists understand faith to have several dimensions (Rom 10:12–17; John 3:16; 6:69; 8:24; 20:30–31; Acts 16:31). There is a cognitive element, or awareness of the content of God's promises proclaimed in the gospel. One is made aware of the Good News through means such as the proclamation of the word or testimony of persons. In addition, there is an intellectual dimension to faith, the acknowledgment of the trustworthiness of the gospel message. The trust or commitment dimension of faith is an act of the will whereby a person appropriates the knowledge gained and believed. At this level of faith one moves beyond affirmation of belief, such as believing that the claims of Christ are trustworthy, to a trust in him. In this trust relationship one cultivates the mind and spirit of the will of Christ. This is at times spoken of as the "mystical union" with Christ. Baptists do not mean this in a sense in which the human being is absorbed; rather, it is a union in which Christ lives through us in the present.[21] William Brackney has spoken of the Baptist emphasis on voluntarism, which he suggests "relates to that which proceeds from the will or from one's own choice or consent. To put it another way, that which is voluntary is uncoerced, resulting from independent action or decision of the will."[22] Voluntarism necessitates a personal Christian experience. The implications, of course, are key for understanding the voluntary nature of church membership.

Baptists have often talked about a process of salvation, but it seems to me we have done so in a different way from others. We speak of the fact that we were saved (Eph 2:8–9; 1 Tim 1:15). In this sense we emphasize the completed fact, focusing on the accomplished work of Christ. But we also speak of the fact that we are being saved—we are becoming what we are as we experience Christ in each moment of our lives (1 Cor 1:18; 15:2; Phil 2:12; Heb 2:3; 1 Pet 2:2). Further, we acknowledge that our salvation is not complete—we will be saved; the process will be completed (Rom 13:11; 1 Thess 5:9; 2 Tim 2:10; Heb 9:28).

What Baptists have not emphasized, and which I think is relevant to our dialogue, is a process of becoming a Christian that begins with infant baptism in some traditions. Although I do not think Baptists would want to say that there is not a process of becoming a Christian, historically we have focused almost exclusively on the choice or decision to follow Christ (respond to his call on our lives). Other traditions, I believe, do better at emphasizing the role of the church as a custodian of the faith. In those traditions that relationship is sealed at infant baptism and nurtured so that one affirms this relationship in later years. From my perspective of an outsider, the process of affirmation is one that in the best-case scenario is natural, normal, and maybe not visibly perceptible. In the worst-case scenarios, the "church" may have many on its roll who are not true disciples of Christ.

In at least two ways Baptists have affirmed institutionally a "process of salvation," while at the same time denying it. For example, we have had a strong tradition of Sunday school emphasis for children and adults alike. In practice we have used Sunday school as a means of nurturing a process of salvation so that our children will naturally want to choose to confess faith in Christ. While their wills are pliable, we have sought to be instruments of God in shaping them. In many cases initiation comes not so much as a profound moral crisis, but as a natural affirmation of trust in God's love and desire to be baptized into the church. Many of us who grew up in Baptist homes were enrolled in the Cradle Roll class of Sunday School the week we came home from the hospital. We were regular attenders of Sunday school and other church activities, the result of which for many of us was several hours per week of nurturing in the church. From the days of our birth we heard of God's love and concern for us. Our "initiation" was over a period of years, though most of us still look back to a "moment" of salvation.

Also, there has been a growing trend among Baptist churches to have infant dedication services. Although practices differ among our churches, there seem to be several common themes, including a focus on the commitment of the parents and church to provide a nurturing environment whereby the child will grow one day to make a personal affirmation of faith in Christ.

The Baptist emphasis on the nurturing role of the church has always been juxtaposed with an emphasis on the personal choice or decision. We have done so in part because we believe this is faithful to the biblical emphasis. Baptists have proposed that "the dynamics of a satisfactory religious experience are not centered in the church but, instead, *are centered in human life.* Each person is endowed with capacities which make him competent to meet all the demands with which genuine religion confronts him."[23] The church is certainly crucial in nurturing and encouraging a person's response to God's grace, but Baptists insist that it does not follow that one equates the church and the process of revelation. The Baptist emphasis has sought to retain the individualistic dimension of faith. Unfortunately, in practice this individualistic approach at times has encouraged decisions made in isolation from the community. But in the best sense we have sought to hold a balance between personal decision made in the context of a nurturing community and voluntary involvement in an intentional community of faith.

The modern Baptist tendency to emphasize the dramatic nature of this decision is seen in our focus on a specific moment of salvation such as "walking down an aisle" or "saying a sinner's prayer." The result is that we have failed to make clear that we certainly allow that for some the decision can be quite gradual over an extended period of time, and even quite natural. In our broader heritage we have recognized that for some the decision to respond to the call of Christ is very public, quite sudden, and emotionally charged, while for others the decision is private, gradual, and with little visible emotion. At times certain Baptists have leaned to one extreme or another, but the fact is that we have not endorsed a single pattern of religious experience.

But I hasten to add that almost all Baptists have emphasized the fact that each person must make his or her own personal decision about Christ. The church can nurture, but the individual must decide. You can see how this relates to the earlier discussion on the church. In Baptist life, church membership is for those who have come to the point of spiritual maturity where a relationship with Christ can be affirmed and a decision is made to covenant with a body of believers.

Certainly modern Baptists have been very much affected by the revivalism tradition in this country.[24] Influenced by this movement, Baptists have tended to institutionalize the process of conversion. What emerged historically in a context of spontaneity was soon institutionalized in protracted meetings, then fall and summer revivals, and then responding to a tract with a "sinner's prayer." Thus in our tradition this has served to "shorten" the process of conversion into an immediate event expressed in such phrases as "when I took the preacher's hand" or "when I walked the aisle." At times it may even appear that we have focused less on a process of experience and more on a transaction.

BELIEVER'S BAPTISM

A third piece of the puzzle in thinking about initiation in the Baptist way of life is baptism. Baptists have traditionally preached believer's baptism, seeing it as a New Testament practice (Matt 28:19; Acts 8:35–38; Col 2:12). It is an integral dimension of the concept of regenerate church membership. Thus, typically, Baptists see a person hearing the story of God's grace, responding to that call by faith, making a public confession of that faith, requesting church membership, being baptized in obedience to the command of Christ, and being welcomed into the fellowship of the church.

In addition, for Baptists, baptism must always be examined in the context of a believer's confession. A classic statement for us is Romans 10:9–10. Paul begins by saying confession is a condition of salvation: "If you confess…you will be saved." He ends, though, by saying confession is an expression of salvation: "With the lips confession is made unto salvation." A Baptist understanding is that Paul's point is not that saying so makes it so, but salvation is already so and may be experienced insofar as it is confessed.

The basic meaning of the word *confession* is "to agree with." It is used to denote agreement between two parties. In legal documents it means to give consent to something. It means to acknowledge or declare publicly. In the context of salvation, public confession has three functions in Baptist life. First, public confession is an outward confirmation of an inward experience. Baptists do not believe that is it appropriate to seek to make salvation entirely inward. Confession allows one's experience of salvation to escape from the limitations of personal impressions. To confess is to expose one's spiritual condition to the light of the family of faith. In a sense, it keeps our religion honest. To say nothing is to sidestep responsibility, while to bear witness is to speak of a "binding word" that cannot be retrieved. Second, public confession is also a community commitment in the Baptist experience. To confess is to declare the same testimony as others by affirming a common faith. Third, confession is also proclamation. Paul said we confess not ourselves, but Jesus Christ who lives within us (2 Cor 4:5). Our confession is a word of witness to the world.

For our discussion, I would like to suggest that in the Baptist way of life, baptism is the initiatory form of confession. Baptism symbolizes the spiritual union of a believer with Christ (Rom 6:3–8). It further functions as a public transfer of loyalty, which takes place in a community of like-minded believers concretized in a local congregation (1 Cor 12:13). In Baptist life baptism is oriented toward participation in the community. As a symbol of the new birth, it marks one's initiation into the shared life of that community whose life is shaped by the life, death, and resurrection of Jesus, which are given visual expression in baptism by immersion. Baptism thus is a powerful event for the baptized as a public confession of a new allegiance and a new family. It is also a powerful event for the baptizing community as members of the church are reminded of their own public confessions and assume the responsibility for edification and support of the one being baptized or welcomed into the community of faith. Though Baptists on the one hand have perceived the confession of faith in Christ to be an intensely personal event, it is not a private event. In speaking of the Baptist emphasis on covenant, Charles Deweese argues that "baptism is, in effect, a covenant with God and the church." Thus, traditionally, many Baptist churches actually had baptismal covenants.[25]

ISSUES RELEVANT TO ECUMENICAL DISCUSSION

As I seek to make a few observations related to ecumenical discussion I am even more aware of my limitations both in trying to speak for Baptists and in my limited formal involvement in prior discussions.

I think, of course, that if we Baptists are as scriptural as we like to claim, we must affirm a principle of the unity of the church. We do not understand this to mean institutional unity, but it certainly should involve for us recognition of the many expressions of the one body. Further, we must be engaged (and I feel this is a privilege) in ecumenical discussions.

Several issues are difficult for Baptists. Of course, the one that first comes to mind is the acceptance of other baptisms. Baptists traditionally have had difficulty in accepting the baptism of others due to our emphasis on the mode of baptism (immersion), on the candidates (those old enough to make public confession of faith in Jesus Christ as Savior), and the concept of voluntary membership in the church.[26]

From my perspective, an area of needed dialogue between Baptists and others is issues related to confession of faith as requisite to membership in the church. Mark Heim has pointed out, rightly I believe, that in fact many churches move in the direction of Baptists with various types of confirmation rites and catechumen classes that are required before one can participate in the Eucharist.

And in practice some Baptist churches seem to be backing off from requiring rebaptism for acceptance into church membership. My observation is that several factors are at work. Negatively, some are revising their policies based on pragmatic concerns for church growth, without serious theological reflection. Another factor is the reality that a growing number of families representing two church traditions are involved in Baptist life (e.g., husband = Baptist; wife = Presbyterian). At times in those situations Baptists have found that a family member may not want to be rebaptized and yet functionally that person is involved in the local church as a "member" in just about every other way, including participation in the Eucharist.

Some Baptist churches are beginning to address the issue that a rebaptism that follows many years after a personal confession of faith is in and of itself a variance from the Baptist vision. I think this will be a major topic of discussion for us in the days ahead. I really do not have a prediction as to where this will lead. Of course, knowing our Baptist tradition and structure, we will probably come out in many places.

NOTES

1. Norman H. Maring and Winthrop S. Hudson, *A Baptist Manual of Polity and Practice,* rev. ed. (Valley Forge, PA: Judson Press, 1991), 17.

2. Robert Theodore Handy, "The Philadelphia Tradition," in *Baptist Concepts of the Church,* ed. Winthrop Still Hudson (Philadelphia: Judson Press, 1959), 36. See also Stanley J. Grenz, *Theology for the Community of God* (Nashville: Broadman & Holman, 1994), 610–12, for a discussion of the Baptist understanding that the "true church is essentially people standing in voluntary covenant with God."

3. Stewart A. Newman, *A Free Church Perspective: A Study in Ecclesiology* (Wake Forest, NC: Stevens Book Press, 1986), 3.

4. John Smyth, *The Works of John Smyth,* ed. W. T. Whitley (Cambridge: Cambridge University Press, 1915), 403.

5. John Smyth, *Short Confession of Faith in XX Articles* (1609), art. 12.

6. *New Hampshire Confession* (1833), art. 13.

7. *The Baptist Faith and Message* (1963), art. 6.

8. Miroslav Volf, *After Our Likeness: The Church as the Image of the Trinity* (Grand Rapids, MI: William B. Eerdmans, 1998), 36.

9. Some, such as those in the Landmark tradition, do not recognize the universal church. However, they do not represent mainline Baptist thought. For more on the Landmark influence on Baptist thinking about salvation, see Bill J. Leonard, "Southern Baptists and Conversion: An Evangelical Sacramentalism," in *Ties That Bind,* ed. Gary A. Furr and Curtis W. Freeman (Macon, GA: Smyth & Helwys, 1994), 9–22.

10. *The Baptist Faith and Message* (1963), art. 6.

11. The role of baptism in this intentional faith commitment will be examined later.

12. Grenz, *Theology for the Community of God,* 710.

13. Two observations need to be made. First, there are some Baptist churches that practice a more open membership and do not require baptism, but this does not seem to me to be either the historical Baptist approach or the norm. Second, there is a growing

trend among Baptists to baptize younger and younger children. For example, Southern Baptists baptized 3,873 preschoolers (ages five and under) in 1996. I suspect that one reason for the latter is in part due to a lack of a Baptist theology of children.

14. William R. Estep Jr., "Respect for Nonconformity Permeates the Baptist Conscience," in *Defining Baptist Convictions: Guidelines for the Twenty-first Century,* ed. Charles W. Deweese (Franklin, TN: Providence House, 1996), 80.

15. Baptists often refer to this as "the age of accountability." There is no agreement as to the exact age.

16. Of course a major issue for contemporary Baptists is maintaining this ideal when besieged by a trend to uncommitted church membership.

17. Charles W. Deweese, *Baptist Church Covenants* (Nashville: Broadman Press, 1990), vi.

18. See Warren McWilliams, "The Church Seeks to Be Regenerate," in *Defining Baptist Convictions,* ed. Deweese, 124ff. He observes that covenants in Baptist life have been used at the formation of new churches, admission of new members, covenant renewal meetings, and in cases of church discipline.

19. Baptists have agreed that the elect receive God's grace, but they have disagreed as to how people are chosen to receive grace: that is, the doctrine of election. One camp of Baptists has affirmed that Christ died for the sins of the world and that theoretically at least, any person can turn from sin and be saved. Another camp has believed that Christ died only for the elect and not for all people. The elect are those who were chosen by God, by name, before creation.

20. *The Baptist Faith and Message* (1963), art. 4.

21. Clearly, a more extensive discussion of salvation would need to address such issues as conviction and repentance. I have deliberately limited my discussion to those dimensions of the salvation experience that seem to be relevant to the initiation discussion.

22. William H. Brackney, "Voluntarism Is the Flagship of the Baptist Tradition," in *Defining Baptist Convictions,* ed. Deweese, 86.

23. Newman, *A Free Church Perspective,* 46.

24. For extended discussion on his influence see Leonard, "Southern Baptists and Conversion," in *Ties That Bind,* ed. Furr and Freeman, 16–17. In this essay Leonard discusses various traditions that have had an impact on the practice and understanding of conversion in Baptist life. Those include (1) the Regular Baptist Calvinist tradition, (2) the Separate Baptist tradition with its focus on a dramatic, often emotional, encounter with Christ, (3) the Landmark tradition of Baptist churches as the only true churches of Christ, (4) the Revivalist tradition, (5) the Sunday school tradition, which has emphasized children making faith their own, but as a willing confirmation of simple trust in God's love, and (6) the Fundamentalist tradition, which has tended to add intellectual assent to a list of propositions to faith.

25. Charles W. Deweese, "Believer's Baptism is Covenant," in *Defining Baptist Convictions,* ed. Deweese, 105.

26. For an excellent discussion of some of these issues as well as a proposed solution, see S. Mark Heim, "Baptismal Recognition and the Baptist Churches," in *Baptism and the Unity of the Church,* ed. Michael Root and Risto Saarinen (Grand Rapids, MI: William B. Eerdmans, 1998). Heim suggests that a "fuller model of Christian initiation" might involve baptism, personal confession, and participation in the Eucharist.

INITIATION INTO CHRIST IN THE WESTERN CATHOLIC TRADITION

Jeffrey Gros, FSC

In this pairing of Roman Catholic and Southern Baptist, we were asked to address our agreements, disagreements, and needs for clarification on the appropriate mode of initiation, with special reference to Baptism. In Catholic ecclesial self-understanding, four principles need to be taken into account in articulating the present position of the church on initiation into Christ:

- Catholicism affirms that the church of Christ *subsists* in the Catholic Church, and that it is in "real, if imperfect, communion" with other Christian churches.

- The Catholic Church is a communion of churches with a variety of evangelistic and liturgical traditions, of which the largest is the Latin West with a history of Rome-centered evangelization and liturgical centralization. This essay will only treat Western practice in Christian initiation.

- For the Catholic Church, initiation into Christ is essentially ecclesial and ecumenical: "To believe in Christ means to desire unity; to desire unity means to desire the Church; to desire the Church means to desire the communion of grace which corresponds to the Father's plan from all eternity. Such is the meaning of Christ's prayer: *Ut unum sint.*"[1] Therefore, for both Catholics and for those who would understand Catholicism, the ecumenical principles of the Catholic Church, the results of dialogues in which it has been engaged, and its hermeneutical horizon of the goal of full communion among Christians, must be taken into account. There is no biblical Christology or soteriology, in the Catholic view, without an ecclesiology.

- The Catholic Church is in the early stages of catechetical, ecclesiastical, liturgical, and evangelical renewal initiated by the Second Vatican Council (1962–65). Therefore the levels of reception of various reforms, the appropriate diversity developed from the principles of subsidiarity and inculturation, and the renewed focus on the priesthood of all believers, create a diversity of church practice in initiating the individual into Christ that can only be hinted at here.

In this essay we will look at Catholic understandings of evangelization and initiation, the catechetical and liturgical renewal of initiation, and the ecumenical context of understanding Catholic identity and initiation thereunto.

EVANGELIZATION

To understand Catholic approaches to evangelization, we will need to understand the traditional style of initiation and the theology of infant baptism, the renewed approach to evangelization, and the focus on adult Christianity with the rites that accompany this initiation.

The experience of the Catholic Church in the United States is that the vast majority of its members have been initiated through the family, first by infant baptism, then through nurture in a Christian family, and later in the setting of Catholic parishes and schools. Full initiation, as it is understood today, includes water baptism, confirmation, and first communion.

This initiation has varied greatly through the centuries according to circumstances. In the first centuries of the Church, Christian initiation saw considerable development. A long period of *catechumenate* included a series of preparatory rites,

which were liturgical landmarks along the path of catechume-
nal preparation and culminated in the celebration of the sacraments of Christian initiation. (No. 1230)[2]

Where infant Baptism has become the form in which this
sacrament is usually celebrated, it has become a single act
encapsulating the preparatory stages of Christian initiation
in a very abridged way. By its very nature infant Baptism
requires a *post-baptismal catechumenate*. (No. 1231)

Born with a fallen human nature and tainted by original sin,
children also have need of the new birth in Baptism to be
freed from the power of darkness and brought into the
realm of the freedom of the children of God, to which all ...
are called.[3] The sheer gratuitousness of the grace of salvation
is particularly manifest in infant Baptism. The Church and
the parents would deny a child the priceless grace of becoming a child of God were they not to confer Baptism shortly
after birth.[4] (No. 1250)

Baptism is the sacrament of faith.[5] But faith needs the community of believers. It is only within the faith of the Church
that each of the faithful can believe. The faith required for
Baptism is not a perfect and mature faith, but a beginning
that is called to develop. (No. 1253)

For all the baptized, children or adults, faith must grow *after*
Baptism. (No. 1254)

In the reform of the Catholic Church in the years since the
Vatican Council, several factors have influenced Christian initiation. In this section, we will focus on the renewal of evangelization, the restored *Rite of Christian Initiation of Adults* (RCIA), and
the sacramental understanding of the church that underlies them.

As Catholics understand the gospel, evangelization includes
not only *kerygma* but also *didache* and *diaconia*. There is no conversion to Christ without conversion to the church as the sacrament of his presence on earth and to its mission that has a
social-ethical, dialogical, and ecumenical content.[6] Since 1975,
there has been much talk about the *new evangelization,* which

includes not only proclamation but also inculturation, ecumenical collaboration, and new approaches to the "old" Catholic cultures of Europe and Latin America.[7]

Evangelization, catechesis, and initiation for Catholicism are always communitarian, which is to say sacramental. One of the central elements of the renewal of evangelization and initiation since the council has been the reform of all of Catholic worship, and especially the *Rite of Christian Initiation of Adults* as central to baptismal worship.[8] There is some argument continuing as to whether we now see adult baptism as *normative*. However, the rite and the initiation process do recognize that historically and theologically adult initiation preceded infant baptism, which derives from it.[9]

For the unbaptized adult, initiation takes place through a series of pedagogical and ritual stages culminating in the profession of faith, water baptism, confirmation, and first communion, all normally within the celebration of the vigil of Easter.

If the truth be known, the majority of "new Catholics" are either uncatechized baptized Catholics or other Christians who are either baptized and uncatechized or active believers. In the latter case, the rites are very explicit that "anything that would equate candidates [for full communion in the Roman Catholic Church] with those who are catechumens is to be absolutely avoided."[10] The official Catholic text goes on to say that no burden greater than necessary is to be laid on the candidate for full communion, and that care should be taken in all of the rituals to honor the Christian character of the baptized.

Much work needs to be done in clarifying this practice in the Catholic community, since the new rites of initiation have become quite extensive and an important dimension of evangelical and liturgical renewal.[11] However, even with proper account being taken of the churches from which people come to full communion with the Catholic Church, formation is important for initiation to the ecclesial self-understanding of Catholics, their ecumenical commitments, and the level of relationship with the church of the candidates' origin.

The church as a community initiates, by a series of postbaptismal reflections, those who have been converted to Christ by spiritual nurture, breaking open the word of God, incorporating into the ritual-communal life of the community, providing opportunities for Christian service and reflection, full sacramental integration into the community, and finally a period of reflection on what the Holy Spirit has done through the process.

The vision of this process is to initiate one into a regular sacramental life whereby one is nourished on a regular basis by the word of God and its preaching and by the communal sacramental life of the church centered on the Lord's Supper. Initiation is neither a liturgical rite nor the decision of an individual, but it is a process by which the Spirit nourishes a grace-inspired response to Christ in the community culminating in the participation in Christ's death and resurrection and continued through living as the new creation in the church.

CATECHETICAL AND LITURGICAL RENEWAL

As a church that focuses on the centrality of the weekly celebration of word and sacrament in the community, initiation is directed toward full incorporation into the life of Christ. It is focused on the spiritual, liturgical, and ethical as well as on the cognitive, on the life of the community as well as on the conversion of the individual.

Liturgical space as well as liturgical texts are renewed as the rites are reformed. Many churches have removed altar rails separating the people of God from the sanctuary, most have provided ambos for lay readers complementing the pulpit for gospel reading and proclamation. Some have introduced immersion baptistries or prominent fonts with "living" water, and most have moved them into the church proper either at the entrance or near the sanctuary. In all of this, the theology of initiation, the ongoing call to conversion, and interiorizing the adoption that began in baptism are central.

Catechetical renewal emphasizes the biblical and ritual dimensions of Christian development, both prior to baptism for adults and for those incorporated into the church as infants. Catechetical directories are available.[12] Concern for the content of the faith produced a *Catechism of the Catholic Church,* which was finished in 1992.

ECUMENICAL PRINCIPLES UNDERLYING CHRISTIAN INITIATION

For the Catholic Church, our common baptism is a basis for the ecumenical commitment of all who are initiated into the church. In this section a brief overview will be given on the ecumenical principles inherent in Catholic baptismal faith and the results and responses of the Catholic Church in ecumenical dialogue, along with a note on the implications of religious liberty for Christian initiation.

The commitments of the Catholic Church articulated in the council have been further deepened and specified in subsequent official teaching, and codified in the 1993 *Directory for the Application of Principles and Norms on Ecumenism:*

> The ecumenical movement is a grace of God, given by the Father in answer to the prayer of Jesus and the supplication of the Church inspired by the Holy Spirit....Those who are baptized in the name of Christ are, by that very fact, called to commit themselves to the search for unity. Baptismal communion tends toward full ecclesial communion. To live our Baptism is to be caught up in Christ's mission of making all things one.[13]

The *Directory* goes on to explicate what the initiated Christian, and specifically the Roman Catholic, is challenged to ecumenically by becoming part of Christ and his mission in the church.

This direction is further supported by Pope John Paul II in his 1995 encyclical, which reiterates the conviction of the Vatican Council:

> All those justified by faith through Baptism are incorporated into Christ. They therefore have a right to be honored by the title of Christian, and are properly regarded as brothers and

sisters in the Lord by the sons and daughters of the Catholic Church.[14]

Specifically, the *Directory* emphasizes the importance of bringing this common baptismal faith to consciousness:

> By the sacrament of baptism a person is truly incorporated into Christ and into his Church and is reborn to a sharing of the divine life. Baptism, therefore, constitutes the sacramental bond of unity existing among all who through it are reborn....It is therefore of the utmost importance for all the disciples of Christ that...the various Churches and Ecclesial Communities arrive as closely as possible at an agreement about its significance and valid celebration....It is strongly recommended that the dialogue concerning both the significance and the valid celebration of baptism take place between Catholic authorities and those of other Churches and Ecclesial Communities at the diocesan or Episcopal Conference levels.[15]

The second implication of ecclesial initiation into the Catholic Church, relative to ecumenism, is initiation into its relationships with other churches and the results of dialogues with them. Pope John Paul II has made it clear that the results of the World Council and bilateral dialogues must become a "common heritage."[16]

The most wide-ranging approach to initiation with which Catholics should become familiar as they are initiated into their own church is *Baptism, Eucharist and Ministry* of the World Council and its evaluation by the Catholic Church and its ecumenical partners.[17] The official Catholic response to this text is the first reaction to an ecumenically produced document since the Council of Florence (1439), to my knowledge, and therefore carries the limitations and promises of such an innovative venture.[18]

The confessional state, or the Catholic "culture," can no longer be relied upon to provide the nurture and external support for that faith into which the Christian is to be initiated.[19] Religious liberty becomes a factor in Catholic sacramental practice. Catholics are more reluctant to baptize infants of families who have not demonstrated their ability to mediate the faith of the community to their child. We recognize that people, in good faith, will choose other positions and communities than those that the Catholic Church affirms to be true to the gospel. Catholics see themselves on the same footing in society as other persons.

For the Catholic Church and other churches, receiving new members is inviting them into Christ and into a process guided by the Holy Spirit, a church *semper reformanda,* always striving to be more faithful to Christ's mandate toward deepened faith, mission, and unity. As Pope John Paul II reminds us: "Two thousand years after Christ's coming, Christians unfortunately present themselves to the world without the full unity he desired and for which he prayed.…The grace of Baptism itself is the foundation on which to build that full unity to which the Spirit continually spurs us."[20]

NOTES

1. John Paul II, *Ut unum sint: On Commitment to Ecumenism (UUS),* par. 9, available on the Vatican website at http://www.vatican.va/holy_father/john_paul_ii/ encyclicals/documents/hf_jp-ii_enc_25051995_ut-unum-sint_en.html.

2. *The Catechism of the Catholic Church* (Washington, DC: United States Catholic Conference, 1994).

3. Council of Trent (1546): DS [Denzinger-Schönmetzer, *Enchiridion Symbolorum* (1965)] 1514; cf. Col 1:12-14.

4. CIC [Codex Iuris Canonici], can. 867; CCEO [Corpus Canonum Ecclesiarum Orientalium], cann. 681; 686, 1.

5. See Mark 16:16.

6. Paul VI, *Evangelization in the Modern World* (Washington, DC: United States Catholic Conference, 1975).

7. John Paul II, *Linking Evangelization and Ecumenism,* reprinted in *Origins* 16, no. 9 (August 1, 1996): 139–41.

8. International Commission on English in the Liturgy, *Rite of Christian Initiation for Adults* (Washington, DC: United States Catholic Conference, 1988). Cf. Aidan Kavanagh, *The Shape of Baptism: The Rite of Christian Initiation* (New York: Pueblo, 1978); Paul Bradshaw, "Christian Initiation," in *The New Dictionary of*

Sacramental Worship, ed. Peter Fink (Collegeville, MN: Liturgical Press, 1990), 601–12.

9. *Catechism,* nos. 1232–33.

10. "Reception of Baptized Christians into the Full Communion of the Catholic Church," in *Rite of Christian Initiation,* no. 477.

11. Ronald A. Oakham, *One at the Table: The Reception of Baptized Christians* (Chicago: Liturgical Training Publications, 1995).

12. *General Directory for Catechesis* (Washington, DC: United States Catholic Conference, 1998).

13. Pontifical Council for Promoting Christian Unity, *Directory for the Application of Principles and Norms on Ecumenism, 1993* (hereafter *Directory*), par. 22, available on the Vatican website at http://www.vatican.va/roman_curia/pontifical_councils/chrstuni/general-docs/rc_pc_chrstuni_doc_19930325_directory_en.html.

14. *UUS,* par. 13.

15. *Directory,* pars. 92–94.

16. *UUS,* pars. 24, 80.

17. In Lukas Vischer and Harding Meyer, eds., *Growth in Agreement: Reports and Agreed Statements of Ecumenical Conversations on a World Level* (New York: Paulist Press, 1984). *Baptism, Eucharist and Ministry: Report 1982–1990* (Geneva: World Council of Churches, 1990).

18. Max Thurian, ed., *Churches Respond to BEM: Official Responses to the "Baptism, Eucharist and Ministry" Text,* vol. 6 (Geneva: World Council of Churches, 1988), 1–40; *"Baptism, Eucharist and Ministry:* An Appraisal," Vatican Response to WCC Document, *Origins* 17, no. 23 (November 19, 1987).

19. Jeffrey Gros, "Christian Baptism: The Evangelical Imperative," in *Baptism and Church: A Believers' Church Vision,* ed. Merle D. Strege (Grand Rapids, MI: Sagamore Books, 1986), 173–92.

20. John Paul II, "Baptism is Foundation of Communion," *L'Osservatore Romano* (English edition), no. 16 (April 22, 1998): 11.

RESPONSE

Paul E. Robertson

I appreciate Jeff Gros's clear presentation on initiation in the Western Catholic tradition. His paper surfaces several areas of mutual understanding as well as points of disagreement, but with a respect for our differing traditions.

As I have reflected on my initial paper and his response, I feel that it might be appropriate to remind myself as well as non-Baptists of the difficulty of caricaturing Baptists. In an essay entitled "Baptist Identity" in *Baptists around the World,* Albert Warden observed that there are three deeply divided parties among Baptists. The first he identified as mainline ecumenical bodies such as the American Baptist Churches/USA. Those in this group represent a wide range on a theological spectrum, tend to permit open membership, are often deeply concerned for social issues, and are supportive of the ecumenical movement. The second group, which Warden called conservative evangelicals, contains the main bulk of Baptists in this country. This group operates in a more conservative theological framework, tends to be more conservative on social issues, and for the most part is not too involved in councils of churches either nationally or locally. The third group is identified by Warden as separatist fundamentalists who are militantly opposed to theological liberalism, hold conservative views on social issues, and condemn the ecumenical movement.

As for me, I find myself situated in a denomination that fits into the second category. In the 1960s my denomination seemed to be leaning toward the end of the spectrum where the first group is located (I am one Baptist who was and is sympathetic to that move), but in the 1970s and 1980s it has reversed that leaning and probably is even leaning toward the other end of the spectrum. In spite of these differences there is a commonality among us, although I readily recognize that at times the ties seem elusive to those looking at us from the outside.

With that brief note, let me respond more directly to Gros's paper in the three areas that are to guide our responses.

AREAS OF AGREEMENT

Certainly, with Catholics we affirm the importance of the church and right thinking about the nature of the church. It appears to me that both see the need for growth. Baptists especially are struggling to learn how to appreciate the universal perspective of the church and the diversity therein. Catholics, as I perceive them, are seeking to appreciate more the congregational emphasis.

I hope I am faithful to Baptists in saying that both we and Catholics desire "unity" in the church. Many Baptists I think resonate with the joy of ecumenical dialogue, but at the same time they resist any sense of the need of institutional unification. Unfortunately, from my perspective, many Baptists are still unwilling to dialogue with those of differing understandings of the Christian faith.

Baptists would appreciate the emphasis on the "reimaging of the whole church as missionary" and the focus on "evangelization" as suggested in this paper. Although there would be differing definitions of *evangelism* among Baptists, probably most would focus on the leading of one who has no personal relationship with Christ to be a person who has faith in Christ. Although I am not familiar with Gros's use of the term *evangelization,* among Baptists the ideas that Gros seeks to include in the term are consistent with a Baptist understanding of the mission of the church as including *kerygma, didache,* and *diaconia,* with the possible exception of the deemphasis on individual decision, which will be discussed later.

I found intriguing the fact that Catholics are dialoguing on the role of adult baptism as "normative." For the unbaptized adult there is an "intense time of ritual and spiritual preparation." Baptists have informally had this emphasis in our tradition. We have sought to encourage those persons who make professions of faith to be involved in various discipleship activities of the church, most notably Sunday school and discipleship training. However, we are struggling with the realization that we have done better at getting people in the door than we have in helping them grow in Christ. We are masters of programming, but we do not fare so well when it comes to fostering Christian growth. A sobering statistic for us is that in many established Baptist churches, only about 50 percent of the membership is involved, even nominally, in the ongoing life of the church. I must admit that I simply did not understand Gros's point of absolutely avoiding language that equates "candidates" "with those who are catechumens." Thus, we too are finding the need to develop "intense times of ritual and spiritual preparation." For us that seems to be participation in a new member training (some of it prebaptism and premembership) for those desiring to come into the membership of the local congregation. We agree that this training is more comprehensive than mere doctrinal instruction and is inclusive of spiritual transformation. Like Catholics, we believe this growth does not take place in isolation, but rather in community. It is a process that is nurtured by the Spirit.

I find it interesting that liturgical space is being renewed as rites are reformed. I think we find ourselves in agreement on the emphasis on the people of God doing the work of God.

I certainly appreciate the reform of worship that includes more Bible reading in worship. For years I have felt a strange paradox in that Baptists like to claim to be people of the Book, yet in a majority of our churches often only a few verses of scripture might even be read on a given Sunday. I only hope that Baptists will do better here as well.

I found much agreement with Gros in emphasizing salvation from our confessional perspectives. I think we both affirm that justification by faith alone is at the heart of the gospel. We both reject "easy believism" on the one hand and antinomianism on the other. (I find the recent statement by some Evangelicals and Catholics "The Gift of Salvation" to be a helpful contribution to understanding, cooperation, and further dialogue.) I suspect that some of our misunderstandings of each other are the different ways in which we use words. Most often in Baptist life we use *salvation* to point to the moment of salvation. At other times, however, we will refer to the ongoing process of *being saved* or even to the fact that in the future we *will be saved.*

AREAS OF DISAGREEMENT

Baptists would agree that initiation into Christ is "ecclesial and ecumenical." However, the use of the word *essentially* would cause concern for some. In the Baptist tradition there has always been an emphasis on the key role of the church in initiation, though at times it has been obscured. But that has been balanced, when it is done best, with an individual emphasis. Our way of thinking might be something like this, in terms of initiation: Christ ➤ individual or individual/church ➤ church.

Likewise, Baptists would disagree that "evangelization, catechesis, and initiation" are "always communitarian, which is to say sacramental." To be sure, Baptists have at times been guilty of a "conversionistic, individualistic reductionism." But ideally we have sought to balance individualism with a healthy understanding of the role of the church as a community of faith. I would agree that the community emphasis is needed, but must communitarian mean sacramental?

As we would expect, the role of baptism continues to be an area of disagreement. Gros sought to be helpful in suggesting that it is best for us to talk of "infant" and "adult" baptism. For Baptists, this seems to blur the issue. For us, the issue is not best stated as "infant" versus "adult." More appropriate for us might be "believer" versus "unbeliever." We hold that baptism is for those who have come to an "age of responsibility" and are thus able personally to confess faith in Christ. Thus, in our tradition, the issue is not one of rebaptism but of one's legitimate baptism, which is to be a believer's baptism by immersion. Many, if not most, Baptists historically have said that a baptism that is not a believer's baptism by immersion is not really a baptism at all. But, as I suggested in my paper, this is an area needing further serious reflection in Baptist life. Like Catholics, Baptists believe that nurturing the spiritual development of new members is a solemn responsibility of the church and we too have much to learn in this area.

AREAS OF NEEDED CLARIFICATION/DIALOGUE

The idea of "full initiation" as including "water baptism, confirmation, and first communion" was intriguing. Although we have far different understandings of the recipients of baptism, it seems that the Catholic perspective of water baptism and confirmation (in the sense of its role of incorporation into the adult Christian community) might be close to our profession of faith. In our case, we would also see profession of faith and water baptism as preceding participation in the Lord's Supper, although I suspect that most Baptists would not speak of a first participation in partaking of the Lord's Supper as prerequisite to full initiation. That is not to say that we do not emphasize participation in the Lord's Supper, but practical emphasis has been more on the conversionist experience. In terms of the relationship of participation in the Lord's Supper and church membership, I think most Baptists would speak of personal faith and baptism as prerequisites to church membership. In that sense, church membership becomes prerequisite to participation in the Lord's Supper. I don't know that Baptists even speak of participation in the Lord's Supper as prerequisite to full membership. This is not because Baptists take such participation lightly, but it is almost assumed that one in membership in the church will want to participate.

Seeing baptism as the basis for ecumenical commitment will be an ongoing struggle for Baptists, due to our emphasis on a believer's baptism. From a pastoral perspective, I understand the Catholic concern for rebaptism. Indeed I am concerned for the alarming number of rebaptisms even of Baptists. But I suspect that accepting the baptism of unbelievers (infants in particular) will be a problem for most Baptists. I rather think that most Baptists would focus ecumenical concern around a common faith in Jesus Christ as Savior.

The emphasis on the sacramental nature of the church seems to be an area of ongoing dialogue. Just what does it mean to say one has a sacramental view of the church and another does not have that emphasis? Is it possible to have a "high" view of the church and not have a sacramental view?

I think both the Baptist and the Catholic emphasis on initiation would begin with God's call in a person's life. I suspect that we need more dialogue on the role of human works in this process. As you know, Baptists themselves have dual birthmarks in Arminianism and Calvinism, which can lead to our sending out confusing signals. Can Baptists and Catholics learn from each other on the role of faith? Have Baptists failed to appreciate the communal dimensions of faith? Have Catholics failed to recognize the responsibility of the individual in the role of faith? Speaking for myself, and I think many Baptists, I look forward to the dialogue.

RESPONSE

Jeffrey Gros, FSC

Paul Robertson's paper is very helpful for clarifying the issues of common ground as well as delineating differences, not only with Roman Catholic ecclesiology and initiation practice, but also with Orthodox and Reformation churches as well. The issues raised in the sections on church, salvation, and baptism are clear and to the point, and the issues raised in the last section should be good bases for discussion.

AREAS OF RESONANCE

While the content is different, "the nature of the church has been of crucial importance" for both of our traditions, and I would suggest for all serious Christians, certainly for those in the ecumenical movement. A "high" ecclesiology, be it Baptist or Catholic, is a hallmark of the biblical Christian.

"The New Testament designates both the people of God in their totality and any local congregation of his people," as the church, the *ekklesia*. While Catholics may place more emphasis on the universality or catholicity of the church, both dimensions remain in a dynamic tension. It is important for Catholics to recognize that churches that are congregational in polity, like Baptist churches, can be catholic in their interdependence. Certainly local responsibility and accountability, subsidiarity, and inculturation are values that can enrich Catholic spirituality from the best of the Baptist tradition.

"The 'profession of faith' as the key initiatory rite" is central to the Catholic celebration of initiation, even for infants. The Nicene Creed is proclaimed on behalf of the infant, when the faith of the community supplies for the lack of conscious faith of the child.

For Catholics "regeneration, or the new birth, is a work of God's grace whereby believers become new creatures in Christ Jesus." In fact, this is so firm a conviction that we trust to baptize infants, who receive their gift of faith from God through the symbolic (sacramental) action of the community.

The three elements of faith, though developed differently in Catholicism, can be readily affirmed: (1) cognitive, (2) intellectual, and (3) trust or commitment.

While uncomfortable with the "born again" expectations in some evangelicalism, including Baptist, Catholics resonate with the fact that appropriation of baptismal faith "can be quite gradual over an extended period of time, and even quite natural." Like Baptists, for Catholics "baptism must always be examined in the context of a believer's confession." For Catholics baptism has also the aspects of (1) public confession, (2) community commitment, and (3) public proclamation, though, as will be noted below, with quite different emphases.

Catholics and Baptist agree, "In [the Christian] life baptism is oriented toward participation in the community." In fact, this is so firm a conviction that the guarantee of a Christian upbringing is enough to assure a congregation of the appropriateness of incorporating an infant into participating in the sacramental life of that community—and the Orthodox even more fully by chrismation and Eucharist.

POINTS OF DISSONANCE

Catholics do not believe that "the true church is found where persons voluntarily are standing in covenant relationship with God and one another." The covenant and the church is a gift from God in which both sinners and saints may be found, and is grounded on a continuity of faith, sacramental life, and visible structures of communion continuing from the apostles.

For Catholics, the church is not made up of individual believers; rather, individual believers belong to the people of God, universal in time and space, gifted with the justification of Christ, the content of the Christian faith, the sacramental life of the community, and the differentiated ordering of ministries among the whole people of God. "The universal church consists" not "of all those in relationship to Christ as Savior." Indeed many in the church on earth may have fallen away from this relationship, while many other Christians who do not pertain to the church may be holier and closer to Christ than its members.

The church is not, but is called to be, "an intentional faith community." For this reason, after the persecutions abated in the fourth century, many monastic movements sprang up and still continue among Catholic, Orthodox, and some Reformation churches to provide a context for more intentional Christian living within a more diverse and inclusive church.

While profession of faith is central to Catholic identity, we define *faith* as a gift from God, so that the ability to "make a conscious declaration of faith" is not essential for initiation into the church.

While the demands of "covenantal responsibility" are not as key as the honoring of the free initiative of God in the community in the process of initiation, we have much to learn from the discipline of the believers' churches, Baptists among them. Indeed, we can say "only true disciples of Christ are church members," but we would recognize even among the biblical disciples of both Testaments those whose salvation depended on the unmerited love for the sinner mediated through the nurture and rituals of the disciplined community. There is always a tension between discipline and inclusiveness.

While affirming the unmerited grace of God in Jesus Christ, Catholics would not say that "human works or effort have no role in salvation." From the Catholic perspective this would deny the doctrine of creation and free will as well as the ability of God's free grace to engender works of grace and even collaboration in the work of sanctification and the ethical life. The current *Joint Declaration on the Doctrine of Justification*[1] between Catholics and Lutherans demonstrates the common ground on faith and works that is emerging.

Each person is challenged to make "his or her own decision about Christ," but neither the integrity of the church nor the faith of the individual can be judged by the outward form that decision is to take. The church is founded on Christ, not on the decision. The identity of the Christian, for the Catholic, is founded on the gift of grace, the sacramental life of faith, the disciplined life, but not on some dramatic experiential moment.

The issues of public confession, inward experience, community commitment, and proclamation find different expression in Catholic than in Baptist understanding of initiation. While they are all present, God's initiative in the baptizing community and the community's public confession of the faith as a corporate body supply for the weakness of the individual or the lack of full consciousness of the infant. The sacraments themselves and the people of God in history are proclamations of the word of God in the world just as surely as the verbal proclamation of the cognitive content is of the Christian faith.

For the Catholic, "baptism is, in effect, a covenant" *from* God *in* the church. This does not exonerate Catholic communities from their responsibility for discerning the readiness of families to really transmit their faith to children put forward for baptism. Rather it places a heavier responsibility on all members of the community to witness to this covenant love and to mediate the faith celebrated in baptism, especially as an adult, appropriated faith.

POINTS OF NON-SONANCE

We need to explore what it means to have "insisted on the freedom and responsibility of the individual as being central in all matters of faith, beginning with human participation in revelation and becoming articulate in the voluntary aspects of association in church membership." If this means an affirmation of both grace and freedom, then Baptists may be closer to Catholics than either of us is to classical Lutherans and Calvinist Christians.

The definitions of church and faith need to be clarified before we rule one another out. It is not clear what the implications are of the statement: "The church does not determine faith, but nurtures it and later supports it." It is not clear how this corresponds to the centrality given to church in the first page of the essay.

More clarity is necessary to determine the relationship of "voluntarism" to a doctrine of grace. Catholics are usually characterized as Arminian but seem more focused on a grace-centered doctrine of church than I seem to find in the Baptist self-explanations.

The understanding of salvation here seems more dynamic than the "once saved, always saved" rhetoric sometimes heard about, and occasionally from, Baptists. How does this process language integrate with the "born again" character of much Baptist expectation for salvation?

Robertson has raised some very important issues for clarification and discussion. We have much to learn from each other, much mutual stereotyping to dispel, and many occasions for common witness and our common Christianity. The delicate issues of proselytism, the nurture of interchurch—Baptist and Catholic—families, and work in the public order on issues that divide us and divide our communities from others beg for our common witness. We find the rebaptism issue very troubling, as Baptists find the nominal Catholicism of many a counterwitness to a disciplined church. However, we find the positive witness of honest dialogue like this, common families in our congregations and parishes, and the common gospel in which our conscientious differences are rooted, a witness to the Holy Spirit that draws us together despite our differences.

NOTE

1. Lutheran World Federation and the Pontifical Council for Promoting Christian Unity, *Joint Declaration on the Doctrine of Justification* (Grand Rapids, MI: William B. Eerdmans, 2000).

DIALOGUE 6

THE TEACHING AUTHORITY OF THE CHURCH: A DIALOGUE BETWEEN THE STONE-CAMPBELL RESTORATION AND THE LUTHERAN TRADITION

THE PLACE OF AN AUTHORITATIVE TEACHING OFFICE IN THE CHRISTIAN CHURCH (DISCIPLES OF CHRIST)

Michael Kinnamon

This is a topic about which I have thought a good deal in the past.[1] I believe that these reflections adequately represent the Disciples tradition, and I hope that they will serve to provoke discussion. With that end in mind, I will present my argument/ analysis in four points.

 1. *Authority as a problem for Disciples.* Every church must face the responsibility of teaching the Christian faith in ways that are authoritative for its members. As I see it, a church teaches authoritatively when—through public statements, approved forms of worship, authorized acts of service and witness, or confessional formulas—it claims to interpret authoritatively the Christian faith and, thereby, provides guidance for agencies of the church and individual believers as they confront the challenges of the contemporary world. The Christian Church (Disciples of Christ), however, has not adequately developed instruments, procedures, or criteria[2] for authoritative teaching and, as a result, is likely to face a number of obvious difficulties in the coming years:

- In the absence of authoritative teaching through delegated structures, such teaching will be increasingly undertaken by individuals or groups that are not necessarily accountable to the total community. Decisions about what the church believes, how it worships, and the shape of its ministry are already made by editors of influential publications, national and regional staff, local clergy, independent organizations, and seminary professors.

- In the absence of authoritative teaching by the church, we are likely to sense ever greater "loss of identity" among Disciples. Two lines frequently heard in our congregations are "We don't know what we believe" and "Everybody here is free to believe what he or she wants." If the claims of personal (or local) perspective are not brought into dialogue with the authoritative claims of the whole community, then the church is bound to lack direction and cohesion.

- In the absence of authoritative teaching by the church, the prophetic role by local ministers is likely to be even further blunted. As long as pastors are accountable only to the congregation, and as long as congregations have unfettered power to dismiss pastors who do not please them, we can hardly expect ordained ministers to speak with prophetic authority, no matter how idolatrous the community may become.

- In the absence of means for authoritative teaching, Disciples will be unable to respond effectively to ecumenical initiatives. What good does it do, for example, for the Disciples Council on Christian Unity to write a favorable response to BEM's convergence on baptism if those congregations that remain "closed membership" (i.e., requiring for membership baptism by immersion) are not directly challenged to grow beyond that position?

As many of you know, Jim Jones had ministerial standing in the Disciples of Christ, standing that was never challenged or revoked. The tragedy of Jonestown underscores my conviction that the Disciples lack effective means for determining and communicating the limits within which diversity of belief and practice is acceptable, even enriching, but beyond which the fundamental identity of the community is subverted. Our general minister and

214

president at the time of Jonestown, Kenneth Teegarden, wrote in 1975 that, "[b]eyond the scriptural confession of faith in Jesus as the Christ and one's personal Lord and Savior, the Christian Church has no yardsticks of orthodoxy"[3]—and, thus, no means for authoritative shepherding of groups such as the People's Temple. The response of our General Assembly following Jonestown—to decide that a Disciples minister who is not employed in an approved ministry will not be continued in standing—simply shows that, when a church fails to assert legitimate teaching authority, it is often forced to respond legalistically to events that deserve pastoral, educational attention.

I begin by airing such dirty laundry because it helps point toward a kind of thesis for this paper. While Disciples (in my judgment) bring many gifts to ecumenical dialogue, on the question of authority we have much to learn from our ecumenical partners. Or perhaps I should say that we have much to learn from one another. While some of you may be concerned about freeing the individual from the tyranny of the church, many Disciples are now concerned about freeing the church from the tyranny of the individual.

2. Themes from Disciples history. I like the way that Bible scholars Mary and Dale Patrick put it: "When it comes to sniffing out heteronomy, Disciples are blue-ribbon bloodhounds in the ecumenical kennel."[4] Our movement began in the early nineteenth century as an "experiment in liberty" that eschewed creeds, ministerial order, and liturgical uniformity. Confessions and ecclesial hierarchy, we contended (with some historical justification), are responsible for divisions in the body of Christ. The church needs to get behind these "human inventions," to restore the essential pattern or system of New Testament Christianity as the basis of the church's unity and for the sake of its proclamation. Scripture, therefore, is the source and norm of all teaching. And within scripture is a simple, timeless gospel that is quite clear to the reason of believers—if only they are allowed to read the Bible unencumbered by clerical imposition or the accretions of theological tradition. The conscience and insight of each believer are worthy of respect. When decisions do need to be made for the common good, they should be made democratically within local communities of faith.

I want to add two qualifications to this rather standard description. First, the founders of the Disciples movement, especially Alexander Campbell, were looked to as authoritative leaders and interpreters of the faith by their followers. Subsequent generations witnessed an institutionalization of ecclesial authority (e.g., in mission societies, state secretaries, and the international convention); but, after the passing of the first generation of leaders, there was no obvious place to look for teaching authority among Disciples.

Second, the freedom proclaimed by these Disciples founders was the freedom to confess the gospel without constraint, but the point was confession of the Gospel. As Churches of Christ historian Leonard Allen puts it, theirs was a "freedom for holiness" rooted in the restoration of the church to those foundations laid for it in the New Testament alone. Restoration, in other words, was the principle that, in the mind of our nineteenth-century ancestors, made possible the balance between freedom and obedience to the gospel. The problem, as Allen points out, was a "persistent temptation to view Restoration as an accomplished fact"[5]—which directly undermined the commitment to freedom. Beyond that, Restorationism was based on Enlightenment assumptions that seemed increasingly suspect with the rise of modem historical consciousness. Thus, the Disciples stream of this movement jettisoned the idea of Restoration (with good reason, I believe), but with nothing to replace it. In such a situation, freedom easily turns into subjectivistic license.[6] Disciples leaders hoped to address this issue when the church restructured (a decade-long process that culminated in 1968). The restructuring was based on the idea of "free and voluntary relationships" among three "manifestations" of church—the local, the regional, and the general—each with its own "authority, rights and responsibilities."[7] It should be pointed out that the newly created General Assembly was charged "to manifest the wholeness and unity" of the church—which means, writes Jim Duke, that "the exercise of teaching authority is the Assembly's stock-in-trade." Having said that, however, Duke goes on to observe "that the Assembly's competency to deal with these matters is shrouded in so many clouds of unknowing that, for the sake of the well-being of the church, it should not dare attempt to 'teach the faith with authority' unless or until more adequate provisions for decision-making are available"![8] For one thing, the normal resolution process has been ill suited for the sort of study, testing, and consensus building that responsible theological judgments require. For another, it is unclear whether General Assembly actions truly represent the voice of the general community and whether they are intended to speak for or to the church as a whole. Some congregations take General Assembly statements very seriously; others (most?) generally ignore them completely.[9]

3. *Presuppositions for acceptable teaching authority among Disciples.* Many contemporary Disciples, in my experience, share both my longing for authoritative teaching and my appreciation for the best of our heritage—including our historic fear of the abuses of authority in the church. The intersection of these concerns leads to the question: What would authoritative teaching that is sensitive to the Disciples heritage look like? I will suggest six points:

- Authority, for Disciples, must always be dispersed and shared. The Spirit, we argue, is given to the whole church and, thus, the discernment of truth needs to take place through the interaction (as opposed to the individualistic judgments) of all its members. Authoritative teaching, in short, must be based on broadly participatory structures.

- Authoritative teaching will always seek to be faithful to the witness of scripture. "The norm for authority," writes William Baird in his excellent booklet on the issue, "is the personal revelation of God as witnessed by the apostles."[10] We now realize, in a way our founders did not, that scripture cannot and should not be divorced from the church's ongoing experience of God-in-Christ (i.e., tradition); but the scriptural witness has, for us, a strong priority. Authoritative teaching, in short, must be carefully, deliberately exegetical.

- Authoritative teaching will encourage diversity. If we accept (1) that the truth of the gospel is our goal and (2) that no group or tradition possesses it absolutely (good Disciples assumptions), then it follows that we need to become a covenanted community of "unlikeness" (Jew and Greek) precisely for the sake of truth. In practice this means that Disciples will leave a wide range of decisions to personal judgment, but judgment that is shaped by the church's authoritative proclamation of the gospel.

- Since Disciples strongly affirm that the church of Jesus Christ is one, authoritative teaching among us will pay close attention to the voice of the universal Christian community (as expressed, e.g., through instruments and statements of the ecumenical movement).

- Authoritative teaching in the Disciples can only be understood as a process of guidance and reconciliation that does not, except in extreme cases, imply sanction or exclusion. The real authority of a given teaching, Disciples will always insist, lies in its immediate authenticity, its capacity to convince and, in this way, bind the conscience. Coercion begins where genuine authority ends.

- Disciples will also insist that all decisions made by, or teachings offered by, the church are fallible, reformable, and ultimately subject to God's judgment.

It is important to note that the Disciples Commission on Theology, both in its "Word to the Church on Authority" (1983)[11] and a widely influential conference on Disciples identity and mission held at Christian Theological Seminary in 1987,[12] called for development of a process of authoritative teaching. Since that time, steps have been taken in this direction:

- Under the leadership of General Minister and President Richard Hamm, the church has been led to rethink the way decisions are made in General Assembly. What Dr. Hamm calls a "process of discernment" is now being used to authorize intensive study—in congregations, regions, general units, and seminaries—of carefully chosen critical issues (e.g., the authority of scripture, the church's response to racism, and the role of homosexuals in the ministry of the church). If and when the General Assembly takes action on these issues, such action should be grounded in broad theological reflection and will, it is hoped, be more readily received throughout the denomination. In July, the Disciples Administrative Committee gave preliminary approval for the development of a "Commission on Faith and Understanding," which would oversee this decidedly democratic approach to authoritative teaching.

- Disciples regional ministers, under the impact of the ecumenical convergence on ministry, have begun to speak of their role as at-least-somewhat-authoritative teachers of the faith.

The Commission on Theology has also suggested:

Regional ministers have the task, individually and collegially, to proclaim, teach and pass on the apostolic faith as it is witnessed to in Scripture and Tradition, thus assuring continuity of witness from generation to generation. They also bear the responsibility of helping the church to understand the changing situations it faces in its own life and in the world, and to interpret the Christian faith appropriately and intelligibly in ever-new situations.[13]

One obvious problem is that most current regional ministers have been selected for their ability to manage program, not their knowledge of the apostolic tradition. It will take a generation, I suspect, before this is substantially changed.

4. *An attempt at signaling broader implications.* The great ecumenical task in the United States, Reinhold Niebuhr once wrote, "is to find an institutional form broad enough, and a comprehension of the Christian faith rich enough, to give a solid basis for the instruments of grace which the historic church has rightly developed and, at the same time, to appreciate the validity of the 'sectarian' protest against the corruptions which periodically appear

in these means of grace."[14] I want, briefly, to flesh out this familiar church/sect dichotomy (though in order to avoid the negative connotations associated with the term *sect,* I will describe it as a tension between the *affirming* church and the *protesting* church).

Protesting churches have consistently rejected any tendency to exalt the fallible, relative structures and practices of our ecclesial earthen vessels. To paraphrase Niebuhr, they have been more conscious of the corruptions of church order, theological formulation, and liturgical structure than appreciative of them as means of grace. Protesting churches know that ministerial hierarchy can threaten the freedom of all Christians to interpret scripture and to be seen as a community of diverse and complementary gifts. This has usually led to a preference for lay ministry (or, at least, for the limiting of clerical authority) and congregational policy. They know that creedal affirmations can be absolutized, detracting from the immediacy of religious experience (the ongoing work of the Holy Spirit) and, in this way, sapping the vitality of faith. They know that liturgical forms can become empty rituals and that sacramental actions can be experienced in nearly magical terms. Thus, they prefer spontaneous prayer (or, at least, prayer prepared for each worship occasion) and forms of worship that are close to the model of scripture.

Where the protesting churches have a keen sense of corporate sinfulness, the affirming churches have a deep awareness of individual fallenness and of our consequent need for structures through which we encounter God's sustaining grace. Where protesting churches emphasize the necessity of a faithful response to God's saving acts, affirming churches stress the initiative of God, which may touch the lives of saints and sinners, the committed and the lukewarm. Where protesting churches fear that an overemphasis on order can destroy freedom in Christ, affirming churches fear that disorder can destroy our continuity in the one apostolic faith.

These Christians and their churches know that if ordained ministers are not allowed and enabled to exercise oversight and to teach the faith, the church may lack ethical and theological discipline. They know that without liturgical structure worship can become banal and sentimental, relying more on the performance of the leader than on the full biblical witness. They know that without theological affirmations that attempt to express the catholicity and continuity of Christian faith, churches can be tempted to take their bearings from secular culture. They know that if the congregation is made the locus of authority the unity of the church across time and space (of which the bishop is a prime symbol) may be minimized.

My fear is that, with regard to the question of authority, the Disciples have neither preserved the power and legitimacy of our original protest nor developed an appropriate teaching office in light of our altered understanding of church. This is a prime example of where the ecumenical movement could play an important role in a church's internal renewal.

NOTES

1. See, e.g., my article "Authority: Reflections on the Future of the Disciples Tradition," *Mid-Stream* 26 (1987): 332–38. Some of what follows is from that article.

2. The question of criteria is not really raised in this paper.

3. Kenneth Teegarden, *We Call Ourselves Disciples* (St. Louis: Christian Board of Publication, 1975), 51.

4. Dale Patrick and Mary Patrick, "Fundamental Issues of Authority in the Church Today," *Mid-Stream* 26 (1987): 324.

5. C. Leonard Allen, "Congregational Life and Discipline: An Historical Perspective," *Mid-Stream* 26 (1987): 381.

6. This is one reason why the ecumenical attempt to articulate the apostolic faith is so important for the Disciples.

7. "The Design for the Christian Church (Disciples of Christ)," *Yearbook and Directory of the Christian Church (Disciples of Christ) 2004* (Indianapolis: Office of General Minister and President, 2004), 612.

8. James O. Duke, unpublished paper presented to the Commission on Theology and Christian Unity of the Council on Christian Unity, Christian Church (Disciples of Christ), Indianapolis, 1982.

9. The "Design" for the restructured church includes a "Preamble," which in recent years has come to serve the Disciples in ways that confessions of faith are typically used: as an element in corporate worship, as an educational resource, at times of ordination. Still, no Disciple would see the Preamble as a test of fellowship, as a necessary and definitive summary of the Christian faith.

10. William Baird, *What Is Our Authority?* (St. Louis: Christian Board of Publication, 1983), 10.

11. The report is printed in ibid., 39–44.

12. The reports and background papers for this conference are printed in the July 1987 issue of *Mid-Stream.*

13. D. Newell Williams, "A Word to the Church on Ministry," in *Ministry among Disciples: Past, Present and Future* (St. Louis: Christian Board of Publication, 1985), 54.

14. Reinhold Niebuhr, "The Ecumenical Issue in the United States," in *Essays in Applied Christianity* (New York: Living Age Books, 1959), 269.

THE PLACE OF AN AUTHORITATIVE TEACHING OFFICE IN THE EVANGELICAL LUTHERAN CHURCH OF AMERICA

Philip Krey

My topic in this paper is the place of an authoritative teaching office in the Evangelical Lutheran Church in America. The understanding of the authoritative teaching office among the various traditions in the ELCA range from the congregationalism of some Midwestern manifestations of Norwegian Lutheranism in a predecessor church body to the more clerical and episcopal tradition of Eastern Lutheranism rooted in the Muhlenberg tradition.[1]

In this paper I will argue that the authoritative teaching office in the Evangelical Lutheran Church in America is in a state of ferment in a new church with many institutions and persons contributing to the teaching of the church. The North American democratic and diverse context, having created an institution governed by concerns for representation in gender, race, and lay status, represents a powerful force on the theological and reform proposals to the ELCA. Nevertheless, this diversity of sources for the teaching authority is governed by a constitutional principle of the universal church represented in the local church and the local church represented in the universal. The locus of the teaching authority in the ELCA is not discontinuous with the Lutheran confessional and historical traditions, although it is in tension ecumenically and in its relationships with other churches.[2]

THE CONFESSIONS

Theologically and confessionally, the authoritative norm in the ELCA is the gospel that is the "power of God for salvation to everyone who has faith,"[3] proclaimed in the scriptures as law and gospel and witnessed by the Lutheran Confessions, especially the unaltered *Augsburg Confession* of 1530.[4] All teaching in the ELCA is a witness to Jesus Christ and the gospel.

According to the *Augsburg Confession,* Christ is the sole ruler and authority in the church and all teaching is merely a witness to him and the gospel that is the power of God for salvation. The scriptures, both Old and New Testaments, are normative in teaching, and the Confessions, especially the unaltered *Augsburg Confession,* witness to their truth.[5]

The *Augsburg Confession* and the *Apology* clearly state that it is the responsibility of bishops to teach and judge doctrine but they do not limit this authority to the bishops.[6] The Confessions are also quick to limit the authority of bishops when they teach something contrary to the word of God, when they bind consciences, or make arbitrary rules in matters of worship.[7] The Lutheran movement, so concerned about teaching authority within a system that binds consciences and that confuses the human and the divine, recognized various places of authoritative teaching. Both in the Latin and the German, the Confessions regularly speak of the consensus of the teaching of these churches and use phrases like "To this our teachers reply," a term that alludes to their "pastors and preachers' teaching."[8] But this teaching also represents the faith of the signers of the confession: princes, mayors, and city council members.[9]

THE CONSTITUTION OF THE ELCA

Although the ELCA constitution assigns the responsibility of teaching to the presiding bishop and the bishops of the sixty-five synods, the highest authority is the biannual assembly made up of bishops, pastors, and laypersons "who legislate all matters which are necessary in pursuit of the purposes and functions of this church."[10] In the national church and in its sixty-five synods, 60 percent of councils, committees, boards, and other organizational units are made up of laypersons with assigned percentages for men and women and persons of color and/or persons whose primary language is one other than English. Moreover, as noted above, a commitment to the church's teaching on a local level and on a universal level to the historic communion of the saints and the fellowship of believers and congregations today provides a fruitful tension between the ELCA as a modern representative and bureaucratic institution and a communion with a passion for ecumenism and unity with other Christians. The article on the nature of the church in the *Constitution for Synods* expresses this dynamic:

> All power in the Church belongs to our Lord Jesus Christ, its head. All actions of this synod are to be carried out under his rule and authority. §5.02. The Church exists both as an inclusive fellowship and as local congregations gathered for worship and Christian service. Congregations find their fulfillment in the universal community of the Church, and the universal Church exists in and through congregations. This church, therefore, derives its character and powers both from the sanction and representation of its congregations and from its inherent nature as an expression of the broader fellowship of the faithful. In length, it acknowledges itself to be in the historic continuity of the communion of saints; in breadth, it expresses the fellowship of believers and congregations in our day.[11]

The normal process for any change in teaching or policy in the ELCA is for a study to be launched by a division or commission that includes teaching theologians, bishops, parish pastors, churchwide professionals, experts, and lay leaders chosen according to the criteria noted above. Close attention is given that biblical experts are present in the study, since the scriptures are the source and norm of all teaching.[12] The issue is researched and a draft written by the study commission, and, if it includes an ecumenical issue, in addition to ecumenical leaders of other communions, representatives are consulted of the National Council of Churches USA, the World Council, and the Lutheran World

Federation. Normally a draft of a policy is sent to the seminary faculties and a representative sample of congregations for study and review and it is studied in workshops or forums of the synods in assembly. For a critical development in the church's teaching or a change in the understanding or practice of ministry, for example, a motion must come from the Church Council to the Churchwide Assembly that is the highest legislative authority of the church (12.11). Before it reaches the Churchwide Assembly, however, normally the issue would have been studied, debated, and voted on in synods across the church.

As the nature of the church is described in the ELCA constitution for synods the locus of the teaching authority in the ELCA comes from both above and below; from length and breadth. Thus a clarification or reinterpretation of teaching, which in the Lutheran tradition is a witness to the truth of the gospel of Jesus Christ, can come to the Churchwide Assembly from a number of sources, for example:

- a dialogue sponsored by the Lutheran World Federation, as in the recent Joint Declaration on the Doctrine of Justification

- the World Council of Churches, as in the Lima Document

- the National Council of Churches

- a memorial from a synod

- a congregation protesting a teaching about doctrine or practice, as in the example of the ordination of gays and lesbians

- a division or commission assigned a particular study or a social statement

- a seminary or an individual theologian who raises a controversy or question about a practice or doctrine, as in the case of infant communion (a controversy issuing from a practice at the Lutheran Theological Seminary Gettysburg in the 1980s)

- the Conference of Bishops, as in the ruling of the bishops that all baptisms needed to employ the traditional formula of "Father, Son, and Holy Spirit" and not another formula like "Creator, Redeemer, and Sanctifier"

The locus of the teaching authority in the ELCA calls for intensive education of laypersons who must be persuaded by professional theologians, bishops, bureaucrats, journalists, and other leaders to change policy or the church's teaching. Although some would argue that this modern representative and institutional form allows for the manipulation by a few persons, the brief history of the ELCA in its ecumenical decisions does not bear this out. The decisive votes in the historic ecumenical decisions of the summer of 1997 in favor of proposed agreements on Justification with Roman Catholics and Full Communion with the Reformed Churches, and the narrow failure to muster a two-thirds majority for the "Concordat of Agreement with the Episcopal Church," stemmed as much from the American context, the nature of the predecessor church bodies, and the lack of consensus among bishops and teaching theologians as from the locus of teaching authority in the ELCA.[13] Church leaders pay a price when we do not heed the contextual factors in understanding teaching authority.[14]

ISSUES CONCERNING THE PLACE OF TEACHING AUTHORITY AND THE ECUMENICAL DIALOGUES

The example of thirty years of dialogue with the Roman Catholic Church sponsored by the ELCA and its predecessor bodies raises some significant issues about the locus of teaching authority in the ELCA. Both traditions have accepted a theological propositional form of dialogue and much has been agreed on by theologians in dialogue that "has helped to change attitudes and relations between Lutherans and Roman Catholics not only in the United States but elsewhere."[15] Concerning the topic of this paper, a decision before the formation of the ELCA in the dialogue "The Teaching Authority and the Infallibility of the Church" showed how Roman Catholics could be challenged to consider legitimate the concerns of those Christians who oppose the doctrine of papal infallibility. Lutherans, on the other hand, learned that the church is considered by them to be indefectible as long as this indefectibility is seen as the work of God and not the church itself.[16] In an earlier dialogue on papal primacy, among other things, Lutherans gained a greater appreciation for the role that a single episcopal figure can play in promoting unity. Nevertheless, the cultural, spiritual, and ministerial offices of both churches have grown so divergent that propositional agreements have little impact on the possibility of unity.

In addition, a drift toward congregationalism in teaching and a new kind of localism for the purposes of mission among many congregations in the United States have detracted from the stated constitutional goal of ecumenical dialogue and agreement. At the same time, that proposals like the agreement on Justification are brought to the Churchwide Assembly through the Church Council from the Lutheran World Federation indicates that the tension in teaching authorities between the local and the universal still exists for the good. In other words, a communion of churches is serving as a teaching authority for a national church.[17] The locus of teaching authority in the youthful ELCA is thus in a vigorous state of development.

In conclusion, the noisy debate over episcopacy in the ELCA, given the failure to pass the Concordat of Agreement, holds open the promise that following the Confessions, the office of bishop in the ELCA will continue to develop as a locus of teaching and a symbol of unity in the local church and the church universal. It remains to be seen whether the context of the late-modern world with all its diversity and plurality will lead the ELCA to move toward an ever-increasing dependence on the office of the presiding bishop and the synodical bishops as symbols of unity in teaching. Nevertheless, the locus of teaching authority vested in the office of bishop will not be understood in the ELCA in the sense of *ex cathedra*. The institutional structure of the ELCA redefines that teaching authority by facilitating a pluralistic theological conversation among a number of centers of authority. The authority of the bishop, therefore, is not in making pronouncements but in encouraging a conversation leading to a consensus.

NOTES

1. Henry Melchior Muhlenberg (1711–87) organized the disparate German Lutherans in the colonies into an organized structure for mission with a constitution and an educated clergy in a ministerium.

2. Not everyone would agree with this state of affairs in the ELCA. See the section "Teaching Authority" in *Lutheranism: The Theological Movement and Its Confessional Writings,* by Eric W. Gritsch and Robert W. Jenson (Philadelphia: Fortress Press, 1976); although the following represents a criticism of a predecessor church body, it would also apply to the present situation: "Lutheranism is under the perennial mandate to move from the heresy of institutionalism to the orthodoxy of ecumenism, for Christian truth and Christian unity are always in tension" (200).

3. Romans 1:16 and cited in art. XXVIII of the *Augsburg Confession,* "On the Power of Bishops."

4. "Even though modern historical study and the actual relativity of all language complicates the process of interpretation, The Word of God as it is communicated to us in the Scriptures remains the final judge of all teaching in the Church. The Reformers looked to tradition in the form of creeds and confessions as a secondary guide to the establishment of sound teaching…The creeds and confessions also supply hermeneutical guidance for our reading of the Scriptures today." Paul C. Empie, T. Austin Murphy, and Joseph Burgess, eds., *Teaching Authority and Infallibility in the Church: Lutherans and Catholics in Dialogue VI* (Minneapolis: Augsburg, 1980), 29.

5. *The Augsburg Confession (AC),* in the *Book of Concord: The Confessions of the Evangelical Lutheran Church,* trans. and ed. Theodore G. Tappert (Philadelphia: Fortress Press, 1959).

6. "This power of keys or of bishops is used and exercised only by teaching and preaching the Word of God and by administering the sacraments" (*AC* XXVIII, 6). "According to divine

right, therefore, it is the office of the bishop to preach the Gospel, forgive sins, judge doctrine and condemn doctrine that is contrary to the Gospel" (*AC* XXVIII, 21).

7. "On the other hand, if they teach, introduce, or institute anything contrary to the Gospel, we have God's command not to be obedient in such cases, for Christ says in Matt. 7:15, 'Beware of false prophets.' St. Paul also writes in Gal. 1:8, 'Even if we, or an angel from heaven, should preach to you a Gospel contrary to that which we preached to you, let him be accursed,' and in 2 Cor. 13: 8, 'We cannot do anything against the truth, but only for the truth'" (*AC* XXVIII, 24).

8. See, for example, *AC*, XXVIII, 18, 53. In the preface to the *AC* the teachers are identified: "Wherefore in dutiful obedience to Your Imperial Majesty, we offer and present a confession of our pastors' and preachers' teaching and of our own faith setting forth how and in what manner, on the basis of the Holy Scriptures, these things are preached, taught, communicated, and embraced in our lands, principalities, dominions, cities, and territories" (*AC* Preface, 25).

9. *AC* Conclusion, 7.

10. *The Evangelical Lutheran Church in America Constitutions, Bylaws, and Continuing Resolutions* as adopted by the Constituting Convention of the Evangelical Lutheran Church in America (April 30, 1987) with amendments to August 1997 (§12.11). "This church shall have a presiding bishop who, as its pastor, shall be a teacher of the faith of this church and shall provide leadership for the life and witness of this church" (§13.21). From the *ELCA Constitution for Synods,* "The bishop shall be a pastor who is an ordained minister of the Evangelical Lutheran Church in America. §8.12. As this synod's pastor, the bishop shall be an ordained minister of Word and Sacrament who shall: a. Preach, teach, and administer the sacraments in accord with the Confession of Faith of this church....Practice leadership in strengthening the unity of the Church and in so doing: 1) Exercise oversight of the preaching, teaching, and administration of the sacraments within this synod in accord with the Confession of Faith of this church; 2) Be responsible for administering the constitutionally established

processes for the resolution of controversies and for administering the constitutionally established processes for the resolution of controversies and for the discipline of ordained ministers, other rostered leaders, and congregations of this synod" (§8.11).

11. ELCA Constitution for Synods, §5.01 and §5.02, in the *Evangelical Lutheran Church in America Constitutions, Bylaws, and Continuing Resolutions* as adopted by the Constituting Convention of the Evangelical Lutheran Church in America (April 30, 1987) with amendments to August 1997.

12. During the subsequent review process, if the *Confessions* have not governed the theology of the study, sharp critiques rise from the theologians of the church.

13. An interesting locus of teaching authority was the role of the theological journals in the debate and the ability of some to use electronic media to communicate with assembly delegates at critical times.

14. See Michael Root, "Introduction: The Ecumenical Task before Us: Reception, Consensus, and Communion," in *Lutheran Ecumenism on the Way: Documentation from the Klingenthal Consultation 5–8 June, 1990,* no. 32 (Strasbourg, 1993), 9–12.

15. William G. Rusch, *Ecumenism: A Movement toward Church Unity* (Philadelphia: Fortress Press, 1985), 85.

16. Ibid., 84.

17. Another example of this was the LWF's determination of South African apartheid as a *status confessionis* and contrary to the teachings of the Lutheran churches.

RESPONSE

Michael Kinnamon

RESONANCE

I am grateful to my colleague, Philip Krey, for his fine paper, and in reading it I am struck by the obvious resonance between our two traditions. Such resonance readily divides into three areas.

First, both the Evangelical Lutheran Church in America (ELCA) and the Christian Church (Disciples of Christ), despite diverse histories, are now decisively shaped by the North American context. To be more specific, both churches (a) have developed broadly representative, democratic structures of governance; (b) are sensitive to the diversity of U.S. society, seeking to ensure, for example, that persons of different racial/ethnic backgrounds are fully included in decision making; and (c) tend toward congregationalism or, in Krey's words, toward a "new kind of localism" that reflects the emphasis on autonomy in U.S. church life.

Second, both churches claim the heritage of the Reformation (although Lutherans clearly do so more insistently). The Disciples, like the ELCA, (a) look to scripture as the source and norm of authoritative teaching; (b) regard Jesus Christ as the center of the biblical witness and, thus, as the "sole ruler and authority in the church" (Krey); and (c) are concerned that the church be always reforming since all human authority is fallible and subject to the living Word. It is interesting to note, in this regard, that the doctrine of justification by grace through faith, the central "hermeneutical key" for Lutherans, was also prominent in the writings of early Disciples. Alexander Campbell, for example, referred to it in the Christian System as "the test of a standing or falling church."[1]

Third, both the ELCA and the Disciples are committed participants in the modern ecumenical movement. Neither church can adequately discuss the question of authority without some reference to dialogues or covenants with other churches. Indeed, the results of such dialogues are, in some sense, authoritative for both communities.

DISSONANCE

Despite these important areas of resonance, the Disciples and the ELCA reflect what we might call different "ecclesial gestalts." A wonderfully formulated sentence from Reinhold Niebuhr helps make the point. There are, wrote Niebuhr, churches that "have been more conscious of the corruptions of church order, theological formulation, and liturgical structure than appreciative of them as means of grace." Such churches, among which I would count the Disciples, believe that ministerial hierarchy can threaten the freedom of all Christians to interpret scripture; and, thus, they do not have bishops (or any hierarchical teaching office).[2] Such churches believe that creedal affirmations can be absolutized, detracting from the immediacy of religious experience (the ongoing work of the Holy Spirit); and, thus, they put little weight on historic confessions of faith. Such churches believe that liturgical forms can become empty rituals; and, thus, they eschew official worship books and standardized prayers.

Readers will recognize in this what Ernst Troeltsch describes as the distinction between *church* and *sect*. It is certainly possible to overstate this distinction with regard to the ELCA and the Disciples of Christ. As my paper indicated, Disciples are striving to recover the churchly elements of our heritage, while Lutherans, as Krey's paper showed, are well aware of the dangers of overemphasizing church order. Still, where Disciples have a deeply rooted suspicion of structure beyond the congregation, Lutherans have a basic appreciation of the need for structures and practices through which we encounter God's sustaining grace. In this same vein, the ELCA has a greater appreciation than Disciples for global networks of communion (i.e., the Lutheran World Federation) and for "the historic continuity of the communion of saints" (ELCA constitution).

NON-SONANCE

The ecclesiological difference, noted in the previous section, can't really be called a "non-sonance" since both churches, thanks to their ecumenical commitments, recognize the need to learn from traditions unlike their own. Perhaps the closest we come to non-sonance is a function of history. Lutherans may feel strange to Disciples because of their conscious attachment to a European heritage. Those Disciples with a penchant for history may recall that the Campbells came from Scotland, but we are a decidedly American community. Of course, with each passing generation, so is the ELCA.

NOTES

1. Alexander Campbell, *The Christian System* (Cincinnati: Standard Publishing, 1901), 153.
2. Reinhold Niebuhr, *Essays in Applied Christianity* (New York: Living Age Books, 1968), 267.

RESPONSE

Philip Krey

RESONANCE

It is striking that both churches have a strong principle for church unity—the ELCA in its ecumenical vision and the Christian Church in its self-conception. Nonetheless, both churches exist in the United States of America where there are historic forces that have been church divisive.

Both traditions understand the scriptures as the source and norm of all teaching, and, within scripture, the gospel is proclaimed as the norming norm. Each tradition argues for the perspicuity of the scripture and the need for it to be accessible to everyone and not just the clergy or a learned few. Both traditions insist that authoritative teaching needs to be faithful to the witness of scripture and, to use Kinnamon's phrase, "must be carefully, deliberately exegetical." In fact, ELCA study documents and subsequent statements that are not carefully exegetical are strongly criticized by all parts of the ELCA. In each church, but more exaggerated perhaps in that of the Disciples, there is a suspicion of human traditions or, in Kinnamon's words, "accretions of theological tradition." Nevertheless, the late-modern criticism of reason and the Enlightenment has brought about a new appreciation in both churches for the tradition and the activity of the Holy Spirit in the church's history. Both churches are less confident that reason or, for example, the historical-critical method, can arrive at a definitive reading of the Bible that the medieval church, for example, could not.

The scripture serves as the source for the principle of continual reformation in both churches, and prophetic protest that is biblical retains a strong value. In both traditions there is a healthy suspicion of unquestioned hierarchy and ecclesial structures. The ELCA is, however, more affirming of ministerial hierarchy and structure.

The Evangelical Lutheran Church of America and the Christian Church both lack adequately developed instruments and procedures for authoritative teaching, but in the case of the ELCA this is largely due to its youth as a church, not because it also lacks the criteria as Kinnamon describes the situation of the Disciples.[1] Both churches are moving toward a democratic approach to authoritative teaching that at one and the same time tries to recognize that the universal church of Jesus Christ is one and that diversity and "unlikeness" are essential criteria to be in faithful relationship to this same Lord, Jesus of Nazareth, a Jew. No group or person in the church possesses truth absolutely. True teaching results in the relationships of the various parts of the body of Christ and the church and in relationship to the one Lord.

Both churches seem to have learned that true teaching is relational, participatory, and inclusive. They share the same American context that inspires an antiauthoritarian tendency—perhaps more innate to the Disciples but nonetheless evident among Lutherans who emigrated from Europe to escape authoritarian church structures. What Kinnamon quotes Mary and Dale Patrick as saying about Disciples could also be said of Lutherans: "When it comes to sniffing out heteronomy, Disciples are blue-ribbon bloodhounds in the ecumenical kennel." There is a healthy respect for the prophetic and a concern for the truth in both traditions that resists the establishment of a fixed teaching authority that is not checked by other centers of authority.[2] This represents a deep-seated institutional memory of the causes of the sixteenth-century Reformation and the development of American Restorationist movements over/against the remnants of these perceived causes in nineteenth-century American Protestantism. Consequently, both churches are vulnerable to those groups and individuals—including individual bishops, theologians, and editors of journals who are not necessarily accountable to the community—who will take issues to the church's public via publications, electronic and print, and other means to influence decisions. The ELCA's biannual assemblies and all the other assemblies including synodical, conference-wide, and conferences of the bishops are a check on the American context's pressures toward individualization, personalism, and "subjective license." Nonetheless, both churches do suffer the trend toward localization and regionalism in America that makes it possible for a bishop, congregation, or pastor to ignore the decisions of the church. It needs to be noted, however, that both churches by definition and goal, to use ELCA language, "derive their character and powers both from the sanction and representation of their congregations and from their inherent nature as an expression of the broader fellowship of the faithful."[3]

DISSONANCE

The fundamental source of dissonance occurs in the differences between the ELCA's relationship to the Lutheran Confessions and its catholic appreciation for the liturgical tradition in Christian worship.[4] In the ELCA the confessions that include the ecumenical creeds are normative for faith and authoritative teaching and thus the role of immediate individual experience and individual interpretation of the scripture is greatly lessened. From the Lutheran perspective, the Confessions, including the creeds, summarize the heart of the scriptures and are thus a faithful witness to the scripture unifying the teaching of the church. They were signed by a representative group of ecclesial and civic leaders in 1530 and portray what preachers and lay leaders corporately believed and taught. Thus they prevent the scriptures from being fragmented by personalized readings causing, in part, the innumerable divisions in American Protestantism.

The Confessions are also helpful in linking an American church, the ELCA, to its catholic roots, for example, in their commendation that the office of bishop serves as the locus of teaching authority in the church, albeit subject to the equally confessional critique of abusive authority noted above. (It is important to note the developing office of regional minister described in Kinnamon's paper.) Thus, the teaching authority of ecclesial leaders is not equal to authoritarianism. The Confessions function in the ELCA as a norm to which all teachings must eventually refer to gain the respect of the ELCA. They thus serve as consensus-building documents over the long haul, even though sharp differences in their interpretation arise in controversies.

The liturgies and common service books of the ELCA also serve as a source of unity. Although cultural and regional differences will affect the content of the parts, normally the shape of the liturgy is uniform. This being said, the rapid changes that have influenced Lutheran congregations via the Church Growth Movement have produced a wide variety of worship forms. Individual pastors and congregations irrespective of the catholic liturgical tradition design many ELCA liturgies. This development again calls attention to the importance of the American context for the ELCA.

NON-SONANCE

Perhaps the only issue that does not make sense in the Disciples' tradition from an ELCA perspective is that of "Restorationism" itself. Ironically, Kinnamon argues that it seems to have lost its meaning for the Disciples as well without principle to substitute for it. From a Lutheran perspective the church was no less fallible in its early stages than in its later history. It has always been both unfaithful and faithful in its corporate response to the gospel.

Nonetheless, if restorationism can be perceived as retrieval, the divisions of the early church to one point did not destroy full communion. The surprise of the late twentieth century is that full communion is being restored even on American soil.

NOTES

1. The implications of a confessional church in the American context will be discussed in the subsequent section on dissonance.

2. See n. 7 in my paper that cites the strong suspicion for authority in the *Augsburg Confession* and the need for other loci of teaching authority in the church when bishops go astray. For

example, the striking imbalance of white men versus women and persons of color in the ELCA Conference of Bishops makes it suspect as a final teaching authority in a church that has constitutionally defined itself with a representational principle.

3. I have adapted the ELCA language for grammar. "Congregations find their fulfillment in the universal community of the Church, and the universal Church exists in and through congregations."

4. These issues are identified in Michael Kinnamon's paper among the themes from which the Disciples could benefit in ecumenical dialogue.

DIALOGUE 7

THE AUTHORITY AND FUNCTION OF SCRIPTURE: A DIALOGUE AMONG ROMAN CATHOLIC, LUTHERAN, AND REFORMED TRADITIONS

THE AUTHORITY AND FUNCTION OF SCRIPTURE IN CATHOLIC TRADITION

Theresa F. Koernke, IHM

> In sacred Scripture, therefore, while the truth and holiness
> of God always remain intact, the marvelous "condescension"
> of eternal wisdom is clearly shown, "that we may learn the
> gentle kindness of God, which words cannot express, and
> how far He has gone in adapting His language with
> thoughtful concern for our weak human nature." *For the
> words of God, expressed in human language, have been made
> like human discourse, just as of old the Word of the eternal
> Father, when he took to Himself the weak flesh of humanity,
> became like other human beings.*[1]

It is generally accepted within Catholic circles that all theology is
ultimately an attempt on the part of human beings to make an
account of the relationship between themselves and God whom
they say has revealed God's Self to them. The experience of God's
Self-revelation, and the arrival at insight to which they could not
have come by their own effort, has led our Jewish ancestors to
write that "in the beginning God speaks, and what God speaks
obtains" (Gen 1–2). It is to this initiative of God that humanity
responds, marked by its limited human condition. This acknowledgment of the radically historical locus of divine Self-revelation
makes an account of the authority and function of sacred scripture a delicate matter, precisely because of the fiducial faith
claim: God acts first in creation and redemption; humanity
responds. In short, precisely as persons intimately participating in
history, we make an account of our fiducial faith that it is God

whom we have heard and that scriptural words are not an expression of our self-dilution.

The purpose of this paper is to describe the official understanding of the authority and function of scripture within the Catholic Church. Part 1 briefly elucidates the shifts in that understanding between pre– and post–Second Vatican Council periods, as they are manifest (1) in liturgical practice, and (2) in the theological project. *Shift* is used advisedly, for after closer study of the official documents, one notes a deeper appreciation of the factor of historicity in post–Vatican II thinking regarding the origin of the scriptures. Indeed, *Dei verbum* actually overcomes the two-source theory of revelation, not simply by asserting that the lived experience of the Word in history, that is, the tradition, is transparency for the Self-revelation of God, but also that "sacred tradition and sacred Scripture flow from the same divine wellspring and tend toward the same end" (*DV,* 9). Part 2 summarizes the 1993 publication of the Pontifical Biblical Commission, the *Interpretation of the Bible in the Church.* Part 3 suggests further issues surrounding the authority and function of scripture in ecumenical dialogue.

AUTHORITY AND FUNCTION OF SACRED SCRIPTURE IN LITURGICAL PRACTICE AND THEOLOGY: BEFORE AND AFTER THE SECOND VATICAN COUNCIL

The modern foundations of the document *Dei verbum*[2] of the Second Vatican Council are in the 1943 encyclical of Pope Pius XII, *Divino afflante spiritu,* and the revisions of the liturgy of Holy Week mandated by him. The bishops at Vatican II reaffirmed the divine origin/authority and the corresponding function of sacred scripture in church life, but did so with far more profound awareness of the assets and liabilities of historical criticism, as well as of other theories of interpretation. The deeper appropriation of the origin and meaning of scripture represented by *Dei verbum* is most dramatically obvious in liturgical practice and theological methodology.

LITURGICAL PRACTICE

It has always been true that the performance of any of the liturgies of the sacraments is concretization of the fiducial faith of the church: through the use of material things, verbal and gestural language, and in specific space arranged in a certain way, we have enacted, at every point in history, what we hold to be true about the relationship between God and the world revealed in Jesus the Christ by the working of the Holy Spirit. This foundational intuition about liturgical practice, joined with the awareness of human weakness, is the reason for the many liturgical reforms throughout history. At regular junctures, the church has asked: Is what we do, really, the best expression of the faith of the church according to our best lights at this point in ecclesial history? Indeed, the very recognition of the need for reform presumes the active presence of the Spirit of Christ, giving the church the competence for ongoing interpretation of its life in Christ.

Prior to Vatican II the *Order of the Mass* certainly consisted of lections from scripture, but each was read by the ordained minister in Latin. Indeed, literally every part of the Mass was contained in one liturgical book, the altar missal used by the ordained minister. This fact is itself an example of the operative theology of worship at that time: the ordained minister was thought to be able to "do it all" without the presence of anyone else.[3] Although the liturgical movement in the 1930s and 1940s had placed vernacular translations of both the weekday and Sunday readings in the hands of the faithful, the scope of biblical material was quite narrow. The Gospel of Matthew, with its stress on church order and Petrine authority, dominated that lectionary. This reflects the pre–Vatican II absorption of scholastic metaphysics in all of its many forms into the Catholic theological imagination. That is, this scholastic intellectual paradigm controlled the theology of ordained ministry and its relation to the universal priesthood of all believers and, in turn, revealed operative assumptions about

245

the authority and function of sacred scripture in ecclesial life. As witnessed by the episcopal practice of determining the topic for the weekly sermon, preaching more often than not consisted of moralizing and dogmatizing that did not necessarily reflect the content of the scripture assigned for that day. The force of this patterned worship behavior on the faithful led to their hesitancy to use the scriptures for personal study and prayer.

By contrast, post–Vatican II practices witness to the entire eucharistic liturgy (Mass) in vernacular languages, including new and more comprehensive biblical fare by way of a three-year cycle for Sundays, and a two-year cycle for weekdays. Further, the Sacramentary (presider's book) and Lectionary are now separate liturgical books, and lay lectors are commonplace. Today, therefore, Catholics not only are exposed to vast and varied biblical literature, but they also, by way of their liturgical responses, assert their faith that the living God is addressing them in the proclamation of the scriptures, and that the Christ, "always present in His Church,"[4] continues to interpret their lives to them in and through the proclamation of the gospel. To be sure, increased familiarity with the scriptures, by way of personal study and prayer, highlights the biblical imagery throughout all liturgical prayers and encourages a resurgence of homiletic studies and biblical preaching (*DV,* pars. 21–22).

It would be safe to say, therefore, that the code to deciphering the recognized authority and function of sacred scripture in the life of the church resides in its public worship, what we know as *theologia prima,* or "first theology." At the conclusion of the proclamation of the first and second lections, the reader says "Word of the Lord," to which the assembly responds "Thanks be to [You] God." And after the proclamation of the gospel, the reader says "Gospel of the Lord," to which the assembly responds "Praise to you, Lord Jesus Christ." This dialogical activity— between God and/or Christ through the ministry of the reader *and* the other members of the assembly—is transparency for the fiducial faith of the Church regarding the origin, that is, authority of sacred scripture, and therefore of its function in ecclesial life: God, source of all truth and holiness in creation and redemption, is always present to the people; God continues to reveal God's Self through the proclamation of the sacred scriptures; the eternal Word of God made flesh in the person of Jesus of Nazareth remains intimately bound to the people by the working of the Holy Spirit; the One Word of God continues to speak to people, and under the guidance of the Holy Spirit, the people have the ability to recognize the Word of God, and in the proclamation of the gospel, to recognize and respond to the Christ whom they know in every moment of their lives.[5] In short, the church does not respond "Thanks be to the Book," or "Praise be to you, O Book," but rather acknowledges the initiative of the living Word. These liturgical responses, always retained in liturgical books, have been the most explicit statement of the authority and function of the sacred scriptures in the deep consciousness of the Catholic Church, even though other liturgical practices and systematic theology based on scholastic metaphysics clouded this statement of faith until the reforms of Vatican II.

SACRED SCRIPTURE IN EDUCATION AND IN THE THEOLOGICAL PROJECT

If the usage of scripture in *theologia prima,* public worship, discloses Catholic convictions regarding its authority, such is true as well for *theologia secunda,* that is, other forms of theological accounts in all their manifestations. Prior to Vatican II, the scriptures were used, in large measure, to buttress dogmatic and moral teaching. Further, the biblical text was not read as a primary source of religious education, and university and seminary textbooks supplemented study of the Bible by conservative commentaries intended to guide the vision of the biblical text and to reinforce the prerogatives of the pope and bishops in the interpretation of the scriptures. Again, by contrast and even in the face of a regressively conservative movement at this time, most Catholic theological methodology is marked by beginning with biblical foundations, both by way of historical-critical study of the scriptures as well as by recognizing the transparency of the scriptures as the word of God addressed to us in this historical moment.

Further, in this postmodern[6] world, most Catholic theologians recognize the inadequacy of the Neoplatonic-Aristotelian-scholastic-theological synthesis and its origin in a stratified and patriarchal social construction of reality. Since the church rather uncritically absorbed this social construction into its practice and sustained it for centuries by its language, the serious ongoing deconstruction of that synthesis, and the attempt to articulate the faith of the church in structures and language other than scholastic categories has proven unnerving to many of the faithful, clergy and laity alike. As witnessed by the argumentation in recent papal communications regarding the role of women in liturgical leadership, on the one hand, and the questioning of that argumentation on the part of responsible theologians, on the other, it would be safe to say that ongoing interpretation of scripture and tradition is obvious as never before. The struggle occurs between those who seem to have equated the presumptions of scholastic metaphysics with the meaning of the gospel, and those who do not associate any one philosophical system with articulation of the faith. To the latter, it is remarkable that some Catholic theologians want to either retain or return to the sole use of the scholastic-metaphysics based theology, which enjoyed almost complete hegemony prior to Vatican II, and in which the scriptures are used (unwittingly?) to buttress assumptions inherent in that theological synthesis. Not surprisingly, this synthesis holds to the exclusive prerogatives of the pope and bishops to interpret scripture, and/or of those who agree with this presumed prerogative.

In this matter, it is important to note that, while affirming the responsibility of the magisterium in authoritative interpretation of the scriptures, *Dei verbum* asserts that,

> there exists a close connection and communication between sacred tradition and sacred Scripture. For both of them, *flowing from the same divine wellspring,* in a certain way merge into a unity and tend toward the same end. For sacred Scripture is the Word of God *inasmuch as it is consigned to writing under the inspiration of the divine Spirit....* Thus, led by the light of the Spirit of truth, these successors [of the apostles] can in their preaching preserve this word of God faithfully, explain it, and make it more widely known. (*DV,* par. 9)

It is clear, therefore, that sacred tradition, sacred Scripture, and the teaching authority of the Church, in accord with God's most wise design, are so linked and joined together that *one cannot stand without the others, and that all together and each in its own way under the action of the one Holy Spirit contribute to the salvation of souls. (DV,* par. 10; emphasis mine)

These paragraphs from *Dei verbum* could well constitute a dense description of the official position of the Catholic Church on the authority and function of scripture current in 1965. As a conciliar document, and especially as a dogmatic constitution, the official weight of *Dei verbum* is greater than a papal encyclical or an instruction from the Biblical Commission. However, because of its organic relation to the convictions in *Dei verbum,* and because of its affirmation by Pope John Paul II, the 1993 instruction on the interpretation of the Bible in the church deserves attention.

THE PUBLICATION *THE INTERPRETATION OF THE BIBLE IN THE CHURCH*

The French text *L'Interpretation de la Bible dans L'Eglise* is not a papal publication, but rather a document of the Biblical Commission issued with papal approval on April 23, 1993.[7] This document lists, describes, and evaluates every major methodology of biblical interpretation—literary criticisms, various hermeneutic theories, and contextual criticisms, such as feminist and liberation theology—precisely with a view to adjudicating the contribution and limitation of each method for grasping the religious significance of the text. In the process, this document sets out the current position of the Catholic Church regarding the authority and function of sacred scripture in all facets of its life. Indeed, the origin or authority of sacred scripture—word of God in human words—specifies its function as *norma normans et non normata* (a standard that sets the standard without being subject to any other standard) for belief and practice.

Joseph Fitzmyer's summary of the contribution of this Biblical Commission document is apt here:

the commission comments on the indispensable task that the interpretation of the bible plays in the church. It cannot be fundamentalistic, for one has to reckon with the bible in its relation to the Incarnation. Just as the Eternal Word became man at a given historic epoch, the written word was submitted to human language at a given period. This calls for the recognition that one must continue to use the historical-critical method of interpretation, because God's word has come to us through a series of interventions in the course of human history. The biblical message is solidly rooted in history. Hence the biblical writings cannot be correctly comprehended apart from their historic conditioning. Diachronic (historical) analysis is indispensable for its proper interpretation and synchronic (holistic) modes of analysis, no matter how enlightening, are incapable of replacing it. The synchronic modes (rhetorical, narrative, semiotic, sociological, anthropological, psychological, feminist) offer correctives to the basic method, which has suffered at times from a too narrow use and an insufficient attention to the dynamic character of the biblical text. The interpretation of the bible is a theological discipline, a way of analyzing Christian faith itself to bring it to a deeper understanding, for it shares in the same quest: *fides quaerens intellectum* ("faith seeking understanding").[8]

Conviction regarding the inerrancy of the scriptures is, thus, not locked to the words on the page, and yet the words on the page cannot be simply dismissed or manipulated by any ideology. If the historical-critical method of interpretation has at times been reduced to the function of an "autopsy" of the text, thereby ignoring or forgetting that the text is transparency for the Word, other modes of interpretation, enlightening as they may be, cannot replace it. No other method can grapple with the radical historicity of the locus of the Self-revelation of God in the scriptures and thus acknowledge their authority.

POSSIBLE ISSUES FOR ECUMENICAL DIALOGUE

The years since the Second Vatican Council witness a common lectionary usage among many of the churches and a most-welcome growth in the use of scripture for personal prayer and study among Catholics. However, this study brings two questions to mind:

- What do our respective denominational statements regarding the authority/origin and function of scripture imply about our operative convictions (conscious or preconscious) about the role/value of humanity in the formation of scripture?

- To what extent has the Neoplatonic philosophical factor in our Western scholastic metaphysics (e.g., dis-value of matter and materiality) captured the catholic imagination?

NOTES

1. Vatican Council II, Dogmatic Constitution on Divine Revelation, *Dei verbum (DV),* November 18, 1965, par. 13 (emphasis added). In the present essay, translations of council documents are from Walter M. Abbott, ed., *The Documents of Vatican II* (New York: Herder and Herder, Association Press, 1966).

2. Both *Dei verbum* and *Divino afflante spiritu* are descendants of the November 18, 1893 encyclical of Pope Leo XIII, *Providentissimus Deus.*

3. Even though the popes regularly mandated that at least one other person should be present, the fact that the directive was needed indicates that ministerial priests very often did not have anyone else present when they celebrated the Eucharist. The vestige of this pastoral oxymoron remains in the 1970 Sacramentary of Pope Paul VI as the *Missa sine populo* (Mass without the people).

4. Vatican Council II, Constitution on the Sacred Liturgy, *Sacrosanctum concilium (SC),* December 4, 1963, par. 7.

5. Referencing Denziger, nos. 1785, 1786, par. 6 of *Dei verbum* says: "'God, the beginning and end of all things, can be known with certainty from created reality by the light of human reason' (cf. Rom. 1:20); but the Synod teaches that it is through His revelation 'that those religious truths which are by their nature accessible to human reason can be known by all persons with ease, with solid certitude, and with no trace of error, even in the present state of the human race.'" See Heinrich Denziger, *The Sources of Catholic Dogma,* trans. Roy J. Deferrari from the 30th edition of *Enchiridion symbolorum* (St. Louis: Herder, 1957).

6. Acknowledging the myriad descriptions of *postmodern,* my meaning here refers to the current situation among philosophers wherein neither scholastic metaphysics nor Newtonian-type science can any longer be seen as sources of an overall or metanarrative of reality.

7. Pontifical Biblical Commission, *The Interpretation of the Bible in the Church* (Vatican City: Libreria Editrice Vaticana, 1993), reprinted in *Origins* 23, no. 29 (January 6, 1994): 497–524.

8. Joseph Fitzmyer, SJ, "'The Interpretation of the Bible in the Church,'" *America* 169, no. 17 (November 27, 1993): 15.

THE AUTHORITY AND FUNCTION OF SCRIPTURE IN THE UNDERSTANDING OF THE LUTHERAN CHURCH– MISSOURI SYNOD

Samuel H. Nafzger

INTRODUCTION

At the heart of the Lutheran understanding of the authority and function of scripture is the centrality of the gospel. Lutherans believe that the heart, core, and center of what we believe, teach, and confess is the good news of the substitutionary life and death of Jesus Christ for the sins of the world. Justification by grace through faith is the central doctrine of the Christian religion on which the church stands or falls. Luther describes the centrality and indispensability of the gospel alone in the Smalcald Articles. In article 2 he states:

> The first and chief article is this, that Jesus Christ, our God and Lord, "was put to death for our trespasses and raised again for our justification" (Rom. 4:25). He alone is "the Lamb of God, who takes away the sin of the world" (John 1:29). "God has laid upon him the iniquities of us all" (Isa. 53:6). Moreover, "all have sinned," and "they are justified by his grace as a gift, through the redemption which is in Christ Jesus, by his blood" (Rom. 3:23–25)....On this article rests all that we teach and practice...(Smalcald Articles, II, 1, 1–3, 5).[1]

The words of this article, in a sense, form Luther's last will and testament. He says in the preface: "I have decided to publish these articles so that, if I should die before a council meets (which I fully expect...) those who live after me may have my testimony and confession...to show where I have stood until now and where, by God's grace, I will continue to stand" (preface, 3). At the heart of the Lutheran confession is the conviction that justification is by grace alone through faith alone.

THE FUNCTION OF SCRIPTURE: THE GOSPEL ALONE

Lutherans believe, teach, and confess that salvation is the free gift of God's grace (undeserved mercy) for Christ's sake alone. "Since the fall of Adam all men who are born according to the course of nature are conceived and born in sin," the Lutherans confessed before Emperor Charles V in Augsburg, Germany, in 1530 (*Augsburg Confession [AC]* II, 1). This "inborn sickness and hereditary sin" makes it utterly impossible for people to earn forgiveness. If salvation were dependent on human initiative, there would be no hope for anyone. But God forgives our sins, says Luther in his *Large Catechism* (1529), "altogether freely, out of pure grace" (*LC* III, 96). The basis for the grace of God that alone gives hope to sinners is the life, death, and resurrection of Jesus Christ.

Lutherans believe that the scriptures teach that God's grace in Christ Jesus is universal, embracing all people of all times and all places. There is no sin for which Christ has not died. Says the *Formula of Concord* (1577), "We must by all means cling rigidly and firmly to the fact that as the proclamation of repentance extends over all men (Luke 24:47), so also does the promise of the Gospel....Christ has taken away the sin of the world (John 1:29)" (*FC,* Solid Declaration XI, 28). Therefore, there need be no question in any sinner's mind whether Christ has died for each and every one of his or her personal sins.

While God's grace is universal and embraces all people, Lutherans believe that the scriptures teach that this grace can be appropriated by sinful human beings *only* through faith. Here is where Luther's decisive break came with the understanding of the doctrine of justification that had generally prevailed in the Western church during the Middle Ages.

Luther had learned from Augustine that only the grace of God could save him. But Luther's rediscovery of the gospel in all its clarity took place when he came to see that he did not first have to do something to merit God's saving grace. Philip Melanchthon, Luther's colleague at the University of Wittenberg, writes in the *Augsburg Confession:* "Our churches also teach that men cannot be justified before God by their own strength, merits, or works, but are freely justified for Christ's sake through faith when they believe that they are received into favor and that their sins are forgiven on account of Christ, who by his death made satisfaction for our sins. This faith God imputes for righteousness in his sight (Rom 3:4)" (*AC* IV, 1–3).

The implications of salvation "through faith alone" permeate everything Lutherans believe and teach. For example, we believe that the conversion of sinners is a gift of God and not the result of any human effort or decision. Lutherans therefore confess in the words of Luther's explanation to the third article of the Apostle's Creed: "I believe that I cannot by my own reason or strength believe in Jesus Christ, my Lord, or come to Him; but the Holy Ghost has called me through the Gospel" (*Small Catechism* II, 6).

Lutherans are by no means anti-intellectual, and we thank God for our reasoning ability. We use it to seek to understand, to present, and to defend what we believe, but we do reject all suggestions that scientific evidence or rational arguments can lend any credibility to Christian truth claims. By the same token, we uphold the importance of emotion and feeling in the life of the Christian, but we steadfastly repudiate any reliance on conversion experiences or "charismatic gifts" for the certainty of salvation. We believe that the scriptures teach that the sole object of saving faith is the cross of Jesus Christ and his resurrection, and that it is only by the miraculous power of God the Holy Spirit that the Christian can say "I believe." Faith is not a human achievement but a gift from God.

"Through faith alone" also implies that it is only through the proclamation of the gospel—in word and sacrament—that the Holy Spirit gives the gift of faith. The proclamation of the gospel word in public preaching therefore occupies a central position in our Lutheran theology. Lutheran churches are preaching churches. But we are also sacramental churches, for the sacraments—baptism and the Lord's Supper—are the gospel made visible. Moreover, it is only through the gospel that Christians receive the power and will to do the good works, which must necessarily flow from the lives of those who are brought to faith.

THE AUTHORITY OF SCRIPTURE: SCRIPTURE ALONE

Luther's insight that salvation comes by grace alone through faith alone cannot be divorced from "on the basis of Scripture alone." For it was directly as a result of his commitment to scripture as God's completely reliable word that Luther came to rediscover justification by grace alone through faith alone.

Together with his contemporaries, Luther held that the Bible is the word of God and that it does not mislead or deceive us. But unlike his opponents, Luther rejected the notion that an infallible magisterium of the church is necessary for the right interpretation of the Bible. Scripture *alone,* said Luther, is infallible. The institutional church and its councils, commissions, theologians, and faculties can and do err. But scripture, says Luther, "will not lie to you" (*LC* V, 76).

While maintaining a deep appreciation for the church catholic, Lutherans believe that scripture alone—not scripture and tradition, scripture and the church, scripture and human reason, or scripture and experience—stands as the *final* standard of what the gospel is, and we believe that

> the prophetic and apostolic writings of the Old and New Testaments are the only rule and norm according to which all doctrines and teachers alike must be appraised and judged, as it is written in Ps. 119:105, "Thy Word is a lamp unto my feet and a light to my path." And St. Paul says in Gal. 1:8, "Even if an angel from heaven should preach to you

a Gospel contrary to that which we preached to you, let him be accursed." (*FC,* Epitome Rule and Norm, 1)

A HUMAN BOOK

The Bible is a collection of thoroughly human documents written by human beings living in history—"the prophetic and apostolic writings of the Old and New Testaments" (*FC* Epitome Rule and Norm, 1). These writings of the prophets and the apostles bear the marks of their human authorship. They were shaped by their historical circumstances, cultural milieus, educational backgrounds, and natural gifts and abilities of their human authors. These writings reveal their thought processes, temperaments, endowments, interests, purposes, perspectives, writing styles, and even limitations (e.g., Paul's lapse of memory in 1 Cor 1:16). Their authors reflect widely divergent callings in life—kings, peasants, fishermen, physicians, judges, historians, and scholars.

The vast majority of the writings included in the canons of the Old and New Testaments possess the characteristics of occasional writings, prepared in response to specific historical circumstances. There is nothing in any of them to suggest that the Holy Spirit gave their authors a heavenly vocabulary or a celestial grammar. Included in the biblical canon is a literature rich in variety and genre—prose and poetry, historical narrative and prophetic oracle, proverb and parable, prayers and liturgical readings, letters and legal contracts, creeds and hymns, sermons and doctrinal treatises, and allegories and fables. The authors of these writings used ordinary human language, subject to the regular principles of grammar and syntax, and they employed the literary forms and devices used in contemporary literature for effective communication. Some authors of biblical material expressly indicate that they did research and made use of sources, both oral and written, on the basis of which they prepared their written accounts (e.g., Num 21:14; Josh 10:13; Luke 1:1–4).

In addition, the scriptural documents of the Old and the New Testaments also have a history of their own. These texts came into existence over a period of more than one and a half millennia.

They were handed down with great care from generation to generation by scribes and copyists. None of the original manuscripts of the writings of the Old and New Testament has been preserved. While variations due to errors in the transmission process appear in the extant copies of the biblical writings, there is no hint in any of these writings that the original documents were "written in heaven" or that the Bible is not what it appears to be—a collection of writings authored by, preserved by, and handed down by human beings.

THE INSPIRED WORD OF GOD

The human authors of the scriptural documents see no conflict in identifying the product of their speaking and writing with the very word of God itself. Moses, God's spokesman, tells the people "all the words of the Lord" (Exod 24:4), and what he said was received by them as that which "the Lord has spoken" (Exod 24:7). That which Moses wrote down was to be regarded as the "statutes and the ordinances" of God himself (Deut 4:1–2). "The Spirit of the Lord speaks by me," says King David, "his word is upon my tongue" (2 Sam 22:2). When the High Priest Hilkiah found "the book of the law in the house of the Lord" (2 Kgs 22:8), the prophetess Huldah introduces its content with the words "thus says the Lord" (2 Kgs 22:18–19). The oracles of the prophets were written down at the counsel of the Lord (Isa 8:1). The book of Amos, the shepherd prophet, begins with this introduction: "the words of Amos, who was among the shepherds of Tekoa…Thus says the Lord" (Amos 1:1–3).

Consistent with this self-understanding of selected portions of writings included in the Old Testament canon is the appraisal of its entire corpus by the authors of the New Testament. "All Scripture (*pasa graphee*) is inspired by God" (*theopneustes,* "God-breathed") (2 Tim 3:16). Written by human beings, their authors "spoke from God" as "men moved by the Holy Spirit" (2 Pet 1:21). The claim of divine inspiration is the distinguishing feature of those writings recognized by the early Christians as the scriptures.

Similarly, the authors of the writings that came to be recognized as the New Testament do not hesitate to regard what they wrote as "words not taught by human wisdom but taught by the Spirit" (1 Cor 2:13). The very formation of the New Testament canon represents the conviction of the early church that these writings, in keeping with Christ's promise to his disciples that he would send the Counselor "to teach you all things, and bring to your remembrance all that I have said to you" (John 14:26; cf. 16:12–15), were likewise "inspired by God," that the words of the apostles were, like those of the prophets, the very words or oracles of God.

The sixteenth-century Lutheran confessors were convinced that the scriptures of the Old and New Testaments claimed for themselves divine inspiration, a conviction that they shared with their Roman Catholic and Reformed opponents. While the authors of the documents included in the *Book of Concord* do not set forth a finely worked-out doctrine of the inspiration of scripture, their constant working assumption is that the prophetic and apostolic writings of the Old and New Testaments are uniquely the word of God. Together with the Nicene Creed, the Lutheran reformers confess their faith that the Holy Spirit "spoke by the prophets." The words of Holy Scripture did not fall "from the Holy Spirit unawares" (Apology IV, 107). Repeatedly the terms *word of God* and the *Scriptures* are used interchangeably. They maintain that there is a "distinction between the Holy Scriptures of the Old and New Testaments and all other writings" (*FC* Epitome Rule and Norm, 7).

The inspiration of scripture, according to its self-testimony, is the work of the Holy Spirit and therefore beyond the ability of human reason to understand. The testimony of its inspiration, however, must be distinguished from theories regarding the way this inspiration was effected. Scripture nowhere explains the *how* of inspiration, but it does point to a variety of ways in which God has chosen to speak his word in human words (see Exod 17:14; Jer 30:2, 36:2; Rev 1:1).

The conviction that scripture is the word of God inspired by the Holy Spirit, is an article of faith, based on the self-testimony of the biblical writings themselves. Christians accept this claim of scripture because they have first been brought to faith in Jesus

Christ, and not because they can prove or demonstrate it. And because they have been brought to faith in this gospel of Jesus, the Christ, they accept its claim to possess divine authority for their proclamation of the good news.

CONCLUSION

Confidence in the authority of the Bible is not possible apart from faith in Jesus Christ. Christians believe what the scriptures teach because they first believe in Jesus Christ. *Christ* is the object of faith, not the Bible. The inversion of this order compromises the centrality of the gospel and results in rationalistic biblicism, as if a demonstration of the Bible's truthfulness—perhaps a piece of Noah's ark, for example—could provide a foundation for faith in the gospel. But the Bible remains a dark book apart from faith in Christ, for he is its true content. When sinners are brought to faith in him, however, Christ points them back to the writings of prophets and apostles as the sole authoritative norm for the content of the gospel.

Intra-Lutheran differences today find their source primarily in connection with the nature of the authority of scripture. While all Lutheran churches profess allegiance to "scripture alone," they do not all agree on what this means in practice. Missouri Synod Lutherans and the twenty-eight other Lutheran churches from around the world that belong to the International Lutheran Council believe that when the complete truthfulness of the Bible is denied, its authority is undermined, and this in turn endangers justification by grace alone through faith alone.[2]

The Holy Scriptures, the very words of God, alone serve, therefore, as the final standard for what we believe, teach, and confess—even about contemporary issues such as the ordination of women to pastoral office and the practice of homosexuality.[3] But the gospel alone is the key that unlocks the contents of the Bible. To make the gospel its own norm is to end up with a kind of fideistic "gospel reductionism." But to substitute the Bible as the ground of faith is to end up with a rationalistic biblicism.[4] Both errors make human reason the norm of the gospel and undermine the authority of scripture and its proper function in the church.

NOTES

1. In the present essay, translations from Lutheran confessional texts are from Theodore G. Tappert, with Jaroslav Pelikan, Robert H. Fischer, and Arthur C. Piepkorn, trans. and eds., *The Book of Concord: The Confessions of the Evangelical Lutheran Church* (Philadelphia: Mühlenberg Press, 1959).

2. From its very beginning, The Lutheran Church–Missouri Synod has taught that the scriptures and the Lutheran Confessions teach the inerrancy of the scriptural writings of the prophets and the apostles. See C. F. W. Walther (the first president of the LCMS), who writes in *Lehre und Wehre,* February 1875, 35: "Whoever believes with all his heart that the Bible is God's Word cannot believe anything else than that it is inerrant." In the face of attacks on the veracity of scripture and its complete truthfulness, the LCMS has reaffirmed its traditional position on the inerrancy of scripture. In 1973 it adopted *A Statement of Scriptural and Confessional Principles,* which states: "With Luther, we confess that 'God's Word cannot err' (*LC* IV, 57). We therefore believe, teach, and confess that since the Holy Scriptures are the Word of God, they contain no errors or contradictions but that they are in all their parts and words the infallible truth. We hold that the opinion that Scripture contains errors is a violation of the *sola scriptura* principle, for it rests upon the acceptance of some norm, or criterion of truth above the Scriptures."

3. See, e.g., Krister Stendahl, *The Bible and the Role of Women* (Philadelphia: Fortress Press, 1966), 7. Stendahl reports that when all the teachers holding academic positions in the field of New Testament studies at Swedish universities (except one) protested the recommendation that women should be permitted to serve as pastors, the members of the committee readily conceded that the apostle Paul's writings forbade this. But the committee did not feel that they should seriously consider the possibility that Paul's opinion as expressed in his New Testament

writings ought to be accepted as normative for all times. See also Walter Wink, "Biblical Perspectives on Homosexuality," *Christian Century* (1979): 1082–86. Wink freely grants that the Bible condemns the practice of homosexuality, but he concludes that the Bible is not correct in so doing.

4. See Carl F. H. Henry, *God, Revelation, and Authority,* vol. 1 (Waco, TX: Word Books, 1976), 215. Lutherans would not agree with Henry's claim that "divine revelation is the source of all truth, the truth of Christianity included; reason is the instrument for recognizing it; Scripture is its verifying principle; logical consistency is a negative test for truth and coherence a subordinate test."

THE AUTHORITY AND FUNCTION OF SCRIPTURE IN THE UNITED CHURCH OF CHRIST

Clyde J. Steckel

HISTORICAL TRADITIONS OF SCRIPTURAL AUTHORITY

In 1957 two Protestant denominations in America, the Congregational and Christian Churches and the Evangelical and Reformed Church, entered into full union, becoming the United Church of Christ. The sixteenth-century Protestant traditions represented by those churches included Calvinist (or Reformed) streams represented by English and New England Puritans and Separatists, a German Reformed stream from the Rhineland, German Lutherans from the Church of the Prussian Union, and Free Church streams from the Second Great Awakening on the American frontier. All of these traditions continued the Protestant Reformation emphasis on the sole authority of the scriptures for ordering faith and life. The Reformed and Lutheran streams also contributed confessional and catechetical interpretations of the scriptural word of God, though with the clear understanding that these confessions were always subordinate to scriptural authority.

In the preamble to the constitution of the United Church of Christ, adopted in 1961, the following scriptural affirmation appears in the third sentence of the second paragraph of the preamble, though the christological theme controlling the entire paragraph should be understood as scripturally grounded.

> It [the United Church of Christ] looks to the Word of God
> in the Scriptures, and to the presence and power of the Holy
> Spirit, to prosper its creative and redemptive work in the
> world. It claims as its own the faith of the historic Church
> expressed in the ancient creeds and reclaimed in the basic
> insights of the Protestant Reformers. It affirms the responsi-
> bility of the Church in each generation to make this faith its
> own in reality of worship, in honesty of thought and expres-
> sion, and in purity of heart before God. (*Constitution and
> Bylaws,* 2001 edition, 2)

In practical terms, these traditions and constitutional affirmations are expressed in preaching and teaching that are explicitly based in scripture, including the use of the common
lectionary; in the insistence that ordained church leaders must be
educated in the scriptures; and in the ordination question, "Do
you, with the church throughout the world, hear the word of God
in the scriptures of the Old and New Testaments, and do you
accept the word of God as the rule of Christian faith and practice?" (*United Church of Christ, Book of Worship,* 1986, 407). Some
members of the UCC have worried that the verbs to look and to
hear as in "looks to" (constitution) and "hear the word of God"
(ordination service) are not sufficiently strong and clear affirmations of the final authority of scripture. But the majority, I think,
would regard these as descriptive verbs about the ways we live
with and honor the scriptural word, without sliding into either a
biblical literalism or a confessional absolutism that would be foreign to our convictions.

While the *Statement of Faith* of the United Church of Christ
(adopted by the General Synod in 1959 and recommended for use
in common worship and for study) does not contain specific references to scriptural authority, it does speak of God's "righteous
will declared through prophets and apostles," how God the creator "sets before each one the ways of life and death," and how
God has "come to us and shared our common lot, conquering sin
and death and reconciling the world" in Jesus Christ. These affirmations are at the heart of the biblical message.

Because of the ecclesiological conviction in the United Church
of Christ that the local congregation is the basic unit of the church,

denominational structures like associations, conferences, and the General Synod can issue no determinative statements on behalf of the whole church, though in our polity of covenant all these expressions of the church are to work together in mutual respect and trust. It must therefore be clearly understood that the following summary statements on the authority and function of scripture in the United Church of Christ are the reflections of this author—member, ordained minister, and theological professor in that church. This is not an official or otherwise authorized statement.

Keeping that caveat in mind, I would summarize the United Church of Christ understanding of the authority and function of scripture in the following ways. The texts commonly named as the books of the Old and New Testaments are authoritative for the communities following Jesus Christ in three ways: (1) authoritative for the practice of Christian life and faith in the world; (2) authoritative for shaping the content of Christian belief and the dynamics of faith; and (3) for the proper ordering of the life and mission of the communities of Christ's followers.

These texts have been authoritative through the centuries as Christ's followers have found in them the living Word, Jesus Christ, in whom their lives are judged and redeemed from sin and death; the creative, providential, and fulfilling purposes of God in all of creation and human history; the empowerment of the Holy Spirit in the life and worship of the church where Jesus Christ is both the head and the foundation; the mission of the church in the world; and each person's life of faith. Confessing this authority, the believer and the church declare these texts to be divinely inspired in ways not attributed to other texts, however profoundly illuminating these other texts may be.

This divine inspiration of the texts of scripture has been variously construed, ranging from divine or spiritual dictation of every word to the writers, to identifying the individual insights of writers as spiritually guided. In the modern period of Western civilization, the tools of critical textual analysis have been applied to scriptural texts, though not by all, and not in the same way. Some churches, including the United Church of Christ, hold that critical analysis opens fresh insight into the Word. Others believe that critical scholarship undermines or even destroys sound belief.

Now that Western civilization has moved into postmodernity, new critical tools are brought to scriptural scholarship, as well as renewed interest in premodern or antimodern interpretations. It is difficult to foresee whether a new consensus will emerge replacing modernity. The traditions embraced in my own denominational heritage, the United Church of Christ, have for the most part embraced the critical interpretive methods of modernity, and have been open to new insights from postmodern criticism, particularly critiques arising from historically oppressed peoples. Especially vexing has been the status of personal or communal experience in scriptural authority. What does one do, for example, if a Christian believer or community has "experiences" that persuade them of the reality of soul reincarnation? There appears to be no scriptural warrant for such belief; indeed scriptural anthropology does not appear to allow such belief at all. Then what? A more deeply divisive question touching on scriptural authority is the question of homosexuality. Scriptural texts have been cited in proof of divine judgment on homosexuality. Other texts are cited that affirm diverse sexual orientations. Each side brings forward not only scriptural texts but also experiences (testimonies of either the curse or gift of sexual orientation, social science, and genetic studies) in support of its beliefs. How is scriptural authority to function in relation to this matter? On top of that, pluralism and a toleration of diverse views are so strongly prized in modern society and in my own church traditions that pastors, theologians, and other church leaders often feel constrained from asserting scriptural authority against anything. How these difficulties of applied scriptural authority will be resolved lies beyond the scope of my imagination or the brief compass of this discussion.

FUNCTIONS OF SCRIPTURE

Communities of Christ's followers read and study the scriptures, hear them preached, pray with scriptural language and images, and celebrate the sacraments of baptism and the Eucharist, all under the inspiration of the Holy Spirit. In these encounters with the living Word, Christ's communities experience forgiveness and reconciliation; their faith is refreshed and illumined; their beliefs are clarified; and their lives as a Christian community and individual believers are instructed and encouraged. The promise of the gospel renews hope that the rule of God in all creation will be fulfilled.

At every scale of size and complexity—the individual believer, the local congregation, denominational and ecumenical organizations, the worldwide Christian movement—these same functions of scripture can be discerned. These diverse expressions of Christian communal and individual life will find scriptural life in them addressed to their particular callings. Individual believers who read, study, and pray the scriptures will discover riches of insight and courage. Teachers and schools will find their formational, instructional, and research functions guided and grounded in scriptural truth. Mission organizations will discover the method and content of their mission quickened in scriptural encounters. Those who care for the formal embodiments of the scriptural message, through framing and reframing creedal and confessional statements, liturgies, and hymnals as well as curricular materials, will endeavor to reflect the scriptural message in that work. Those who guide the churches in ethical reflection and action in the world will seek fidelity to the scriptural word. Also those who care for the organizational life of the church will endeavor to honor scriptural principles in devising and administering such institutions.

It is not easy to remain scripturally attentive and faithful. It is easy to draw from the latest social science research or the newest methods of organizational reform. While the human arts and sciences can be useful in scriptural discernment, they can never be allowed to become predominant in shaping beliefs or actions in the communities of Christ's followers. This is a particular temptation for those under the sway of modernity.

SUMMARY AND CONCLUSION

Scriptural authority is grounded in the faith that God's word in Jesus Christ meets us in the texts of scriptures, with the illumination of the Holy Spirit, a word in which we stand forgiven, redeemed, surrounded by divine grace, and empowered for mission in the world. The communities following Jesus Christ seek to honor that authority in faithful worship, in forming and reforming traditions faithful to the scriptural word, and in both witness and missional service in the world, so that God's realm of justice, love, and peace grows ever toward its ultimate completion and fulfillment.

RESPONSE TO NAFZGER

Theresa F. Koernke, IHM

This response includes (1) mention of ten points of consonance or agreement in Dr. Nafzger's paper. Then there follow (2) reference to points of dissonance or disagreement, and (3) points of non-sonance or serious puzzlement. The second sentence of Nafzger's vigorous work reads, "Lutherans believe that the heart, core, and center of what we believe, teach, and confess is the good news of the substitutionary life and death of Jesus Christ for the sins of the world." My sense is that the understanding of *substitutionary* is the code for appreciating all else.

POINTS OF CONSONANCE

Using Nafzger's wording, the following enumerates points of consonance, that is, words, phrases, and sentences that sound consistent with Catholic teaching. Catholic theology (1) has always taught that justification comes to sinful humanity through the utter gratuity of God's grace that enables us to respond in faith. Thus, (2) no person can earn forgiveness; salvation comes from God through the life, cross, and resurrection of Jesus Christ and the offer of salvation is to all persons and all times; the grace of the life, death, and resurrection of Jesus Christ can be appropriated by sinful human beings only through faith and there are no human works that can merit God's saving grace, that is, conversion is a gift of God and not the result of any human effort or decision; the Holy Spirit calls us through the preaching of the gospel. Therefore, (3) scientific evidence or rational arguments do not prove the credibility of Christian truth claims. Because (4) all scripture is inspired by God, containing words not taught by human wisdom but taught by the Spirit; the scriptures (5) are the *norma normans et non normata* (a standard that sets the standard without being subject to any other standard). That being given, the scriptural writings (6) bear the marks of their human authorship, that is, their historical circumstances, cultural milieus, educational backgrounds, and natural gifts, abilities, and limitations; there is nothing to suggest that the Holy Spirit gave the authors celestial grammar; there is a variety of literary forms. Thus, (7) Christ is the object of faith, not the Bible; to substitute the Bible as the ground of faith is to end up with a rationalistic biblicism. Christians (8) receive the power to do good works that flow from a life of faith and (9) the Spirit enables Christians to remember what Jesus Christ has taught. In the course of history, it is clear that in some matters (10) the institutional church and its councils, commissions, theologians, and faculties can and do err, but scripture "will not lie to you."

POINTS OF DISSONANCE

Catholic theology would name a "primordial" faith-competence of human beings precisely in virtue of the goodness of humanity as creation by God. In other words, all human beings are *capax Dei,* capable of responding to God by God's grace because they are made to respond to God. Faith, as used in Nafzger's paper, as I read it, refers solely to a "fiducial" or trusting faith act, the human response to God enabled by the grace of the Holy Spirit bestowed by God through Christ. Agreed, but there is a certain dis-ease that arises from a sense that the doctrine of total depravity of humanity is at the root of the statements that salvation comes through grace alone, faith alone, and scriptures alone. There are senses in which Catholic theology could say this as well. While Catholic theology would agree that humanity is seriously weakened by its sinful condition, the incarnation of the One Word of God has revealed that it is precisely in the human situation that God has revealed God's Self. And, if one takes this seriously, it is a statement about the radical goodness of humanity and that, even given the darkness that is ours because of our sinfulness, the ongoing competence to respond to the living Christ throughout history is assured by the gift of the Holy Spirit. This tradition is a worthy source of knowledge about God's will.

Further, Catholic theology would agree that baptism and the Lord's Supper are "the gospel made visible." But here, again, arises the question of the ongoing presence and activity of the living Christ by the power of the Spirit to the body of Christ, the church. In the face of the almost overwhelming influence of Neoplatonic categories on the Christian imagination that lead to localizing the risen Christ "in heaven," Catholic theology itself has struggled until recently to articulate lucidly that, as the Constitution on the Sacred Liturgy has said, Christ is always present in his church. This radical knowledge was at the root of the statement of the Council of Trent that the church, intimately united to the living Christ, has the competence to interpret key moments in Christian life by way of the liturgies of the sacraments. These actions, including baptism and the Lord's Supper, are "the gospel made visible" through the presence and activity of Christ by the power of the Spirit.

In the context of asserting that salvation comes through faith alone, rather than through "merits or works," Nafzger states that Luther broke with the understanding of "the doctrine of justification that had generally prevailed in the Western church during the Middle Ages." There may well have been some medieval persons who taught and/or thought that one could manipulate God by the "works" of the sacraments because of a faulty grasp of the meaning of "sacraments are efficacious of God's grace *ex opere operato* (from the work worked or done)." However, what Catholic doctrine says is that, when the liturgies of the sacraments are celebrated, they are always efficacious of the grace of God *ex opere operato passionis Christi* (in virtue of the saving passion of Christ) and that that grace must be freely responded to in faith. There is no cheap grace. Again, perhaps because of the conceptual difficulty of imagining the ongoing presence and power of the Christ to his church by the power of the Spirit, undue attention was paid to the doing of the rite, rather than to the source of the meaning of the rite. It is my understanding that Luther did not use the original texts of Thomas Aquinas and, for that reason, may have presumed that the church actually taught a rite-bound and corrupt understanding of *ex opere operato*. The corrupt understanding said that the simple "doing of the work of the rite" had some sort of manipulative effect on God. The widespread perverted practices of some persons ought not to be confused with what the Catholic Church taught and teaches.

POINTS OF NON-SONANCE

If, as Nafzger says, the scriptures are marked by the historical situation of the authors, are we to presume that all the social-historical factors and assumptions surrounding their lives are in no way present in their words? If real persons are the inspired authors of the scriptures, it seems puzzling to presume that some of those social factors and assumptions are beyond negative critique. For example, if a given author assumed that the patriarchal social order is "the way it ought to be," and if we now know that the church rather uncritically absorbed that patriarchal structure and the philosophical categories that defended it, would it not be true to the gospel who is Christ to name that fact without fear of denying the gospel? Are we today to presume that the revelation in Christ is beyond deeper appropriation in current situations never imagined by the biblical authors? Are we limited to "the words on the page" as we struggle to make an account of the hope that is in us? Is the gospel who is Christ to be "identified with the scriptures"? It is puzzling, for example, to read that the gospel is Jesus Christ, and then to read that women may not be called to orders because we cannot find specific reference in the scriptures. That being said, some Roman officials as well give in to literalism.

And finally, the word *substitutionary* as it refers to the life, cross, and resurrection of Jesus Christ presents a major puzzlement. Does it mean that the humanity of Jesus Christ is not like my humanity? Does it mean that what has transpired in the life of Jesus tells me nothing about my humanity? Does it mean that the death of Jesus has appeased the anger of God? For what has the life, cross, and resurrection of Jesus Christ substituted? As mentioned earlier,

I have a sense that a notion of the total depravity of humanity is key to this doctrine, and that the doctrine may be more closely tied to the legal metaphors of Anselm of Canterbury in *Cur Deus Homo* than to the meaning of the scriptures.

CONCLUSION

It is pleasing to be able to agree at so many points. And yet, I do not find a distinction in the paper between (1) naming the broken moral condition of humanity in need of God's grace, and (2) the testimony of scripture that all creation and humanity are good. Nafzger's assertion that the biblical authors are marked by historical limitations, on the one hand, yet his clinging to the "words on the pages," on the other hand, leads me to hope to engage in conversation about the meaning of the incarnation, of the ongoing presence of Christ to the church, and the roots of the doctrine of substitutionary atonement.

RESPONSE TO STECKEL

Theresa F. Koernke, IHM

Professor Steckel's account of the full union in 1957 of several Reformation churches is a marvelous example of the inherent impulse toward the visible unity of the One Church of Christ. The following response to his paper includes (1) mention of points of consonance or agreement, (2) points of dissonance or disagreement, and (3) points of non-sonance or puzzlement.

POINTS OF CONSONANCE

That God addresses Christians in the living Christ through the power of the Holy Spirit in the proclamation and preaching of the scriptures resounds in Catholic teaching, as evidenced in the documents of the Second Vatican Council (1962–65), especially *Dei verbum* (Dogmatic Constitution on Divine Revelation), *Lumen gentium* (Constitution on the Church), and *Sacrosanctum concilium* (Constitution on the Sacred Liturgy). These documents retrieve and reassert what the Reformation churches have long preserved, that is, the biblical foundation of worship and the theological project as a whole. And the use of the common lectionary is, in my view, a gift of the Spirit in our movement toward visible unity.

Further, the use of historical-critical methods as a means of plumbing the scriptural texts is certainly consistent with the development of the biblical movement among Catholics, especially since the encyclical of Pope Pius XII, *Divino afflante spiritu* (Inspiration of the Divine Spirit, 1943), *Dei verbum* of the Second Vatican Council, and the 1993 statement, approved by Pope John Paul II, of the Pontifical Biblical Commission, "The Interpretation of the

Bible in the Church." Each of these documents agrees on the importance of avoiding either biblical literalism or confessional absolutism.

Finally, Steckel's reference to the challenge of preaching the cross in an age of individualism that resists normative principles can be found in almost every document in Catholic circles.

As I reflect on the influence of the Western metaphysical system that has underpinned our thought patterns and interpretation of the scriptures, individualism appears to me to be part and parcel of that tradition. Granting the impact that it has had on Catholics as well, I cannot help but wonder whether the Reformation church critique of individualism might not be a particularly difficult challenge when one thinks of the kind of emphasis placed on individual autonomy within these churches.

POINTS OF DISSONANCE

Steckel's statement that the local congregation is the basic unit of the church and that church conferences do not have a determinative role for the whole church may well be an expanded example of the individualism of a congregation. It seems inconsistent to say that the United Church of Christ has no common position when there is a clear statement that the scriptures are authoritative (1) for the practice of Christian life, (2) for shaping Christian belief and the dynamics of faith, and (3) for proper ordering of the life and mission of the communities.

A question comes to mind here: What constitutes the One Church of Christ? Is it only a spiritual reality? Granting the fact that the pyramidal image of reality has unduly influenced the practice and organizational structure of the Catholic Church, the documents of the Second Vatican Council have retrieved biblically based communion ecclesiology, a circular image in which one perceives that the One Church of Christ is intimately bound to the ever-present Christ. This image of the church places ordained ministry as servant of the activity of the Spirit in the church as a whole. Thus, bishops' conferences and other such groups make (ideally) decisions not for the whole but in dialogue with the whole church. The intense and thoughtful theological reaction to Pope John Paul II's statement against the ordination of women (*Sacerdotalis ordinatio,* 1994) would be a clear example of the fact that the pyramidal image of the church is being deconstructed and that a communion-of-persons-in-Christ image is once again slowly taking hold of the Catholic imagination and practice.

If one holds that the living Christ is always present in his church by the power of the Spirit, then one can assert that the church, the body of Christ in history, has the competence to address the word of the gospel to crucial moments in life, even beyond the celebration of baptism and the celebration of the Lord's Supper. One need not find explicit references in the scriptures to a specific command, even though the Catholic Church is still struggling with this kind of biblicism. Again, how one comprehends the church makes all the difference in this world.

POINTS OF NON-SONANCE

In reflecting on what puzzles me in Steckel's paper, I again return to the issue of the autonomy of the individual and individual congregations. While it is clear that personal commitment is important in living the Christian life, it seems to me that Robert Bellah's critique of "idiosyncratic individualism" in *Habits of the Heart* is apt. We do not believe alone. Catholic theology has more recently retrieved (by way of Karl Rahner and others) the notion of "primordial" faith of human beings. Here one sees that, in virtue of creation by God, all persons are made by God to know and respond to God. As baptized Christians we are inserted into a set of relationships with Christ and one another by the power of the Spirit. And, in the context of growing up in this group, one comes to make fiducial, that is, trusting faith decisions. These faith acts are obviously influenced by the cultures in which one lives, and we have all been negatively, in my view, influenced by the individualism inherent in the Western metaphysical tradition in which we swim, with all respect to the great Karl Barth. This individualism is, in my view, inimical to St. Paul's instruction in 1 Corinthians 10–11: partaking of the body of Christ is a partaking of Christ and his members; we are not related to the Christ as individuals alone.

CONCLUSION

Is the One Church of Christ an aggregate of individuals, each of whom makes trusting faith decisions during the course of their lives? Even though the Catholic tradition itself tended to see the consequence of baptism in this way for a long time, the retrieval of communion ecclesiology since the Second Vatican Council has released the force of St. Paul's root insights about the nature of the church: What I do is always as a member of the body that gives me my self, tells me who I am—in Christ with others for the sake of the good of the world. What I hold to be true must always be placed in conversation with the tradition and with those who struggle to believe in today's world.

Bishops, at their best in a communion ecclesiology, are always involved in a three-way relationship between the plumbing of the scriptures (using the best means of understanding them) as the norm of faith, the lived experience of the faithful, and themselves as teachers of the faith. Clearly, the history of the Church witnesses to the sad consequence of the pyramidal image of reality inherent on the Western metaphysical system, a system that gave us the image of and practice in the Church of a monarchy. The protesting Reformers did well to reject this monarchical notion of governance, as Catholics are struggling to do today. But also inherent in that philosophical system (absorbed unwittingly) is individualism. Have some of the Reformation churches rejected monarchy in the church, while holding on to another facet of that philosophical system (individualism) that inhibits acknowledging the radical interrelationship of persons with Christ in the church?

Steckel's thoughtful paper encourages me to engage in conversation on the origin of the church, the relationship between scripture and tradition, and authority in the church.

RESPONSE TO KOERNKE

Clyde J. Steckel

My reading of Koernke's paper, "Authority and Function of Scripture in Catholic Tradition," brought me great appreciation and, I hope, increased clarity of understanding. Following the "Fordian" method I will speak of points of agreement or convergence, points of divergence or disagreement, and points that are puzzling. Happily the points of agreement far outnumber the other points.

POINTS OF CONSONANCE

Two points of agreement appear in the first paragraph, namely, that "an account of the authority and function of sacred scripture [is] a delicate matter," and the faith claim that God acts first in creation and redemption, to which human beings respond. On this first point, I fear my own paper, due to its brevity and summary character, is not as delicate as it should have been. My only excuse, beyond my own human frailty, is the daunting task of dealing with such a multiplicity of traditions in a relatively small Christian denomination, the United Church of Christ. On the second point, I not only applaud Koernke's emphasis on divine initiative, I also want to raise my own alarm at some of the theological trends today in many Christian traditions, where a neo-Pelagian or neo-Arminian spirit (I apologize for these polemical terms; they are used for economy only) seems to be growing, in which the critical action identified is human action—not, as it should be, receiving and celebrating God's new realm, but laboring mightily to bring it about. To be sure, mighty labors are needed. But the mightiest deed of all, God's restoration in Jesus Christ, has been done.

A third point of consonance appears where the author speaks of "a deeper appreciation of the factor of historicity in post–Vatican II thinking regarding the origin of the scriptures." My own church tradition shares in that understanding of historicity. We have grave difficulties within my denomination and in ecumenical dialogue where that principle is not shared, where the scriptures are set off, outside the domain of critical historical inquiry.

A fourth point of consonance appears in the discussion of the liturgical praise to the Word, not to the Book, as an indicator of the inspired, sacred character of scriptural texts. It is because they bear, they disclose, they re-present the living Word, Jesus Christ, as they are read and preached, sung, and kept at the heart of prayer.

A fifth point of consonance appears where Koernke describes the liberation of scripture from traditional metaphysics and the official interpretations of pope and bishops. My own tradition is historically also metaphysically cautious. In every generation new philosophies or ideologies (many are old ones in new guises) claim center stage theologically. But our historic loyalty to Jesus Christ as the Word in scripture and as the sole head of the church keeps us critically distant, as we also try to claim new insights that are judged scripturally valid. It is wonderful to see the Roman Catholic post–Vatican II tradition claiming a similar scriptural relativization.

My sixth and final point of consonance appears where the author says, "Conviction regarding the inerrancy of the scriptures is, thus, not locked to the words on the page, and yet the words on the page cannot be simply dismissed or manipulated by any ideology." It is this last point that is particularly challenging in my kind of "free" church tradition. We do dismiss the words, we do manipulate the words ideologically, and yet I am persuaded that we know we should not and must not.

POINTS OF DISSONANCE

The first point of dissonance appears with the phrase, "the official understanding of the authority and function of scripture within the Catholic Church." We could never speak that way in my church. We speak about degrees of authority, authority for whom and where. All our expressions of the church—individual, local church, associations, conferences, the General Synod are scrupulously careful not to speak *for* any other body. On the other hand, we have statements of belief and practice, a book of worship, and hymnals that are widely used and that build a community consensus, without compelling anyone's conscience. This consensus constitutes a shadowy kind of "official" understanding, I think, though many would be understandably reluctant to try to say precisely what that is.

A second point of dissonance appears with the discussion of liturgical practice as the locus of understanding scriptural interpretation. Perhaps it is most clear to say that the centrality of scriptural vernacular translations in the life of the whole community began to characterize the kind of Reformed and free church traditions of the sixteenth century that make up the historical fabric of my own church. Liturgical life was to be subjected to scriptural scrutiny and reformed accordingly. Much of the rich tradition of Western worship was rejected at that time—now, more of our shared liturgical heritage is being recovered.

A third point of dissonance is suggested in the summary of the report of the Pontifical Biblical Commission. The notion that "every major methodology of biblical interpretation" could be adjudicated regarding the contributions and limitations of each method would be foreign to my own church tradition. It is not that we do not do that in a variety of ways, ranging from church-wide theological commissions to the weekly work of interpreting the scriptures in teaching and preaching by the clergy to the continuing faith formation of each individual believer. But we clearly do not have authoritative ecclesial adjudications of new methods of scriptural interpretation. Our bias, I fear, leads us to embrace new methods uncritically.

POINTS OF NON-SONANCE

A phrase that is new to me, "fiducial faith," appears twice in the first paragraph and again later in the text. These multiple usages at key points lead me to think that it is a technical term of some importance. As an adjective modifying faith, *fiducial* faith would seem to imply that there were other kinds of faith. I need clarification on this point.

The other puzzle relates to Koernke's closing questions. They seem more addressed within and to her own Catholic tradition. In my own tradition we may overly value human contributions to the formation of scripture and insufficiently the divine, Spirit-inspired dynamic of that formative process. On her second question about Neoplatonist metaphysics and the denial of matter and materiality, surely all our Western Christian traditions manifest that heresy, though not always on the foundation of Neoplatonism.

RESPONSE TO NAFZGER

Clyde J. Steckel

INTRODUCTION

Though the United Church of Christ and the Lutheran Church–Missouri Synod might seem far apart on theological and social viewpoints, their shared sixteenth-century Protestant Reformation heritage produces a number of consonances, seen in my paper and the one by Sam Nafzger. Particularly the centrality of the gospel of Jesus Christ, justification by grace through faith, and an interpretation of scripture that affirms the fully human character of the writings and the writers, mark out a substantial area of agreement. On other matters, however, like the human role in salvation; the place of tradition, reason, and experience; or other ways the gift of faith might be mediated than through the scriptures, the two papers display a number of dissonances.

CONSONANCES

Grounded in European continental and English Reformed traditions, with substantial Lutheran elements, the UCC heritage has stressed the centrality of faith in Jesus Christ as the key to scriptural authority. Justification by grace through faith is also a shared Reformed and Lutheran conviction, prized in the UCC. Nafzger sets forth these affirmations in the first page of his essay.

Nafzger affirms the universal gracious embrace of all creation and humanity by God in his paper, a conviction held in the UCC.

The UCC faith traditions would also agree with Nafzger's statement of the Lutheran rejection of human works (reason, conversion, works of righteousness) as producing or influencing salvation in any way. It is grace alone. UCC traditions have always rejected Pelagian or Arminian views. That is not to say that a holy life or works of righteousness are unimportant, but they are always understood as grateful responses to the gift of grace.

Nafzger's statements about the fully human character of scriptural writing would also agree with UCC views. Also the way he speaks of scriptural inspiration by the Holy Spirit, without trying to explain that in detail, would characterize a UCC approach to that subject.

Nafzger's concluding admonition about avoiding either a "gospel reductionism" or a "rationalistic biblicism" would resonate with UCC views, though the examples he uses would be problematic for the UCC.

DISSONANCES

First of all, many in the United Church of Christ would not adhere to the notion of the "substitutionary life and death of Jesus Christ." We would affirm that the death and resurrection of Jesus Christ effect salvation and the restoration of humanity and all of creation, and that the fallen, broken, and sinful character of creation and humanity can only be remedied in Jesus Christ. But we would not think of this estrangement from God as requiring the payment of satisfaction to an aggrieved deity, for which only the death of the sinless son of God can atone. Rather we would think of divine grace as a gift from a loving, suffering, and aggrieved God longing for full communion with the estranged creation, a gracious love in which Jesus Christ embodies fidelity to God's realm of justice and peace. He suffers and dies in loyal obedience to that divine vocation, and is raised from death to new life *on our behalf* not as a price to be paid, but as the initiator and sign of that new realm we enter by following him in the way of compassion, prophetic witness, and courageous struggle in the way that leads to the cross and the empty tomb. *On our behalf* expresses this miracle of trusting and following Jesus Christ more truly and powerfully than "substitutionary life and death," in our view.

A second point of dissonance, or at least one requiring more extensive clarification, is the human role in salvation. The classical sixteenth-century Reformation formula, "by grace through faith," has suggested a passive or receptive human role in salvation. Both Lutheran and Reformed theologians sought to avoid any opening for human action cooperating with grace or completing the action of grace. The logical consequence of any such admission, in scholastic thinking governed by the rules of deductive logic, would be to weaken or dilute the sovereignty of grace.

Both the Lutheran and Calvinist traditions tried to clarify the human role by emphasizing the Pauline/Augustinian doctrine of election, or as it became elaborated in Calvinism, predestination. If God's loving but also inscrutable will had already determined who would be saved, then human effort to attain or even demonstrate salvation was futile. Trust, gratitude, and hope were the only theologically appropriate responses to the divine initiative. One should live gratefully, justly, and lovingly in response to the gift of grace. But these responses did not count in salvation.

In the postmodern world of the twenty-first century, such propositionally formulated truths deduced from core faith affirmations no longer hold sway. Experiencing God's freely given grace and seeking to follow its leading are better expressed in metaphoric, poetic form, where a rich diversity of meaning can be discerned, rather than in the effort to formulate unequivocal religious propositions. This postmodern diversity of interpretation does not mean that anything goes in stating the faith of the church. But it does mean that we can affirm both divine initiative and human response in ways that guard the boundaries of each, while avoiding the logical terrors of the sixteenth and seventeenth centuries.

A third dissonance, akin to the one just discussed, would be UCC thinking about the authority of tradition, reason, and experience in relation to scriptural authority. As noted in the introduction to my essay on the United Church of Christ, the preamble to the constitution of the United Church of Christ affirms the word of God in the scriptures of the Old and New Testaments, the ancient ecumenical creeds, the insights of the Protestant reformers, and the efforts of the church in every generation to make the historic faith its own in honesty of expression. Thus scripture, tradition, and human experience are understood to be parts of a whole and continuing process of faith formation, expression, and action. *Sola scriptura,* as an affirmation of the foundational authority of the scriptures, is in keeping with those UCC convictions. But *sola scriptura* as an exclusion of other authorities is not.

A fourth UCC dissonance with the Nafzger paper would relate to its assertion "that it is only through the proclamation of the Gospel—in Word and Sacrament—that the Holy Spirit gives the gift of faith." Most in the UCC, I believe, would find this an excessively restrictive limitation on the freedom of God to give faith in ways beyond our human reckoning.

CONCLUSION

As noted earlier, Nafzger concludes his essay with the admonition to avoid gospel reductionism and rationalistic biblicism. But in that same paragraph he speaks about the authority of the scriptures concerning "contemporary issues such as the ordination of women to pastoral office and the practice of homosexuality." Many in the UCC would regard those Lutheran Church–Missouri Synod teachings as examples of the kind of rationalistic biblicism Nafzger wants to avoid. Our appeal is to scripture, to the word of God set forth in scripture, not to a collection of specific verses appearing to condemn the ordination of women or a homosexual orientation. Many such collections of verses addressing many topics appear in scripture and could be elevated to biblical law. But the gospel forbids that, and instead calls for an inclusive, nonjudgmental, loving, and compassionate invitation to all.

CONCLUDING SUMMARY

In reviewing the three essays addressing the authority and function of scripture, the responses, and the discussion at the

Ecclesiology Study Group, I am moved to offer two observations, one about affinities appearing in the written texts, and one addressing possible misunderstandings evident in the discussion.

Comparing the three essays originally presented, I am struck first with what may seem a paradox, namely, that the predominantly Reformed theological heritage in the United Church of Christ seems in some ways more like modern Roman Catholic traditions than the Lutheran heritage as embodied in the Lutheran Church–Missouri Synod. If that intuition is apt, there are no doubt many reasons for a Reformed and Roman Catholic affinity, including developments taking place since the sixteenth-century Protestant Reformation. But I wonder if there is not a more ancient reason for this affinity. Is it not possible that Calvin's grounding in humanism and the way he developed the notion of the knowledge of God available through the light of human reason may have more in common with Thomas Aquinas, whereas Luther's grounding in the Augustinian tradition makes him more theologically centered in the revelation graciously bestowed in Jesus Christ? On major Reformation doctrinal points—grace, justification, sanctification, the radical freedom of the gospel word in the church and over the church, the priesthood of all believers—Calvin and Luther were in accord. But their contrasting theological methods, as well as their differing social contexts and personalities, should make us cautious about claiming too much commonality. These three essays and our subsequent discussions have provided fresh reminders about the complexity of lining up modern Christian traditions in neat streams of historical derivation with their familiar similarities and contrasts.

My second concluding observation arises from the discussion in the Ecclesiology Study Group. Some members of that group wondered whether my views truly represented the UCC. One member reported an ecumenical dialogue in which a UCC panelist asserted that the scriptures would be simply set aside if they seemed not to support a position taken on other grounds, such as reason or experience. While I acknowledged that such a statement might well be made by a UCC person, I did not regard it as a representative position, nor was it anything I would ever say.

Which of us, then, speaks for the United Church of Christ?

For persons in churches with an authoritative teaching office (Roman Catholic) or confession of faith (Lutheran), it must seem that churches without defined courts of last resort would be open to a diversity of belief in which logically contrary views could be held side by side. I cannot speak on behalf of other so-called free church traditions, but on behalf of my own ecclesial tradition, I can say that while we prefer to emphasize core convictions and remain open about boundaries, it is not the case that anything at all could be believed in the United Church of Christ. In addition to the constitutional and ordinal traditions of scriptural authority cited at the beginning of my essay, the United Church of Christ also sets limits on absolute congregational (or individual) autonomy in that same constitution. In that document the committee on ministry of each association determines fitness for ministerial standing and the standing of local churches in the UCC. While the ethos of our church embraces openness and diversity (convictions maintained in the work of these committees), no local church or candidate for ordination would receive standing if clearly non-Christian theological claims were put forward. Fortunately the strength of our shared convictions and their expression in preaching, teaching, and worship keep us more centered, more on track than might be expected in an ecclesial life that stresses freedom and autonomy. We view freedom and autonomy within the network of covenant relationships representing our relationship with the God we know in Jesus Christ and our relationship with all parts of the Christian family. That covenant network both centers us and helps us agree on our boundaries, even though we are loathe to define those boundaries too tightly.

DIALOGUE 8

ESCHATOLOGY AND MISSION: A DIALOGUE BETWEEN ANGLICAN AND ADVENTIST TRADITIONS

ESCHATOLOGY AND MISSION IN THE ANGLICAN TRADITION

O. C. Edwards Jr.

It would come as a surprise to many Anglicans to learn that they had a distinctive doctrine of eschatology, mission, or anything else, so aware are we of an intention to perpetuate the historic faith of the undivided church.[1] The only stated norm of doctrine for us is Holy Scripture.[2] The sixth of our Thirty-nine Articles, for example, says that "whatsoever is not read therein, nor may be proved thereby, is not to be required of any man, that it should be believed as an article of the Faith, or be thought requisite or necessary to salvation." For all practical purposes, however, what Anglicans assume the scriptures to teach are the doctrines reflected in the *Book of Common Prayer (BCP)*. It is true for us, as perhaps for few others, that *lex orandi,* the law of prayer/public worship, is *lex credendi,* the law of faith. The way to find out what Anglicans believe is to study the *BCP.*

The basic assumption of our eschatology is that history will come to an end when the divine purpose in creation has been accomplished. An important element of this is the notion of the parousia, although I doubt most contemporary Anglicans would envision that idea in all the concrete and dramatic detail that, for example, John Wesley supplied in his sermon the "Great Assize."[3] Rather, with a post-Copernican, if not postmodern, agnosticism of specifics, we assume that whatever that means will occur.[4]

One of the best places to find Anglican teaching is in the collects, the short prayers that "collect together" the emphases of the liturgy for a feast in the church year. For the doctrine under consideration, the collect for the First Sunday in Advent is a case in point:

> Almighty God, give us grace to cast away the works of dark-
> ness, and put on the armor of light, now in the time of this
> mortal life in which your Son Jesus Christ came to visit us in
> great humility; that in the last day, when he shall come again
> in his glorious majesty to judge both the living and the dead,
> we may rise to the life immortal; through him who lives and
> reigns with you and the Holy Spirit, one God, now and for
> ever. Amen.

Assumed in all this is the reality of judgment and that the
period on which that judgment will be based is this life. Oddly
enough, the word *hell* seldom appears in the Prayer Book. My
impression is that, outside of biblical passages quoted, there are
only three places where the word occurs. One is in the older translation of the creed[5] and another is in the third of our Articles of
Religion (*BCP*, 868), a comment on this creedal passage insisting
that the descent into hell occurred without enlarging upon it. The
third is in the catechism, where it is said, "[b]y heaven we mean
eternal life in our enjoyment of God; by hell we mean eternal
death in our rejection of God." What hell consists of is not spelled
out in any detail; there are even some Anglicans who would entertain the possibility that since, as St. Augustine pointed out, evil
does not exist in itself but is rather the absence of good, damnation could simply be a retreat into nonbeing. But even if hell is an
eternal state of damnation, the abiding Anglican emphasis would
see its worst punishment to be the loss of communion with God
rather than any lesser torment that could be added to that. As
John Donne said:

> What Tophet is not Paradise? What brimstone is not
> amber? What gnashing is not a comfort? What gnawing of
> the worm is not a tickling? What torment is not a marriage
> bed, to this damnation to be secluded eternally, eternally,
> eternally from the sight of God? Especially to us. For as the
> perpetual loss of that is most heavy with which we have been
> best acquainted and to which we have been most accus-
> tomed, so shall this damnation, which consists in the loss of
> the sight and presence of God, be heavier in us than others,
> because God hath so graciously and evidently and so
> diversely appeared to *us*.[6]

By the same token, the great joy and reward of heaven is seen to be basking in the presence of God. Anglicans have little interest in what Reinhold Niebuhr referred to as "the furniture of heaven and the temperature of hell." Their emphasis is like that of Richard Baxter:

> As all good whatsoever is comprised in God, and all in the creature are but drops in this ocean; so all the glory of the blessed is comprised in their enjoyment of God and if there be any mediate joys there, they are but drops to this. If men and angels could study to speak the blessedness of that estate in one word, what could they say beyond this, that it is the nearest enjoyment of God?[7]

The yearning for this blessedness is expressed in a number of collects in such statements as "increase and multiply upon us your mercy; that, with you as our ruler and guide, we may so pass through things temporal, that we lose not the things eternal" (prayer for the Sunday closest to July 27). Behind all this there is an utter presupposition of justification by grace through faith. The prayer for the Sunday nearest September 14 is as follows:

> O God, because without you we are not able to please you, mercifully grant that your Holy Spirit may in all things direct and rule our hearts; through Jesus Christ our Lord, who lives and reigns with you and the Holy Spirit, one God, now and forever. Amen.[8]

Further, the motivation for the Christian life in this world is not assumed to be basically a matter of being admitted to heaven or avoiding hell. Rather, it is to recognize that such behavior is the beginning of the life in God of which heaven is only the consummation. Here truly, "virtue is its own reward." This understanding is very much like the Johannine awareness that eternal life begins when one is united to Christ. Thus the collect for the Sunday nearest August 31 asks God to "graft in our hearts the love of your name; increase in us true religion; nourish us with all goodness; and bring forth in us the fruit of good works."

Involved in all these matters is a profoundly corporate understanding of Christian existence both in this life and in the life to come. One of the rubrics for the rite for the sacrament defines baptism as "full initiation by water and the Holy Spirit into Christ's Body the Church" and goes on to label the bond thus established as indissoluble. And the catechism says that it is the sacrament "by which God adopts us as his children and makes us members of Christ's Body, the Church, and inheritors of the Kingdom of God." Thus heaven is not understood as personal reward so much as it is the consummation of the life of the church, the goal to which the pilgrim people of God have been headed all along. The catechism thus says that by "resurrection of the body" we mean "God will raise us from death in the fullness of our being, that we may live with Christ in the communion of the saints." The communion of saints is defined as "the whole family of God, the living and the dead, those whom we love and those whom we hurt, bound together in Christ by sacrament, power, and praise." And the life everlasting means "a new existence, in which we are united with all the people of God, in the joy of fully knowing and loving God and one another."

In the light of this eschatology, what can be said about missions and evangelization? On the whole, the motive for evangelization and mission among Anglicans is not so much to snatch people from the fires of hell as it is to see that they do not miss out on the supreme privilege they were created to enjoy, life forever with God in the loving presence of all the people of God. This may be seen in this prayer for mission in the rite for Morning Prayer:

> O God, you have made of one blood all the peoples of the earth, and sent your blessed Son to preach peace to those who are far off and those who are near: Grant that people everywhere may seek after you and find you; bring the nations into your fold; pour out your Spirit upon all flesh; and hasten the coming of your kingdom; through Jesus Christ our Lord. Amen.

To this may be added the collect for a votive eucharist "Of the Reign of Christ":

Almighty and everlasting God, whose will it is to restore all things in thy well-beloved Son, the King of kings and Lord of lords: mercifully grant that the peoples of the earth, divided and enslaved by sin, may be freed and brought together under his most gracious rule; who lives and reigns with you and the Holy Spirit, one God, now and forever.

To summarize Anglican understandings of eschatology and mission, I can think of nothing better to do than quote from Thomas Browne's *Religio medici:*

I thank God, and with joy I mention it, I was never afraid of Hell, nor never grew pale at the description of that place. I have so fixed my contemplations on Heaven, that I had almost forgot the idea of hell, and am afraid rather to lose the joys of the one, than endure the misery of the other: to be deprived of them is a perfect Hell, and needs, methinks, no addition to complete our afflictions. That terrible term never detained me from sin, nor do I owe any good action to the name thereof. I fear God, yet am not afraid of Him: His mercies make me ashamed of my sins, before His judgments afraid thereof....I can hardly think there was ever any scared into Heaven; they go the fairest way to Heaven that would serve God without a Hell; other mercenaries, that crouch into Him in fear of Hell, though they term themselves the servants, are indeed but the slaves, of the Almighty.[9]

NOTES

1. As Stephen Sykes has pointed out, however, we do not teach everything that was taught in the early church. Thus the principles by which we choose to pass on certain teachings and not others become our distinctive doctrinal emphases. *The Integrity of Anglicanism* (New York: Seabury, 1978).

2. While the rise of modern biblical criticism means that establishing the normative doctrine of scripture is a much more complex task than the Reformers realized, the latest revision of the American *Book of Common Prayer (BCP)* (New York: Church Hymnal Corp.; Greenwich, CT: Seabury Press, 1979) still requires

those being ordained to declare that they "do believe the Holy Scriptures of the Old and New Testament to be the Word of God, and to contain all things necessary to salvation" (526, 538).

3. This may be found in a great number of editions, among them Albert C. Outler and Richard P. Heitzenrater, eds., *John Wesley's Sermons: An Anthology* (Nashville: Abingdon, 1991), 311–23.

4. Such a willingness to accept an assertion without sweating the details has been characteristic of us for a long time. Many have not wished to advance, for instance, in defining the nature of our Lord's presence in the Eucharist much beyond a little verse attributed to Queen Elizabeth I: "He took the bread and brake it / His was the Word that spake it / And what that Word doth make it / I believe and take it."

5. The 1979 American *BCP* has several rites in both traditional and modern English versions. The traditional form of the Apostles' Creed contains the words "he descended into hell" while the modern reads "he descended to the dead." This is understood by many as the harrowing of hell, Christ's preaching to the Old Testament saints and thus offering them salvation through himself, on the basis of 1 Peter 3:19: "he went and made a proclamation to the spirits in prison, who in former times did not obey" (cf. Matthew 27:52; Luke 23:43).

6. Sermon LXXVI, in *Donne's Sermons: Selected Passages,* ed. L. P. Smith (Oxford: Oxford University Press, 1919), 208–11. Quoted in Anglicanism, in *The Thought and Practice of the Church of England, Illustrated from the Religious Literature of the Seventeenth Century,* ed. and comp. Paul Elmer More and Frank Leslie Cross (New York: Macmillan, 1957), 337. This anthology is an invaluable guide to the thought of classical Anglicanism.

7. *The Saint's Everlasting Rest,* quoted in *Anglicanism,* ed. More and Cross, 327. It could be argued that Baxter was not an Anglican because he became a Nonconformist at the time of the Restoration, but his thoughts can be echoed in many passages from those who remained within the established church.

8. See also the collects for the Sunday closest to September 21, and the Monday and Wednesday in Holy Week.

9. The title has nothing to do with Florentine dynasties, but means something like "the faith of a physician." The passage, quoted from *Anglicanism,* ed. More and Cross, 338, appears on page 58 of the Everyman edition of *Religio medici. (The Religio Medici and Other Writings of Sir Thomas Browne* [London: J. M. Dent; New York: E. P. Dutton, 1909]).

SEVENTH-DAY ADVENTIST PERSPECTIVE ON ESCHATOLOGY AND MISSION

Denis Fortin

The relationship between eschatology and mission is a focus point in the theology and practice of Seventh-day Adventists for whom the proclamation of the good news of salvation in Christ is closely related to their understanding of biblical eschatology, in particular, their belief in the second advent of Christ. Based on Jesus' promise to his disciples the night of his betrayal that one day he would return to take his disciples to his Father's heavenly mansions (John 14:1–3), Seventh-day Adventists believe the fulfillment of this promise is linked to the preaching of the gospel. Jesus himself made this association: "And this Gospel of the kingdom will be preached in all the world as a witness to all the nations, and then the end will come" (Matt 24:14).

Early Christians also combined the two events. Paul's encouragement to Titus echoes the words of Jesus and highlights his belief in the second advent of Jesus: "For the grace of God that brings salvation has appeared to all men, teaching us that, denying ungodliness and worldly lusts, we should live soberly, righteously, and godly in the present age, looking for the blessed hope and glorious appearing of our great God and Savior Jesus Christ" (Titus 2:11–13). Through the centuries, this blessed hope and promise have been a strong motivating factor for Christians to preach the gospel to all nations.

As their name proclaims, Seventh-day Adventists believe in the second *advent* of Christ. Our Fundamental Belief #12 partly states "The second coming of Christ is the blessed hope of the church, the grand climax of the Gospel. The Saviour's coming will be literal, personal, visible, and worldwide....The almost complete fulfillment of most lines of prophecy, together with the present condition of the world, indicates that Christ's coming is imminent. The time of that event has not been revealed, and we are therefore exhorted to be ready at all times."[1]

Clearly, Seventh-day Adventist eschatology is premillennial; it is shaped by a belief in an imminent second advent of Christ, to be followed by the millennium and the final judgment of God. This blessed hope is at the center of a Seventh-day Adventist approach to mission.

Emerging in the mid-1800s as an outgrowth of the Second Great Awakening, the Seventh-day Adventist church whole-heartedly embraces salvation in Jesus and the need for personal piety and spiritual growth in the Christian life. With their theological roots traced also to Pietist and Wesleyan understandings of the process of salvation, the Seventh-day Adventist belief in an imminent second advent of Jesus Christ inspires its members to go into all the world to preach the good news of salvation in Jesus.

"INTO ALL THE WORLD"

In his parting words, Jesus left with his apostles the great gospel commission: "Go and make disciples of all nations" (Matt 28:19). Every modern generation of Christians has been challenged by these words of the Master. And so have Seventh-day Adventists. They believe that the gospel of Jesus Christ is to be carried to all men and women in the world, encouraging them to accept Jesus as Savior and Lord and to become responsible members of his church, led by the Holy Spirit as they engage in a life of witness. More than just a formal acceptance of Jesus as Savior, this approach to mission calls upon men and women to dedicate their lives totally to the service of God's will as revealed in scripture.[2]

Because in it God has revealed his will, scripture plays an important role in the salvation of human beings. It speaks of the eternal truths about God and his character, Christ, humanity, sin, salvation, eternal life, and ethical conduct in a world of sin. All these subjects are of significant interest to human beings and aim to answer vital questions related to the very essence of human life. While our secular society offers conflicting and inconsistent views of the purpose for human life and destiny, Seventh-day Adventists believe that the Bible, as God's infallible word, offers to all the knowledge of a saving relationship with Jesus Christ in which humankind regains its true sense of purpose and destiny. Biblical doctrines and truths are, therefore, important and vital elements of this relationship with Jesus as Savior and Lord. Seventh-day Adventists affirm with Peter's words to the Sanhedrin, "Nor is there salvation in any other, for there is no other name under heaven given among men by which we must be saved" (Acts 4:12).

PROPHETIC IDENTITY

The Bible and the great gospel commission are significant elements in a Seventh-day Adventist approach to mission. Furthermore, its missiology is also based on a strong sense of prophetic self-understanding and identity.[3] Adventists see themselves as heirs of the Reformation, and especially the great principles of *sola scriptura, sola gratia, sola fide, solo Christo.* Teachings that others may view as distinctive of Adventists are seen by them as the continuation of the Reformation's recovery and restoration of biblical truth. Adventists also see the Christian Church as part of an ongoing spiritual struggle between good and evil. Christ's victory at Calvary and his Lordship over the church assure the ultimate triumph of good and the end of evil. In this struggle between good and evil, Christ uses various agencies, and Seventh-day Adventists understand themselves as one of these agencies—but not the only one.

In the scriptures, the books of Daniel and Revelation, and other texts in the Synoptics and Pauline writings, are significant to Seventh-day Adventists. As interpreted within a historicist and biblicist hermeneutics, these passages establish that God has a special people at the end of time to preach to the world the message of the imminent and literal second advent of Jesus. Although they attach great importance to these prophetic texts, this does not mean that they regard them as their only focus or wish to isolate them from the rest of scripture. Scripture as a whole is their focus and it is only within the context of the whole that they wish to give to the prophetic and apocalyptic texts their due attention.

Adventists see themselves as the fulfillment of the remnant people of God depicted in Revelation 12 to 14. In biblical writings, the term remnant designates a group who survived a crisis (historical remnant), as well as those who are faithful to God (faithful remnant). While the book of Revelation depicts the historical conflicts between the faithful people of God and evil powers working through secular agencies from the time of Christ's first advent until his second advent in glory, Adventists understand that in the final crisis before the return of Jesus, God's faithful remnant will be identified as those who are committed to Christ as Savior and Lord, and who obey the commandments of God and have the faith of Jesus (Rev 12:17; 14:12).

THE THREE ANGELS' MESSAGE

The message of the three angels of Revelation 14:6–13 is also part of Seventh-day Adventist identity to be a worldwide prophetic voice in the end time. Their theology interprets these conflicts between good and evil, between the faithful people of God and the powers of evil in the world, as the results of Satan's hatred for God's will and truth as found in the scriptures. This message of the three angels is meant to call the attention of all inhabitants of the earth, both Christians and non-Christians, to what God considers important in preparation for the second coming of Christ.

Depicted by an angel flying in midair, the first messenger proclaims the everlasting gospel to every nation, tribe, language, and people on earth. This angel represents a group of people on whom God calls to proclaim to the whole world his everlasting gospel. This is the eschatological fulfillment of Jesus' great commission. This first message contains three parts: fear God, the hour of his judgment has come, and worship the Creator God.

"Fear God, and keep his commandments: for this is the whole duty of man," said the Ecclesiastes (12:13). The beginning of wisdom is to fear God, in the sense of honoring his will and commandments, which were given to all humanity by a God of love, to guide us on the path to everlasting happiness and fulfillment. Far from being a means to attain salvation, for this is only attainable by grace through faith in Christ, obedience to God's commandments and instructions is our response to his love and redemption. Thus a true respect of God involves total dedication on the part of his children to willingly obey his will. True love is shown in acts of obedience (John 14:15).

Although God is a God of love, he is equally so a God of justice. The first angel proclaims that the reason why people on earth should fear God is that the hour of his judgment has come. In his justice God will bring an end to evil and sin thus calling the attention of all humankind to his judgment.

Lastly, the first angel shouts that all people on earth should worship God, the Creator: "worship him that made heaven, and earth, and the sea, and the fountains of waters" (14:7). Significantly, this call quotes from the Decalogue's fourth commandment in Exodus 20:11, the only commandment in which God describes who he is. Seventh-day Adventists view this first angel's message as a call to all humanity to worship the only true God on his day of worship, the Sabbath of creation, given to humanity (and not only to the Jewish people) as a memorial of God's creatorship and love. The Sabbath is the good news that tells us of creation and recreation, of our roots and destiny. The overall link between loving God, obeying his will and commandments, and the announcement of his judgment depicts an all-inclusive message of total dedication to God on the part of earth's inhabitants. The message of the first angel is thus interpreted to be an urgent call to all humanity to know God as the God of the everlasting gospel and to worship him on his day, the Sabbath. This is an urgent call before judgment, for time is running out. The end to evil and sin is in sight.

While the first angel gives a positive message of good news that is to go to every inhabitant of the earth, the second and third angels send messages of warning. The second angel follows with a critical message: "Babylon is fallen" (14:8). In its etymological meaning Babylon is a reference to confusion and, in its wider interpretation, this concept refers to religious confusion and apostasy. The angel's warning here contrasts God's everlasting gospel message with the spurious, false, and apostate in religious beliefs at the time of the second advent. The day will come when false religions will be seen to be the vanity they really are, leading to destruction rather than to life.

The third angel's message points to the ultimate showdown between good and evil at the second advent. This message pictures the final end of those who have rejected truth and allowed themselves to be deceived by the beast and its image and who have received its mark. This is a dire message, the strongest warning, but its intent is also to lead people to experience the everlasting gospel described in the first message.

A NEW HEAVEN AND A NEW EARTH

After the proclamation of this three-part message, John depicts the second advent of Christ followed, at the end of the book, by the vision of a new heaven and a new earth. These foretold events have been sources of encouragement and hope for millions of Christians. While our lives on earth have been assaulted by evils of all kinds and have produced untold sorrows, pains, tears, and deaths, the promise is given of a new way of life where God shall wipe away all tears, where there shall be no more death, and neither sorrow, nor crying, nor pain; for all these will have passed away (Rev 21:4). The Christian's hope is this end of all evil and a new eternal life in the presence of God.

More than a denomination, Seventh-day Adventists view themselves as an end-time movement that proclaims God's last-day message. Their sense of mission is taken from these prophecies of scripture. Having experienced the joy of salvation in Christ and believing his prophetic word to us as found in the Bible, Seventh-day Adventists yearn to share this good news with all humankind. It is this strong sense of prophetic identity that is motivating this relatively small group of Christians to reach out with the everlasting gospel to a world dying and lost without the knowledge of salvation in Jesus and of his will.

NOTES

1. For an exposition of Seventh-day Adventist beliefs one can refer to *Seventh-day Adventists Believe...A Biblical Exposition of 27 Fundamental Doctrines* (Hagerstown, MD: Ministerial Association, General Conference of Seventh-day Adventists and Review and Herald Publishing, 1988) and Raoul Dederen, ed., *Handbook of Seventh-day Adventist Theology* (Hagerstown, MD: Review and Herald Publishing, 2000).

2. Other Christian groups have also a similar theological understanding of mission. See Arthur F. Glasser and Donald A. McGavran, *Contemporary Theologies of Mission* (Grand Rapids, MI: Baker Book House, 1983), 26, for their discussion of this theology of mission.

3. This self-understanding was well expressed in the recent report of conversations between the Lutheran World Federation and the General Conference of Seventh-day Adventists in *Adventists and Lutherans in Conversation,* supplement to the *Adventist Review* (June 25, 1998). Some of the points that follow are taken from this document.

RESPONSE

O. C. Edwards Jr.

RESONANCE

Although I knew very little about Adventist teaching, it came as little surprise to me to learn that they and we agree on what I consider to be the basic shape of eschatology and mission. That is, we both believe that the divine purpose in creation will be accomplished and history will come to an end; that human beings will be judged on the basis of their response to God's loving initiative in this life; that their eternal destiny will be decided in that judgment; that those whose judgment is positive will live forever in blessedness with God and the holy people of God; and that those whose judgment is negative will be deprived of that supreme blessedness for which they were created. We share with Adventists a sense of responsibility to carry out the Great Commission. Both churches are convinced that justification is through faith alone, yet both recognize that those who are justified love to obey the commands of God. Both churches believe that salvation is through Christ alone, although some Anglicans, including the present writer, would allow for the possibility that some may be saved without knowing that it is Christ who saved them.[1]

DISSONANCE

When one moves from that basic shape to any particular detail, however, this agreement fades. It is not so much that the two churches have different visions of these details, as that Anglicans have only a very general view of these matters while Adventists

305

have a quite specific understanding of them. These differences are functions of quite separate views of the way in which God reveals God's Self in scripture. While both churches accept the Bible as the only norm of belief, the two interpret it very differently. Denis Fortin speaks of the Bible as infallible. Although he does not say so, my understanding of what he said is that Adventists believe in the plenary verbal inspiration of Holy Scripture. Anglicans, on the other hand, accept the historical-critical method of interpretation and its successors. Let it be clearly understood that our difference here is not over the ultimacy of the Bible as the norm for Christian belief. Both accept that completely. The difference is rather over how scripture communicates its revelation of God and the divine will.

A case in point is the use the Adventists make of the canonical apocalypses, Daniel and Revelation. They consider them to be detailed prophecies of the end-time. If they interpret the prophecies correctly, they will know what is to come and their place in it. We, on the other hand, are much more likely to believe that these apocalypses are the coded communication of oppressed believers and that they express the conditions under which the communities of their writers struggled. The reason that most generations of believers since have thought these books were detailed prophecies of their own time is that all persecutions of the faithful have a great deal in common. Yet, so many loyal Christians through the centuries have considered these to be coded predictions of their own situation and have been disappointed in their expectation of the immediate return of Christ that Anglicans find it hard to believe that Christians today who launch out in this endeavor are more likely to be correct in their expectations than those who have gone before.

Yet, this diminished certainty about the imminence of the parousia does not mean that Anglicans think believers need to be one whit less vigilant or less totally devoted to the fulfillment of the will of God. Acceptance of the salvation wrought by Christ and living in the light and grace that bestows is what life is all about, and whoever misses that misses what they were created to enjoy. Nor do we think that vigilance will necessarily be relaxed because we do not know whether the end of the world is to come soon or late. The inevitability of death means that the end will come to each of us individually with relative speed and certainty, whenever the end comes for the world as a whole, so we all need to be ready all the time.

By the same token, we do not consider the apocalypses less canonical and thus less authoritative than other books in the Bible. They show us the shape of human existence under God whether they furnish us with a detailed timetable of the future or not. We see no need to argue over whether Our Lord's return will be pre- or postmillennial. We would regard it as presumptuous to have a preference; we hope to praise God for however it is done.

It follows then that we have no sense of a special role for our faith community in the end-time. Rather, we are a part of the body of Christ that remembers the Lord's death until he comes. We know that not all are faithful and that those who persevere unto the end will be a remnant of all the millions who have professed and called themselves Christians. Yet we hope and pray that we, Adventists, and all the other children of God will be numbered among the saints.

Two other differences need to be noted. The first is of great importance to the Adventists, namely, that, while Anglicans are aware that Sunday is not the Sabbath of the commandment, they believe that the day of Our Lord's resurrection has superseded it as our holy day of obligation. Also it needs to be said that we regard the Eucharist as a proleptic enjoyment of the blessings of the end-time.

NON-SONANCE

The aspect of Adventist doctrine presented in Fortin's paper that I simply did not understand is connected with his statement that "the Saviour's coming will be literal, personal, visible, and world-wide." It is the last characteristic that puzzles me. Does the statement mean that Our Lord will be simultaneously visible to everyone on our planet at the moment of his return, or does it mean that over a period of time he will cover the globe? If the former, I would like some explanation of how that could happen. I am sure the Adventists have thought that through, but I have not and could use some help in doing so.

CONCLUDING COMMENTS

Because Anglicans believe that what scripture reveals is the basic shape of the consummation rather than a detailed blueprint, we are comfortable with the idea that other Christians may have more precise expectations than we. We just hope that their greater certainty will not cause them to despair of us.

Similarly, the willingness of some Anglicans to believe that hell is not so much eternal torment as a retreat into nonbeing has some overlap with the Adventist doctrine of conditional immortality by which only the redeemed have eternal life while the wicked are annihilated instead of spending eternity in hell.

NOTE

1. In Faith and Order group discussion, Brother Jeffrey Gros, FSC, suggested that one reason for the agreement between Adventists and Anglicans on the basic shape of eschatology is the historical linkage between them through the thought and work of John Wesley.

RESPONSE

Denis Fortin

I have appreciated reading Professor Edwards's paper for the clarity with which he has presented the Anglican understanding of the relationship between eschatology and mission. As we have attempted in these dialogues, I will respond to what I perceive to be points of resonance, or agreements, between our two traditions (if *tradition* is an appropriate qualifier for as recent a denomination as Seventh-day Adventism is), then I will evoke points of dissonance, and, finally, points of non-sonance.

POINTS OF RESONANCE

The first point of resonance I perceive between Anglicanism and Adventism is in the area of the relationship between eschatology and mission. Edwards rightly contends that mission grows out of eschatology and not the reverse. Although eschatology is not the only motivating factor for mission, it is nonetheless one major stimulus that has motivated Christian missionary activities for centuries. Among other factors, there is also the desire to share the good news of salvation with others who may not know the joy and peace that come from a relationship with Christ. Hence, it is very true that "the motivation for the Christian life in this world is not assumed to be basically a matter of being admitted to heaven or avoiding hell." Along the same thought, another point that Adventists would agree with is the view that "evangelization and mission among Anglicans is not so much to snatch people from the fires of hell as it is to see that they do not miss out on the supreme privilege they were created to enjoy, life forever with God in the loving presence of all the people of God."

A second point of resonance is the statement that the Anglican view of eschatology is based on the "utter presupposition of justification by grace through faith." Seventh-day Adventists heartily agree with a christocentric approach to eschatology, an eschatology in which Christ's ministry, death, and resurrection, are the only bases for one's eternal redemption. This approach also gives the proper motivation to mission. Far from being a work of one's own righteousness, eternal salvation is a gift of God.

A third point of resonance is in reference to the parousia. Here Seventh-day Adventists concur to say "the basic assumption of our eschatology is that history will come to an end when the divine purpose in creation has been accomplished." Adventists would qualify this statement, however, by adding the detailed stipulations that the expected parousia is imminent and, supported by many biblical texts, add that it will be a personal, visible, and majestic event featuring the glorious second advent of Christ. Anglicans, on the other hand, might simply say "with a post-Copernican, if not postmodern, agnosticism of specifics, we assume that whatever that [the parousia] means will occur."

POINTS OF DISSONANCE

Perhaps the most apparent point of dissonance between the two papers is one of methodology. While the Anglican tradition may refer to the *Book of Common Prayer* and other traditional and authoritative documents as proper and adequate exponents of biblical doctrines, Seventh-day Adventists choose to point only to scripture as an appropriate basis of doctrines.

A second point of dissonance, in this case one that emerged only in oral discussion in our group, is also to some extent one of non-sonance, the concept of purgatory. Since they reject this doctrine, Seventh-day Adventists would want to know why and how such a concept should be incorporated into the Anglican tradition as there are no references to purgatory in scripture. In fact, the integration of the doctrine of purgatory into an Anglican theology of eschatology would produce many bewildered looks, even though, as Edwards suggested in discussion, it may be considered only as a "pious opinion," that is, it is something one is not forbidden to believe, but one is forbidden to require others to believe it.

Yet, the mention of this doctrine and the idea "that there should be an opportunity after the earthly period of probation is over to be further refined by God's grace," as Edwards put it in our interchange, highlight two different anthropologies. While Anglicanism teaches the traditional dualistic nature of human beings with a material mortal body and an immaterial, immortal soul, Seventh-day Adventists adhere to a holistic view that understands the human soul to be composed of both a physical body and the breath of life. The state of human beings between death and the resurrection is therefore understood to be that of an unconscious sleep, which, in our view, leaves no room for a purgatory.

POINTS OF NON-SONANCE

This last point of dissonance regarding purgatory and anthropology brings up a point of non-sonance regarding Edwards's understanding of eternal death and hell. Given the current debates within Christianity over the nature of hell, Adventists would be puzzled to read Edwards's references to death and would want to understand better what he means by these statements. "By heaven we mean eternal life in our enjoyment of God; by hell we mean eternal death in our rejection of God." "There are even some Anglicans who would entertain the possibility that, since, as St. Augustine pointed out, evil does not exist in itself but is rather the absence of good, damnation could simply be a retreat into non-being." For Seventh-day Adventists, who strongly believe in the conditional immortality of human beings, granted only to the redeemed by grace through faith in Christ, and in the total annihilation of the wicked, such statements seem to indicate an Anglican departure from traditional Christian beliefs.

A second point that Seventh-day Adventists may not understand clearly is the emphasis Anglicanism places on personal eschatology and the lack of detailed references to universal eschatology. Since Adventist identity is closely related to eschatology, Anglicans would need to explain what the basis of their identity is.